Beginning Biblical Hebrew

Beginning
Biblical
Hebrew

Mark D. Futato

Winona Lake, Indiana
Eisenbrauns
2003

Library of Congress Cataloging-in-Publication Data

Futato, Mark David
   Beginning Biblical Hebrew / Mark D. Futato.
      p. cm.
   ISBN 1-57506-022-1 (cloth : alk. paper)
   1. Hebrew language—Grammar.   I. Title.
   PJ4567.3.F88 2003
   492.4′82421—dc21

                                    2003054970

20 19 18   6 7 8 9 10

To my wife, Adele

Many women do noble things,
but you surpass them all.
(Proverbs 31:30 [29])

לֹא לָנוּ יְהֹוָה לֹא לָנוּ

כִּי־לְשִׁמְךָ תֵּן כָּבוֹד

עַל־חַסְדְּךָ עַל־אֲמִתֶּךָ

(Psalm 115:1)

CONTENTS

INTRODUCTION

Goal

Beginning Biblical Hebrew provides students with a thorough introduction to Biblical Hebrew in an easy-to-learn format.

Familiarity with English and Hebrew grammatical terminology is not presumed. All essential terms are introduced throughout the grammar in clear, nontechnical language.

Students will learn the morphology (forms) and syntax (uses) of Hebrew adjectives, conjunctions, nouns, numbers, prepositions, and verbs.

Students will lay a solid foundation for studying the Hebrew Bible by mastering *Beginning Biblical Hebrew*.

Objectives

Upon successful completion of *Beginning Biblical Hebrew*, students will have:

➤ Mastered the pronunciation of Hebrew
➤ Mastered the forms and uses of Hebrew words
➤ Mastered a vocabulary of 400 Hebrew words
➤ Learned how to analyze any Hebrew word
➤ Learned how to translate standard Biblical Hebrew
➤ Grown in an enjoyment of the Hebrew language
➤ Grown in a commitment to use Hebrew in a lifelong study of the Hebrew Bible.

Method

Each lesson comprises three sections: *grammar*, *vocabulary*, and *practice*.

The *grammar* section introduces students to the elements of the Hebrew language in bite-sized chunks. Students will encounter all grammar essential for reading the Hebrew Bible.

The *vocabulary* section introduces students to ten words. The vocabulary is numerically keyed to Raymond B. Dillard, *Hebrew Vocabulary Cards* (Springfield, Ohio: Visual Education Association, 1981), so that beginning students can easily access this aid to mastering their vocabulary.

The *practice* section has four subdivisions:

1. Focusing on New Material isolates the new grammar, so that students can practice working with new elements without the distractions of other material.
2. Reviewing Previous Lessons ensures that students review all learned material on a systematic basis. This subdivision also often prepares students for the next lesson. So, for example, students review the form and uses of the adjective before the lesson on the participle, because of the high level of similarity.
3. Putting It All Together gives students the opportunity to synthesize all that they have learned at any given point.
4. Reading Your Hebrew Bible provides students with experience in the actual text of the Bible in every lesson from Lesson 1 to Lesson 40.

The back of the grammar contains a Hebrew-to-English vocabulary list, an answer key, and morphology charts for the verb.

Everything necessary for mastering the essentials of Biblical Hebrew is found in *Beginning Biblical Hebrew*.

ACKNOWLEDGMENTS

A number of people have made significant contributions to my passion for and ability in Biblical Hebrew. Their contributions to my life have made the publication of *Beginning Biblical Hebrew* a reality.

First and foremost is my wife, Adele. Adele has supported me from the beginning, when as an undergrad I was learning my first Hebrew words and poring over BDB to find entries for weak roots. The sacrifices she made so that I could succeed in my doctoral studies were expressions of a love at which I marvel more and more as time goes by. Adele's encouragement throughout the writing process has empowered me to bring *Beginning Biblical Hebrew* to completion. To Adele I am forever grateful.

There are three others. Willem VanGemeren was my first Hebrew teacher at Geneva College in the mid-1970s. Willem's love for Hebrew kindled my own, and his rigorous demands ensured that I laid a solid foundation. The late Raymond Dillard, one of my professors at Westminster Theological Seminary in the late 1970s, not only encouraged me in my quest to learn Hebrew and other Semitic languages as a seminarian but also played a key role in my fortuitous decision to go to The Catholic University of America to pursue doctoral studies. At CUA I had the great and unexpected privilege of being mentored by Brother Aloysius Fitzgerald. I have had many wonderful teachers along the way. Br. Aloysius surpasses them all. My mastery of Hebrew philology was facilitated to no small extent by Br. Aloysius, one of the truly great masters of Biblical Hebrew.

Finally, I would like to acknowledge all of the Hebrew students I have taught over the years. *Beginning Biblical Hebrew* was shaped in dialogue with a host of wonderful students. I also wish to express my appreciation for James Eisenbraun and his staff. Jim's commitment to excellence in publishing brings years of work on *Beginning Biblical Hebrew* to their culmination.

On the day that I first saw the design for the cover of *Beginning Biblical Hebrew*, I also learned of the passing of Br. Aloysius Fitzgerald from this life to the next. As he honored me with his time and attention as my mentor, I honor his memory with the publication of this grammar. His influence permeates every page. May he rest in peace.

THE ALPHABET

Keys to Success

1.1 **Memorize the letters** of the alphabet so well that you can write them out as fast as you can write your ABCs!

1.2 **Memorize the names** of the letters so well that you can say them as fast as you can say your ABCs!

1.3 The letters of the alphabet are the basic building blocks of the Hebrew language.

1.4 Mastery of the alphabet is the first step to mastery of Hebrew.

1.5 Do not underestimate the importance of knowing the alphabet as well as you know your own name.

1.6 Success begins here!

Alphabet Chart

1.7 English is written from left to right. Hebrew is written from right to left.

1.8 The English alphabet has consonants and vowels. The Hebrew alphabet has consonants only.

1.9 The alphabet chart on the next two pages reads from right to left, so that from the beginning you enter the fascinating world of Hebrew.

➤ Column 1 contains the **sound** you will make for the Hebrew letter.

➤ Column 2 contains the **book print** you will read in this grammar.

➤ Column 3 contains the **final form** (to be explained) for five special letters.

➤ Column 4 contains the **hand print** you will learn to write.

➤ Columns 5–7 contain the order of the **strokes** you will make to form the letters.

➤ Column 8 contains the **name** you will use to identify the letter.

8	7	6	5	4	3	2	1
Name	Stroke #3	Stroke #2	Stroke #1	Hand Print	Final Form	Book Print	Sound
Alef	⊿Ҳ	Ұ⁴	Ұ	Ҳ		א	Silent
Bet		コ	┐	┒		בּ	**B** as in **B**oy
						ב	**V** as in **V**an
Gimel		⅄	Ұ	⅄		ג	**G** as in **G**as
Dalet		Тᴸ	⁼	Т		ד	**D** as in **D**og
Hey		↓┌┐	┐ᴾ	┌┐		ה	**H** as in **H**at
Vav			∫↓	∫		ו	**V** as in **V**an
Zayin		⅂ᴾ	∫↓	⅂		ז	**Z** as in **Z**oo
Chet		↓┌┐	┐ᴾ	┌┐		ח	**CH** as in Ba**CH**
Tet		∪ᴸ	ʾ⁄	∪		ט	**T** as in **T**op
Yod			⅃↓	⅂		י	**Y** as in **Y**ou
Kaf			⊐↓	⊃		כּ	**K** as in **K**ey
		Тᴸ	⁼	┐	ך	כ	**CH** as in Ba**CH**
Lamed	⅃	⅃↓	∫↓	⅃		ל	**L** as in **L**ot

8	7	6	5	4	3	2	1
Name	Stroke #3	Stroke #2	Stroke #1	Hand Print	Final Form	Book Print	Sound
Mem		מ	מ	מ	ם	מ	**M** as in **M**at
Nun	ן	ן	⁀	ן	ן	נ	**N** as in **N**ut
Samech			ס	ס		ס	**S** as in **S**ee
Ayin		ע	ע	ע		ע	Silent
Pey		פ	פ	פ		פ	**P** as in **P**ie
		פ	ף	ף	ף	פ	**F** as in **F**an
Tsade		צ	צ	צ	ץ	צ	**TS** as in Ca**TS**
Qof		ק	ק	ק		ק	**K** as in **K**ey
Resh			ר	ר		ר	**R** as in **R**ug
Sin	שׂ	שׂ	שׂ	שׂ		שׂ	**S** as in **S**ee
Shin	שׁ	שׁ	שׁ	שׁ		שׁ	**SH** as in **SH**e
Tav	ת	ת	ת	ת		ת	**T** as in **T**op

➤ **Memorize the letters** of the alphabet so well that you can write them out as fast as you can write your ABCs!

➤ **Memorize the names** of the letters so well that you can say them as fast as you can say your ABCs!

Five Final Letters

1.10   There are five letters that have a different form when they are the last letter of a word.

1.11   Four final letters have the last stroke going straight down and extending below the line rather than going across the line to the left.

Final Form	Basic Form
ך	כ
ן	נ
ף	פ
ץ	צ

1.12   One final letter is more square than round.

Final Form	Basic Form
ם	מ

Letters with Two Pronunciations

1.13   English has letters with two pronunciations, for example, the letter "c" in city and cat, or the "th" in this and thing. There are six letters that had two pronunciations when Biblical Hebrew was spoken. These letters are referred to by the mnemonic *begadkefat*.

ת   פ   כ   ד   ג   ב   ←

1.14   You are learning the pronunciation of Modern Hebrew. Only three letters have two pronunciations. The difference in pronunciation is marked by a dot in the letter, called *weak dagesh*. With the *dagesh*, the sound is hard; without, it is soft.

	Soft			Hard
V as in **V**an	ב		**B** as in **B**oy	בּ
CH as in Ba**CH**	כ		**K** as in **K**ey	כּ
F as in **F**an	פ		**P** as in **P**ie	פּ

1.15   The weak *dagesh* is also found in the letters ג (*gimel*), ד (*dalet*), and ת (*tav*), but the pronunciation in modern Hebrew is not affected.

Letters That Look Alike

1.16   There are several letters that look alike. You may confuse them at first. Soon they will look as different as O and Q, or U and V, or G and C.

ר	ד
ז	ו
צ	ע

	כ	ב
ת	ח	ה
	ס	ם

Letters That Sound Alike

1.17   English has pairs of letters that sound alike, for example, <u>k</u>ite and <u>c</u>ar, or <u>f</u>ind and <u>ph</u>one.

1.18   There are five pairs of letters that sound alike in Hebrew.

V as in **V**an	ו	ב
CH as in Ba**CH**	כ	ח
T as in **T**op	ת	ט
K as in **K**ey	ק	כ
S as in **S**ee	שׁ	ס

Guttural Letters + Resh

1.19   There are four sounds originally made in the throat, called *gutturals* (from the Latin *guttur* = throat): א (*alef*), ה (*hey*), ח (*chet*), and ע (*ayin*). The letter ר (*resh*) shares characteristics in common with the gutturals. Special characteristics of the gutturals and *resh* will be pointed out in following chapters.

Practice

Focusing on New Material

A. Memorize the names and letters of the alphabet so well that you can write them out as fast as you can say and write your ABCs!

B. Make the sound and say the name of the following letters, reading from right to left.

ד ח ל פ ע א ף צ ם ג ס י כ ת נ   ←

ב ו ס ה ק ר פ ך ט שׁ ן ב ז ץ שׂ   ←

C. Read the two previous lines again and circle the letters in a special final form.

D. Read the two previous lines again and underline the gutturals + *resh*.

E. Read the two previous lines again and draw a box around the *begad-kefat*s.

F. Match the letters that sound alike.

ו	כ
ט	שׂ
ח	ת
ק	כּ
ס	ב

Reading Your Hebrew Bible

G. The following is Gen 1:1–3. Make the sounds and say the names of each letter.

בראשית ברא אלהים את השמים ואת הארץ   ←

והארץ היתה תהו ובהו וחשך על פני תהום   ←

ורוח אלהים מרחפת על פני המים   ←

ויאמר אלהים יהי אור ויהי אור   ←

2

THE VOWELS

A Brief History of Hebrew Vowels

2.1   During the original phase, Hebrew was written without any vowels indicated in the script. The letters צדק could have meant "righteousness," "his righteousness," "they are righteous," etc.

➤ This phase was before King David, ca. 1,400 B.C. to 1,000 B.C.

2.2   During the middle phase, several letters of the alphabet came to be used to indicate certain vowels. The letters צדקו could have meant "his righteousness," or "they are righteous," but not "righteousness." We will refer to these letters used to indicate vowels as *vowel letters*.

➤ This phase was after King David, ca. 1,000 B.C. to 300 B.C.

2.3   During the final phase, "points" were added to the text to eliminate all ambiguity. The word צָדְקוּ could only have meant "they are righteous." We will refer to these points as *vowel signs*.

➤ This phase was ca. A.D. 700 to A.D. 1000.

➤ The scholars responsible for adding the vowel signs to the text are called "Masoretes."

➤ The text of the Bible produced by the Masoretes is called the "Masoretic Text," abbreviated MT.

➤ You are learning to read the Hebrew text from this final phase.

Vowel Names, Signs, Sounds, and Positions

Name	Sign	Sound	Position
1. qamets	ָ	**a** as in f**a**ther	אָ
2. patach	ַ	**a** as in f**a**ther	אַ
3. chatef-patach	ֲ	**a** as in f**a**ther	אֲ
4. tsere	ֵ	**ey** as in h**ey**	אֵ
5. segol	ֶ	**e** as in y**e**t	אֶ

6. chatef-segol	ֱ	**e** as in y**e**t	אֱ
7. chireq	ִ	**e** as in sh**e**	אִ
8. chireq-yod	יִ	**e** as in sh**e**	אִי
9. cholem	ֹ	**o** as in sn**o**w	אֹ
10. cholem-vav	וֹ	**o** as in sn**o**w	אוֹ
11. qibbuts	ֻ	**u** as in r**u**le	אֻ
12. shureq	וּ	**u** as in r**u**le	אוּ
13. qamets-chatuf	ָ	**o** as in **o**dd	אָ
14. chatef-qamets	ֳ	**o** as in **o**dd	אֳ

Vowel Class and Length

2.4   There are three classes of vowels.

➤ "a" class

➤ "i" class

➤ "u" class

2.5   There are four lengths of vowels.

➤ long

➤ medium

➤ short

➤ very short

2.6   A basic knowledge of vowel class and length will help you greatly in learning the various forms of words in future lessons.

Chart of Vowel Class and Length

	"a"		"i"		"u"	
Long	וֹ	cholem-vav	יִ	chireq-yod	וּ	shureq
Medium	ָ	qamets	ֵ	tsere	ֹ	cholem
Short	ַ	patach	ִ	chireq	ֻ	qibbuts
			ֶ	segol	ָ	qamets-chatuf
Very Short	ֲ	chatef-patach	ֱ	chatef-segol	ֳ	chatef-qamets

Notes:

○ The vowels וֹ (*cholem-vav*) and ◌ֹ (*cholem*) are different lengths and classes.

○ Furthermore, ◌ָ (*qamets*) and ◌ָ (*qamets-chatuf*) are two different vowels that look identical; *qamets-chatuf* is rare.

Putting Consonants and Vowels Together

2.7   First pronounce the consonant, then the vowel.

2.8   Most vowels are placed under the consonant: רָ pronounced like *rah*.

2.9   The vowel ◌ֹ is placed above the consonant: תֹ pronounced like *tow*.

2.10   The vowel וֹ is placed to the left of the consonant: תּוֹ pronounced like *tow*.

2.11   The vowel וּ is placed to the left of the consonant: זוּ pronounced like *zoo*.

2.12   Read the following from right to left:

בָּרָא בָּתַח דָּבָר יָבֵשׁ זָקֵן סֵפֶר   ←

אִם עִיר אֲנִי נֶפֶשׁ אֱלֹהִים בֹּקֶר   ←

כֹּהֵן סוּס עָמוּד מָקוֹם אֲנָשִׁים   ←

Vocabulary

daughter	בַּת	414	father, ancestor	אָב	369
he ate	אָכַל	1	mother	אֵם	451
he remembered	זָכַר	32	brother	אָח	372
he is heavy	כָּבֵד	85	sister	אָחוֹת	372
he sent	שָׁלַח	25	son, descendant	בֵּן	380

Notes:

○ The number following the Hebrew word refers to the card number in R. Dillard, *Hebrew Vocabulary Cards* (Springfield, Ohio: Visual Education Association, 1981).

○ The general order of the vocabulary list is nouns followed by verbs.

○ Tips for memorizing vocabulary [from M. Brown-Azarowicz et al., *Yes! You Can Learn a Foreign Language* (Lincolnwood, Ill.: Passport Books, 1986) chap. 3.]

- Memorize words grouped according to related meaning.
- Review 10 minutes after initial learning.
- Review 60 minutes after that.
- Review again 24 hours later.
- Review every 2 days until automatic recall is attained.

Practice

Focusing on New Material

A. **Focus on the sounds of the vowels.** The following are not Hebrew words, but they sound like English words. Pronounce the Hebrew word, then write the English word that sounds the same.

.1	.2	.3	.4	.5
פָל	פַל	פֶּל	פֶל	פֵל

.6	.7	.8	.9	.10
פֵּל	פִל	פִיל	פֹם	פוֹם

.11	.12	.13	.14	.15
פֵּד	פוּד	פָט	פֶט	בָּל

.16	.17	.18	.19	.20
בַּל	בֵּל	בֵל	בֶּל	בֵּד

.21	.22	.23	.24	.25
בָּד	בִּיד	בֹּט	בּוֹט	בָּט

.26	.27	.28	.29	.30
בּוֹט	בָּט	בֶּט	בֶּת	בִּית

B. **Focus on the class of the vowels.** Memorize the vertical columns on the chart on p. 8 before doing this exercise.

1. Circle the "a" vowels: ◌ֻ ◌ְ וֹ ◌ֹ ◌ֶ ◌ִי ◌ַ ◌ֺ וֹ ◌ָ
2. Circle the "i" vowels: ◌ִי ◌ֱ ◌ֹ ◌ֻ ◌ֶ ו ◌ְ ◌ֵ ◌ִ ◌ַ
3. Circle the "u" vowels: ◌ֱ ◌ֻ ו ◌ֹ ◌ֶ ◌ַ ◌ְ ◌ָ ◌ִ ◌ֲ

C. **Focus on the length of the vowels.** Memorize the horizontal rows on the chart on p. 8 before doing this exercise.

1. Circle the long vowels: ◌ְ ◌ֶ ו ◌ַ ◌ֻ ◌ִי ◌ִ ◌ֹ וֹ ◌ָ
2. Circle the medium vowels: ◌ְ ◌ֱ ◌ֹ ◌ֶ ◌ַ ו ◌ֻ ◌ִ ◌ֵ ◌ֲ
3. Circle the short vowels: ◌ֱ ◌ֲ ו ◌ֹ ◌ֶ ◌ְ ◌ַ ◌ָ ◌ִ ◌ֻ
4. Circle the very short vowels: ◌ָ ◌ֱ ◌ֻ ◌ֲ ◌ְ ◌ֶ

Reviewing Previous Lessons

D. Focus on letters with two pronunciations. The following are not Hebrew words, but they sound like English words. Pronounce the Hebrew word, then write the English word that sounds the same.

בַּךְ .5	פּוּל .4	פוּל .3	בֶּט .2	בֶּט .1
פֶּס .10	פֶּס .9	בֶס .8	בֶּס .7	בַּךְ .6

E. Focus on letters that look alike. The following are not Hebrew words, but they sound like English words. Pronounce the Hebrew word, then write the English word that sounds the same.

רֶד .5	רִיד .4	דִיד .3	בֶּס .2	כֶּס .1
כַּר .10	זִיל .9	וִיל .8	תָּל .7	הָל .6
זוֹם .15	פָּצ .14	פֶּע .13	לוֹס .12	לוֹם .11

F. Focus on letters that sound alike. The following are not Hebrew words, but they sound like English words. Pronounce the Hebrew word, then write the English word that sounds the same.

טָל .5	בַּךְ .4	בַּח .3	וֶס .2	בֶּס .1
שֵׁם .10	סֶם .9	קַר .8	כַּר .7	תָּל .6

Putting It All Together

G. The following are not Hebrew words, but they sound like English words. Pronounce the Hebrew word, then write the English word that sounds the same.

קִי .5	שֵׁף .4	בֶּל .3	רֶן .2	גֶּם .1
שִׁי .10	אֶג .9	הֶן .8	שֶׁן .7	נֹת .6
נֶד .15	יְ .14	זוּ .13	ווֹט .12	ר .11
עוֹץ .20	שִׁי .19	ס .18	כֶּק .17	בֶּק .16
שׁוֹל .25	עֶם .24	אֶם .23	לִין .22	וֶת .21
קָץ .30	גֶּט .29	רוּף .28	נִיר .27	נִיד .26

Reading Your Hebrew Bible

H. The following are from Genesis 1 (slightly modified). Read aloud in Hebrew until you can read as quickly as in English.

(Gen 1:1)	בָּרָא אֱלֹהִים אֶת הַשָּׁמַיִם	1.
(Gen 1:4)	אֱלֹהִים אֶת הָאוֹר כִּי טוֹב	2.
(Gen 1:5)	בֹקֶר יוֹם אֶחָד	3.
(Gen 1:11)	הָאָרֶץ דֶּשֶׁא עֵשֶׂב	4.

SYLLABLES, SHEVA, AND STRONG DAGESH

Syllables

3.1 A syllable is a group of letters that are pronounced together in a word. The word "syllable" has three syllables: syl la ble. Just as English has rules governing syllables, so does Hebrew. In Hebrew:

➤ A syllable may not begin with a vowel.

➤ There are two kinds of syllables.

An "open" syllable: consonant + vowel: שָׁ

A "closed" syllable: consonant + vowel + consonant: לַח

Examples:		
שָׁ לַח		שָׁלַח
אָ חוֹת		אָחוֹת
כָּ בֵד		כָּבֵד

➤ The last syllable is usually the accented syllable.

Sheva

3.2 You have learned the three very short vowels ֱ ֲ ֳ . Each of these is made up of a vowel (ֶ ַ ָ) plus ְ which is called "*sheva*." *Sheva* (pronounced *shva*) often occurs alone under a consonant and has two different jobs.

3.3 "Vocal *sheva*" is a very short vowel, pronounced like the first "e" in severe.

← דְּבָרִים   דְּ בָ רִים

3.4 "Silent *sheva*" has no pronunciation and serves to close a syllable.

← מִדְבָּר   מִדְ בָּר

3.5 Telling the difference between vocal *sheva* and silent *sheva* is easy.

13

➤ **One basic rule: "short and silent."**

If a *short* vowel comes before the consonant under which there is a *sheva*, the *sheva* is *silent*.

מְדַבֵּר ← מִדְ בָּר

יַקְטִיל ← יַקְ טִיל

➤ Various applications:

If a *sheva* is under the first consonant of a word, the *sheva* is vocal. (This *sheva* is not preceded by a short vowel.)

דְּבָרִים ← דְּ בָ רִים

If there are two *sheva*s in a row, the first is silent and the second is vocal. (The first is preceded by a short vowel and is silent, the second is not and is vocal.)

יִקְטְלוּ ← יִקְ טְ לוּ

Identify the *sheva*s in the following examples: (answers in footnote[1])

מִלְחָמָה ←

מִזְבְּחוֹת ←

יְדַבֵּר ←

More about Dagesh

3.6   You have learned "weak *dagesh*," which indicates the hard pronunciation of the *begadkefat*s ב, כ, and פ.

3.7   There is also "strong *dagesh*," which looks like weak *dagesh*, but has a different job.

➤ **Strong *dagesh* doubles a consonant**, meaning that there are two consonants present even though only one is written. The word קַטֵּל could be represented in English as *qittail* (*qit tail*), since the strong *dagesh* means that there are two *tet*s (ט). A consonant with strong *dagesh* should be pronounced twice as long, as in the English word mea<u>nn</u>ess.

---

1. Silent, preceded by a short vowel. First is silent, preceded by a short vowel, but second is vocal, not preceded by a short vowel. Vocal, not preceded by a short vowel, since under first consonant of the word.

Telling the Difference between Weak *Dagesh* and Strong *Dagesh*

3.8   If a *dagesh* is in a consonant other than a *begadkefat*, it is strong *dagesh*.

3.9   If a *dagesh* is in a *begadkefat*, it may be weak *dagesh* or strong *dagesh*.

➤ If the sound before the *begadkefat* is a consonant, the *dagesh* is weak.

מִדְבָּר   מִדְ בָּר   ←

Since the sheva is preceded by a short vowel, it is silent and closes the syllable. So the dagesh is preceded by a consonant.

➤ If the sound before the *begadkefat* is a vowel the *dagesh* is strong.

קָדַשׁ   קָדַ שׁ   ←

➤ Identify the dageshes in the following examples: (answers in footnote[2])

מִשְׁפָּט

יְדַבֵּר

מַלְכֵנוּ

> *Guttural Characteristic #1: gutturals (א ה ח ע) and resh (ר) will not have either weak dagesh or strong dagesh.*

Vocabulary

day, time, lifetime	יוֹם	387	God, god	אֵל	450
battle, war	מִלְחָמָה	427	God, gods	אֱלֹהִים	376
king	(מֶלֶךְ) מֶלֶךְ	393	land, earth	(אֶרֶץ) אֶרֶץ	378
kingdom, reign	מַלְכוּת	646	word, matter	דָּבָר	381
city, town	עִיר	397	hand, power	יָד	386

---

2. Weak, follows a consonant. Strong, follows a vowel. Weak, follows a consonant.

Notes:

○ The word אֱלֹהִים is a plural noun. When referring to the one true God, it will be treated as a singular noun; when refering to false gods, it will be treated as a plural.

○ If the accent is on a syllable other than the last, the accented syllable will be indicated by colored type in the vocabulary list only, for example, (אֶרֶץ) אֶרֶץ. Learn the vocabulary with the proper accent.

○ When a word ends in הָ, for example, מִלְחָמָה, the ה is a vowel letter and is silent.

○ Final ךְ usually has a silent *sheva* in it, for example, מֶלֶךְ.

Practice

Focusing on New Material

A. Focus on sheva. Identify each *sheva* as vocal or silent and give the reason.

מִנְחָה	.5	מַקְטִיל	.4	נֶגְדּוֹ	.3	יַקְטִיל	.2	מְדַבֵּר	.1
דְּרָכִים	.10	מִזְבְּחוֹת	.9	דְּבָרִים	.8	בְּרָכָה	.7	כּוֹתְבִים	.6
יְדַבְּרוּ	.15	יְדַבֵּר	.14	סִפְרוֹ	.13	מַלְכוֹ	.12	קָטְלוּ	.11

B. Focus on dagesh. Identify each *dagesh* as weak or strong and give the reason.

מִשְׁתֶּה	.5	נִזְבַּח	.4	אִשָּׁה	.3	קֹדֶשׁ	.2	מְדַבֵּר	.1
חִצִּים	.10	מִזְבְּחוֹת	.9	יִכְתֹּב	.8	עַמִּים	.7	מְדַבֵּר	.6
יְדַבְּרוּ	.15	יְדַבֵּר	.14	נֶגְדּוֹ	.13	מַלְכוֹ	.12	קָטְלוּ	.11

C. Focus on syllables. Divide the following into syllables, pronouncing each word as you go. If there is a strong *dagesh* in a letter, draw a line through that letter.

מִנְחָה	.5	מַקְטִיל	.4	נֶגְדּוֹ	.3	יַקְטִיל	.2	מְדַבָּר	.1
דְּרָכִים	.10	מִזְבְּחוֹת	.9	דְּבָרִים	.8	בְּרָכָה	.7	כּוֹתְבִים	.6
יְדַבְּרוּ	.15	יְדַבֵּר	.14	סִפְרוֹ	.13	עוֹלָמִים	.12	קָטְלוּ	.11

Reviewing Previous Lessons

D. Focus on the class of the vowels.

1. Circle the "a" vowels: ◌ְ ◌ֲ וֹ ◌ֶ ◌ָ יִ ◌ֹ ◌ַ וּ

2. Circle the "i" vowels: יִ ◌ֻ ◌ֵ ◌ֶ ◌ֱ וֹ ◌ָ ◌ֹ ◌ַ

3. Circle the "u" vowels: וּ ◌ֻ ◌ְ ◌ֹ ◌ֵ ◌ֻ ◌ֶ ◌ְ ◌ֱ

E. Focus on the length of the vowels.

1. Circle the long vowels: ◌ֵ וֹ ◌ֻ ◌ָ יִ ◌ֶ ◌ַ וּ ◌ָ ◌ֹ

2. Circle the medium vowels: ◌ְ ◌ֵ ◌ֱ ◌ֹ ◌ַ וּ ◌ֶ ◌ֻ ◌ְ

3. Circle the short vowels: ◌ֶ ◌ְ וּ ◌ֹ ◌ֱ ◌ָ ◌ֵ ◌ֲ ◌ַ

4. Circle the very short vowels: ◌ָ ◌ְ ◌ֲ ◌ֱ ◌ֳ ◌ְ ◌ַ ◌ֶ

Putting It All Together

F. The following are not Hebrew words, but they sound like English words. Pronounce the Hebrew word, then write the English word that sounds the same.

5. קִי	4. לֵץ	3. דָּל	2. גֵּת	1. שֶׁן
10. שִׁי	9. וְשָׁתָה	8. טַרְגֶּת	7. קוֹץ	6. רוּת
15. נֶד	14. לֶתֶר	13. זִירוֹ	12. הִשְׁתּוֹרִי	11. סִיל

Reading Your Hebrew Bible

G. The following is the vocalized text of Gen 1:1–3. Read and reread the text out loud, until you can read it as fast as in English.

1. בְּרֵאשִׁית בָּרָא אֱלֹהִים אֵת הַשָּׁמַיִם וְאֵת הָאָרֶץ

2. וְהָאָרֶץ הָיְתָה תֹהוּ וָבֹהוּ וְחֹשֶׁךְ עַל פְּנֵי תְהוֹם

וְרוּחַ[3] אֱלֹהִים מְרַחֶפֶת עַל פְּנֵי הַמָּיִם

3. וַיֹּאמֶר אֱלֹהִים יְהִי אוֹר וַיְהִי אוֹר

---

3. The *patach* (◌ַ) under the *chet* (ח) in רוּחַ is not a full vowel but is a slight "a" (as in *father*) sound that makes it easier to pronounce a final *chet* (ח) or *ayin* (ע) and is called "furtive *patach*." Furtive *patach* is pronounced before the final *chet* (ח) or *ayin* (ע), is not accented, and is printed slightly to the right to distinguish it from *patach*.

THE NOUN: BASIC FORMS

Gender of Nouns

4.1 A few English nouns show a difference between the masculine and the feminine, e.g., *host/hostess* and *waiter/waitress*.

4.2 All Hebrew nouns are either masculine or feminine.

4.3 Sometimes the thing referred to by the noun is masculine, sometimes feminine:

➤ סוּס is a masculine noun meaning "horse."

➤ סוּסָה is a feminine noun meaning "mare."

4.4 Sometimes the thing referred to has nothing to do with male or female:

➤ דָּבָר is a masculine noun meaning "word."

➤ מִלְחָמָה is a feminine noun meaning "battle."

Masculine Singular Nouns

4.5 Masculine singular nouns are usually "unmarked," i.e, there is no special ending to mark the noun as masculine.

➤ סוּס ('horse') is masculine singular, having no special ending.

➤ דָּבָר ('word') is masculine singular, having no special ending.

> *Masculine is abbreviated m, and singular is abbreviated s;* סוּס *is a ms noun.*

Feminine Singular Nouns

4.6 Feminine singular nouns are usually "marked," i.e, there is a special ending to mark the noun as feminine.

4.7 The most common feminine ending is the הָ ending (the ה is a vowel letter):

➤ סוּסָה (mare) is feminine singular, marked by the הָ ending.

➤ מִלְחָמָה (battle) is feminine singular, marked by the הָ ending.

4.8   Another feminine ending is ת, preceded by various vowels:

➤ בַּת (daughter) is feminine singular, marked by the ת ending.

➤ מַלְכוּת (kingdom) is feminine singular, marked by the ת ending.

> *Feminine is abbreviated f;* סוּסָה *is a fs noun.*

Irregular Singular Nouns

4.9   Some unmarked nouns are actually feminine.

➤ אֶרֶץ (earth) is feminine singular but unmarked.

➤ עִיר (city) is feminine singular but unmarked.

4.10   The true gender of such nouns will often be indicated by context and will be identified in the vocabulary lists.

4.11   Parts of the body that occur in pairs look masculine but are feminine.

hand   יָד

4.12   Here are the nouns learned to this point that look masculine but are feminine:

mother	אֵם
land, earth	אֶרֶץ
hand	יָד
city, town	עִיר

Number of Nouns

4.13   English has a singular and a plural, usually marked by adding -s or -es, e.g., *boy/boys* and *flash/flashes.*

4.14   Hebrew has a singular, a plural, and also a dual.

Masculine Plural Nouns

4.15   Masculine plural nouns are usually marked by the ִים ending.

סוּסִים	סוּס
horses	horse
אֵלִים	אֵל
gods	god

> *Plural is abbreviated p;* סוּסִים *is a mp noun.*

Feminine Plural Nouns

4.16   Feminine plural nouns are usually marked by the וֹת ending.

סוּסוֹת	סוּסָה
mares	mare
מִלְחָמוֹת	מִלְחָמָה
battles	battle

Irregular Plural Nouns

4.17   Some masculine plural nouns look feminine.

אָבוֹת	אָב
fathers	father

4.18   Some feminine plural nouns look masculine.

עָרִים	עִיר
cities	city

➤   *Note that the vowel in the plural of עִיר is different from the vowel in the singular. Vowel changes will be discussed in Lesson 8.*

4.19   The true gender of such nouns will often be indicated by context and will be indicated in the vocabulary.

4.20   Here are the nouns learned thus far that appear to be one gender in the plural but are the other gender.

mp	אָבוֹת	אָב
fp	עָרִים	עִיר

Dual Nouns

4.21   The dual is used to refer to two things, not one or three.

4.22   Nouns in the dual are marked by the ◻ַיִם ending.

4.23   The use of the dual is mostly limited

➤   To nouns that come in natural pairs:

יָדַיִם	יָד
two hands	hand

➤   To certain expressions of time:

יוֹמַיִם	יוֹם
two days	day

Dual is abbreviated d; יוֹמַיִם *is a md noun.*

Summary of Basic Noun Forms

	Plural	Singular
Masculine	סוּסִים	סוּס
Feminine	סוּסוֹת	סוּסָה

Vocabulary

they *m*	הֵם / הֵמָּה (הֵמָּה)	865	he, it	הוּא	860
they *f*	הֵנָּה (הֵנָּה)	866	she, it	הִיא	861
you *mp*	אַתֶּם	863	you *ms*	אַתָּה	858
you *fp*	אַתֵּן / אַתֵּנָה (אַתֵּנָה)	864	you *fs*	אַתְּ	859
we	אֲנַחְנוּ (אֲנַחְנוּ)	862	I	אֲנִי / אָנֹכִי	857

Notes:

○ A *sheva* (ְ) under a final ת is silent, as in אַתְּ.

○ The *fp* forms אַתֵּן / אַתֵּנָה occur only 4 times and 1 time, respectively.

Practice

Focusing on New Material

A. Focus on gender. Read the following Hebrew words; circle the masculine words and underline the feminine words.

1. אֵלִים מֶלֶךְ דָּבָר יוֹם מַלְכוּת אָב בַּת בֵּן מִלְחָמוֹת

2. מִדְבָּר מִנְחָה סֵפֶר דַּלִּים טוֹבוֹת שָׁלוֹם אֱמֶת עַמִּים

B. Focus on number. Read the Following Hebrew words; circle the singular words, underline the plural words, and draw a box around the dual words.

1. אֵלִים יָדַיִם דָּבָר אֱלֹהִים מַלְכוּת אָבוֹת בַּת בֵּן מִלְחָמוֹת

2. מִזְבְּחוֹת עוֹלָמִים עֵינַיִם מִשְׁפַּחַת אֲרָצוֹת אֱמֶת טוֹבִים

C. Focus on number and gender. Read the following Hebrew words and circle the word that is out of place in terms of number or gender.

2. אֵלִים סוּסוֹת טוֹבִים   1. יוֹם מֶלֶךְ מַלְכוּת

4. בַּת אָב אֵם   3. סוּס דָּבָר אֵלִים

6. אֶרֶץ מֶלֶךְ דֶּרֶךְ   5. יָדַיִם מַיִם יָמִים

Reviewing Previous Lessons

D. Focus on *sheva*. Identify each *sheva* as vocal or silent, and give the reason.

5. מַלְכוּת   4. תִּשְׁמַע   3. אֶכְתְּבָה   2. מִלְחָמָה   1. מְדַבֵּר

E. Focus on *dagesh*. Identify each *dagesh* as weak or strong, and give the reason.

5. מִשְׁפָּט   4. קָטֵל   3. אֶכְתְּבָה   2. אִשָּׁה   1. מְדַבֵּר

F. Focus on pronunciation. Read the following English words, written in Hebrew.

5. בֶּתֶר   4. אַלְשׁוֹ   3. סְרִיר   2. גַּרְדֶּן   1. מוּן

Putting It All Together

G. Focus on meaning. Circle the word that does not belong in terms of meaning.

2. אֵל אֵם אֱלֹהִים   1. יוֹם מֶלֶךְ מַלְכוּת

4. בַּת אָב עִיר   3. יָד אָח אָחוֹת

6. אָכַל מֶלֶךְ מִלְחָמָה   5. בֵּן אֶרֶץ בַּת

Reading Your Hebrew Bible

H. The following is Gen 1:1-3.

1. בְּרֵאשִׁית בָּרָא אֱלֹהִים אֵת הַשָּׁמַיִם וְאֵת הָאָרֶץ

2. וְהָאָרֶץ הָיְתָה תֹהוּ וָבֹהוּ וְחֹשֶׁךְ עַל פְּנֵי תְהוֹם

וְרוּחַ אֱלֹהִים מְרַחֶפֶת עַל פְּנֵי הַמָּיִם

3. וַיֹּאמֶר אֱלֹהִים יְהִי אוֹר וַיְהִי אוֹר

1. Read the text out loud and circle all nouns marked as plural or dual.

2. Read the text out loud and underline all words that have a *begad-kefat* letter.

3. Read the text and draw a box around all words *without* a guttural or *resh*.

5

PRONOUNS AND THE DEFINITE ARTICLE

Personal Pronouns

5.1   In the vocabulary of Lesson 4 you learned the Hebrew personal pronouns: הוּא, הִיא, אַתָּה, etc.

Forms of the Personal Pronouns

they *m*	הֵם / הֵמָּה		he, it	הוּא
they *f*	הֵנָּה		she, it	הִיא
you *mp*	אַתֶּם		you *ms*	אַתָּה
you *fp*	אַתֵּן / אַתֵּנָה		you *fs*	אַתְּ
we	אֲנַחְנוּ		I	אֲנִי / אָנֹכִי

Use of the Personal Pronouns

5.2   These personal pronouns are used only as the subject of a sentence, as in the English sentence, "I am a father." This type of sentence uses a verb in English, "am," but not in Hebrew.

   "I am a father."   אֲנִי אָב

5.3   The subject (the part of the sentence about which something is said) is אֲנִי and the predicate (the part of the sentence telling something about the subject) is אָב.

5.4   The word order in Hebrew is variable.

   "I am a father."   אָב אֲנִי

   "She is a mother."   הִיא אֵם

   "You are a son."   בֵּן אַתָּה

24

5.5 The subject agrees with the predicate in number and gender; for example, if the predicate is *fs*, the subject is *fs*; or if the predicate is *mp*, the subject is *mp*.

"You are a daughter."	בַּת אַתְּ
"They are gods."	הֵם אֵלִים

Definite Article

Basic Form

5.6 Hebrew does not have an indefinite article, as does English: "a car" or "an apple." So אָח can be translated "brother" or "a brother," depending on the context.

5.7 The Hebrew definite article is not a separate word, as is the English definite article, "the."

5.8 The Hebrew definite article is always attached to the beginning of a word, and is made up of three parts: (1) ה, (2) a *patach* (◻) under the ה, and (3) a strong *dagesh* in the first letter of the word.

"the horse"	הַסּוּס
"the word"	הַדָּבָר
"the king"	הַמֶּלֶךְ

Definite Article and Gutturals + Resh

5.9 When the gutturals + *resh* were introduced, you learned that these letters have several special characteristics. Guttural characteristic #1 (see p. 15) is that gutturals never have *dagesh*. So the form of the definite article will be slightly different on words beginning with a guttural or *resh*.

➤ On nouns beginning with ה and ח, the article is הַ with no strong *dagesh*—that is, no doubling of the first consonant. These words are treated "as if" the first letter is doubled; this is called "virtual doubling."

"the splendor"	הַהוֹד
"the arrow"	הַחֵץ

➤ On nouns beginning with א, ע, and ר, the article is הָ. To "make up for" the lack of doubling in the first letter, the short vowel ◻ is lengthened to the medium vowel ◻ָ; this is called "compensatory lengthening."

"the father"	הָאָב
"the city"	הָעִיר
"the chariot"	הָרֶכֶב

➤ On nouns beginning with הָ, חָ, and עָ the article is usually הֶ.

"the wrong"	הֶחָמָס
"the mountains"	הֶהָרִים
"the clouds"	הֶעָבִים

Vocabulary

priest	כֹּהֵן	388	man, Adam	אָדָם	371
he walked, went	הָלַךְ	6	man, husband	אִישׁ	375
he took, seized	לָקַח	11	woman, wife	אִשָּׁה	412
he gave, presented	נָתַן	14	house, temple	בַּיִת (בֵּית)	379
he heard	שָׁמַע	26	way, road	דֶּרֶךְ (דֶּרֶךְ)	382

Notes:

○ The plural of אִישׁ is אֲנָשִׁים.

○ The plural of אִשָּׁה is נָשִׁים.

○ שָׁמַע also means "obey."

Practice

Focusing on New Material

A. Focus on the personal pronoun. Translate the following Hebrew sentences.

3. אָב אֲנִי	2. אַתָּה אָב	1. הוּא אָב
6. אֵם אָנֹכִי	5. אַתְּ אֵם	4. אֵם הִיא
9. סוּסוֹת הֵנָּה	8. הֵם סוּסִים	7. הוּא סוּס
12. אֲנַחְנוּ אֵלִים	11. אֵלִים אַתֶּם	10. אַתָּה אֵל

B. Focus on the definite article. Translate the following Hebrew words, paying attention to the presence or absence of the definite article.

1. יוֹם   2. הַיּוֹם   3. אֱלֹהִים   4. הָאֱלֹהִים   5. הַבַּת

6. בַּת   7. הַמֶּלֶךְ   8. מֶלֶךְ   9. יָד   10. הַיָּד

11. אָחוֹת   12. עִיר   13. הָעִיר   14. הַדָּבָר   15. דָּבָר

Reviewing Previous Lessons

C. Focus on letters that sound alike. Circle the letters that sound alike.

1. ב כ ו   2. ס שׁ שׂ   3. ט ת ה   4. כ כ ק   5. צ ח כ

D. Focus on gutturals and *resh*. Circle the gutturals or *resh*.

1. ד ר ךְ   2. ע צ ט   3. ה ת ב   4. מ א ג   5. ל ח ו

E. Focus on gender and number. Identify the gender and number of the following.

1. אָח   2. בַּת   3. סוּסוֹת   4. אֵלִים   5. אֶרֶץ

Putting It All Together

F. Translate the following.

1. אָנֹכִי אָב   2. הָאָב אָנֹכִי   3. אַתָּה הַמֶּלֶךְ

4. הַמִּלְחָמָה הִיא   5. הֵנָּה סוּסוֹת   6. זָכַר

7. הִיא הָאָרֶץ   8. הַבַּת אַתְּ   9. שָׁלַח

10. אֵלִים אַתֶּם   11. נָתַן   12. כָּבֵד

Reading Your Hebrew Bible

G. The following is 2 Samuel 7:1-2.

1. וַיְהִי כִּי יָשַׁב הַמֶּלֶךְ בְּבֵיתוֹ

וַיהוָה[1] הֵנִיחַ לוֹ מִסָּבִיב מִכָּל אֹיְבָיו

---

1. The letters יהוה are the Lord's covenantal name, often translated LORD, in contrast to Lord, and are referred to as the Tetragrammaton, "four letters." According to Jewish tradition, which wishes to revere the divine name, the Tetragrammaton should not be pronounced. The edition of the Hebrew Bible you are

.2   וַיֹּאמֶר הַמֶּלֶךְ אֶל נָתָן הַנָּבִיא

רְאֵה נָא אָנֹכִי יוֹשֵׁב בְּבֵית אֲרָזִים

וַאֲרוֹן הָאֱלֹהִים יֹשֵׁב בְּתוֹךְ הַיְרִיעָה²

1. Read the text out loud and focus on pronunciation.

2. Read the text out loud and circle all words you know.

3. Read the text out loud and underline all words with the definite article.

4. Can you find the name "Nathan"? Draw a box around it.

---

reading places one or more of the vowels from אֲדֹנָי, "my lord," on the Tetra-grammaton. So when you come to the Tetragrammaton, you are to say "Adonai."

2. When the definite article is added to a word beginning with יְ the strong *dagesh* is not added.

6

THE VERB:
QAL PERFECT

Overview of the Hebrew Verb

6.1 The material in this section provides you with an overview of the Hebrew verb. You need to be able to understand and to use properly the following terms: *root*, *pattern*, *conjugation*, *paradigm*, and *parse*.

Root

6.2 The basic building block of a Hebrew word is the "root." A *root* is the core consonants of a word, usually three consonants, minus the vowels and consonantal prefixes or suffixes. Common consonantal prefixes for nouns are מ and ת. Roots are indicated by writing the consonants without vowels, prefixes, and suffixes; for example, the root of מֶלֶךְ ("king") and מַלְכוּת ("kingdom") is מלך.

6.3 As is the case in the previous example, words from the same root usually have related meanings. Adding elements to the root—various vowels or consonantal prefixes or suffixes, for example, וּת in מַלְכוּת—alters the meaning. Endings for gender and number, being suffixes, are never part of the root.

Example #1	Root	זרע	
	Verb	זָרַע	"he sowed"
	Noun	זֶרַע	"seed"
	Noun	מִזְרָע	"sown land"

Example #2	Root	ספר	
	Verb	סָפַר	"he counted"
	Noun	סֵפֶר	"document"
	Noun	מִסְפָּר	"number"

Pattern

6.4   There are seven basic verb "patterns" in Hebrew.[1] A pattern is the root plus the characteristic added elements. The pattern you will learn in this lesson is the *qal* (from the Hebrew word קַל meaning "light" or "simple"), and the *qal* is the simple active pattern.[2] Another pattern, for example, is the *niphal*, which is formed by prefixing a נ to the root and is used for the passive of the *qal*, among other uses.

6.5   Changing from one pattern to another **changes the meaning** of the verb.

Example #1	Root	זרע	
	Qal	זָרַע	"he sowed"
	Niphal	נִזְרַע	"it was sown"

Example #2	Root	ספר	
	Qal	סָפַר	"he counted"
	Niphal	נִסְפַּר	"he was counted"

Conjugations

6.6   There are two types of conjugations for Hebrew verbs: "finite" and "non-finite."

➤ Finite conjugations are conjugated for person, gender, and number; for example, זָרַע is 3rd person, masculine, and singular. There are three basic finite conjugations in Hebrew: *perfect*, *imperfect*, and *imperative*. You are learning one of the finite conjugations in this lesson: the *perfect*.

➤ Non-finite conjugations are not conjugated for person but are conjugated either for gender and number only or not at all. There are three non-finite conjugations in Hebrew: *participle*, *infinitive absolute*, and *infinitive construct*.

6.7   Changing from one conjugation to another **changes the use, that is, the time of or the kind of situation** expressed by the verb; for example, in the *perfect*, סָפַר could be translated "he counted," but translated "he will count" in the imperfect.

---

1. The four primary patterns make up 97% of all verbs in the Hebrew Bible; B. W. Waltke and M. O'Connor, *An Introduction to Biblical Hebrew Syntax* (Winona Lake, Ind.: Eisenbrauns, 1990; hereafter: *IBHS*) §21.2.3e.
2. The *qal* makes up 69% of the verbs in the Hebrew Bible; *IBHS* §21.2.3e.

Paradigm

6.8   A verb "paradigm" is a chart showing verb forms for person, gender, and number. A paradigm of the English verb "to be" would include "I am," "you are," "he/she is," and so on. English paradigms move from the 1st person ("I am") through the 3rd person ("he/she is"). Hebrew paradigms move from the 3rd person through the 1st person. This is because the *3ms* (3rd person masculine singular) is the base form from which the others are derived. In the vocabulary and in Hebrew dictionaries, most verbs are listed according to the *3ms* form. In this grammar, the root used for the paradigms of the regular verb in Hebrew is קטל.

Parsing

6.9   "Parsing" is identifying the elements of a verb. The order for parsing Hebrew verbs is: (1) pattern, (2) conjugation, (3) person, (4) gender, (5) number, and (6) root; for example:

Verb	Pattern	Conj.	Person	Gender	Number	Root
1. הָלַךְ	qal	perfect	3	m	s	הלך

Qal Perfect

Form of the Qal Perfect

6.10   Memorize the following verb paradigm well enough to write it out in Hebrew.

	Verb	Pronoun	
קָטַל	קָטַל		*3ms*
קָטְלָה	קָטְלָה		*3fs*
קָטַלְתָּ	קָטַלְתָּ	אַתָּה	*2ms*
קָטַלְתְּ	קָטַלְתְּ	אַתְּ	*2fs*
קָטַלְתִּי	קָטַלְתִּי	אֲנִי / אָנֹכִי	*1cs*

קָטְלוּ	קָטְלוּ		*3cp*
קְטַלְתֶּם	קְטַלְתֶּם	אַתֶּם	*2mp*
קְטַלְתֶּן	קְטַלְתֶּן	אַתֵּן / אַתֵּנָה	*2fp*
קָטַלְנוּ	קָטַלְנוּ	אֲנַחְנוּ	*1cp*

> The abbreviation *c* stands for "common," that is, a form used in common for both masculine and feminine. The perfect conjugation is abbreviated *pf*.

6.11 The base form of the qal *pf* is the 3*ms* form: קָטַל. The other forms are made by adding suffixes to the 3*ms* form. To highlight the suffixes, they are printed in color. The suffixes are related to the personal pronouns, except in the 3rd person forms.

6.12 In the 2*mp* and 2*fp* forms, the vowel under the first consonant is reduced from the medium vowel *qamets* (◌ָ) to *sheva* (◌ְ), because medium vowels are not allowed in open syllables that are two or more syllables before the accent.

6.13 In the 3*fs* and 3*cp* forms, the theme vowel (see 6.15) reduces to *sheva* (◌ְ).

6.14 The accent is on the next to the last syllable in the following forms: קָטַלְתָּ, קָטַלְתְּ, קָטַלְתִּי, and קָטַלְנוּ. Memorize these forms with the accent.

6.15 There are two types of perfect verbs in the Qal: "action" and "stative." Whether a given verb is action or stative will often be indicated by the vowel under the second consonant, called the "theme vowel." The theme vowel of action verbs is *patach* (◌ַ). The theme vowel of stative verbs is most often *tsere* (◌ֵ), but sometimes *cholem* (◌ֹ). *Tsere* (◌ֵ) as a theme vowel will usually occur only in the 3*ms* form; in the other forms *patach* (◌ַ) will occur; for example: כָּבֵד, but כָּבַדְנוּ.

Use of the Qal Perfect

6.16 The perfect conjugation is used in a variety of ways. Only two uses are introduced at this point: "definite perfect" and "stative perfect."

➤ The **definite perfect**,[3] a use of action verbs, expresses **complete action in the past** and is best translated into English with a simple past tense.

"he ate"	אָכַל
"he walked"	הָלַךְ
"he sent"	שָׁלַח

---

3. *IBHS*, §30.5.1b.

➤ The **stative perfect**, a use of stative verbs, expresses a "**state of being**"; for example, "he is old," and "she is young," and is best translated into English with a present tense. [4]

"he is heavy"   כָּבֵד

➤ The use of the perfect will be the same in all the patterns, with the exception of the stative perfect, which is a use found only in the *qal*.

6.17   Remember: changing from one **pattern** to another changes the **meaning** of the verb, but changing from one *conjugation* to another changes the *use* of the verb, that is, the *time of or kind of situation* expressed by the verb.

Vocabulary

forever, antiquity	עוֹלָם	432	garment, clothing	בֶּגֶד (בֶּגֶד)	455
trust	בָּטַח	67	clan, family	מִשְׁפָּחָה	474
write	כָּתַב	45	prophet	נָבִיא	430
guard, observe, watch	שָׁמַר	61	boy	נַעַר (נַעַר)	477
judge, decide, punish	שָׁפַט	62	soul, self *f*	נֶפֶשׁ (נֶפֶשׁ)	394

Notes:

○ The plural of נֶפֶשׁ is נְפָשׁוֹת.

○ The English equivalent of Hebrew verbs from this lesson on will not be a literal rendering of the 3*ms* form, as has been the case in lessons 1–5, but will be a neutral rendering without reference to person, gender, or number.

Practice

Focusing on New Material

A. Focus on roots. Write the Hebrew root of the following.

5. דֶּרֶךְ   4. דָּבָר   3. אֶרֶץ   2. אָכַל   1. אָדָם

10. שָׁלַח   9. מִלְחָמָה   8. מִשְׁפָּחָה   7. מַלְכוּת   6. מֶלֶךְ

---

4. The stative pf is best translated with a present tense in discourse and a past tense in narrative.

B. Parse the following.

	Verb	Pattern	Conj.	Person	Gender	Number	Root
1.	שָׁלַח						
2.	לְקָחָה						
3.	הָלַכְתָּ						
4.	זְכַרְתֶּם						
5.	שָׁמַעְנוּ						
6.	כָּתַבְתִּי						
7.	בְּטַחְתֶּן						
8.	אָכְלוּ						
9.	קָטַלְתְּ						
10.	קָטַל						

C. Focus on meaning. Cover the left column with a card and translate
the Hebrew in the right column; then slide the card down one line to
verify that your translation is correct.

		1.	לָקַח
1. He took.		2.	לָקְחוּ
2. They took.		3.	לָקַחְתִּי
3. I took.		4.	לָקַחְנוּ
4. We took		5.	לְקַחְתֶּם
5. You (*mp*) took.		6.	לָקַחְתָּ
6. You (*ms*) took.		7.	לָקְחָה
7. She took.		8.	שָׁמְעָה
8. She heard.		9.	זָכְרָה
9. She remembered.		10.	הָלַכְתָּ
10. You (*fs*) walked.		11.	הָלַכְתִּי
11. I walked.		12.	כָּבְדוּ
12. They are heavy.		13.	שָׁלְחָה
13. She sent.		14.	שָׁמַעְנוּ
14. We heard.		15.	אָכַלְתָּ
15. You (*ms*) ate.		16.	זְכַרְתֶּם

16. You (*mp*) remembered.	17.	זְכַרְתֶּן
17. You (*fp*) remembered.	18.	זָכַרְתִּי
18. I remembered.	19.	נָתַן
19. He gave.	20.	כָּבַדְנוּ
20. We are heavy.		

Reviewing Previous Lessons

D. Focus on the personal pronoun. Translate the following Hebrew sentences.

	1.	כֹּהֵן אֲנִי
1. I am a priest.	2.	כֹּהֵן הוּא
2. He is a priest	3.	כֹּהֵן אַתָּה
3. You (*ms*) are a priest.	4.	אֵם הִיא
4. She is a mother.	5.	אֵם אַתְּ
5. You (*fs*) are a mother.	6.	אֲנָשִׁים הֵם
6. They (*mp*) are men.	7.	אֲנָשִׁים אֲנַחְנוּ
7. We are men.	8.	אֲנָשִׁים אַתֶּם
8. You (*mp*) are men.	9.	נָשִׁים אַתֶּן
9. You (*fp*) are women.	10.	נָשִׁים הֵנָּה
10. They (*fp*) are women.		

Reading Your Hebrew Bible

E. The following is Psalm 1:1.

אַשְׁרֵי הָאִישׁ אֲשֶׁר

לֹא הָלַךְ בַּעֲצַת רְשָׁעִים

וּבְדֶרֶךְ חַטָּאִים לֹא עָמָד

וּבְמוֹשַׁב לֵצִים לֹא יָשָׁב

1. Read the text out loud, focusing on pronunciation.

2. Read the text out loud and circle all *qal* pf verbs.

3. Read the text out loud and underline all *mp* nouns.

4. Read the text out loud and draw a box around all nouns with the definite article.

SENTENCES
WITH VERBS

Subject

7.1 The subject may be **specified by the form of the verb alone**. In Hebrew, שָׁלַחְתִּי is a complete sentence, "I sent." The subject, "I," is indicated by the suffix, תִּי.

7.2 The subject may be **specified by the addition of a personal pronoun**. When a pronoun is added, emphasis is being placed on the subject. The sentence אֲנִי שָׁלַחְתִּי means "I (not you or anybody else) sent."

7.3 The subject may be **specified by a noun**, when the verb is 3rd person.

"A father sent."	אָב שָׁלַח
"A mother sent."	אֵם שָׁלְחָה
"Men sent."	אֲנָשִׁים שָׁלְחוּ

7.4 As the previous examples show, the verb and subject—whether a pronoun or a noun—must agree in person, gender, and number.

Direct Object

7.5 The direct object is the **object** (person or thing) affected **directly** by the action of the verb. In "he threw a ball," the direct object is "a ball."

"He sent a horse."	שָׁלַח סוּס
"He sent a garment."	שָׁלַח בֶּגֶד

7.6 There are two kinds of direct objects in Hebrew: "indefinite" and "definite."

➤ The two previous examples are of the **indefinite direct object**, an object that is not definite.

➤ When there is a **definite direct object**, the word אֶת is placed before the object. The word אֶת is not translated but simply indicates the presence of a definite direct object. The direct object marker אֶת will occur in two forms. About 10% of the time, the form is אֵת. About 90% of the time, the form is אֶת־. The bar at the top left of the word is called *maqqef* and functions somewhat like a hyphen in English.

"He sent the horse."   שָׁלַח אֶת הַסּוּס

"He sent the garment."   שָׁלַח אֶת־הַבֶּגֶד

Word Order

7.7   Typical word order in Hebrew is: (1) verb, (2) subject, and (3) direct object.

שָׁלַח הָאָב אֶת־הַסּוּס

"The father sent the horse."

שָׁלְחָה הָאֵם אֶת־הַבֶּגֶד

"The mother sent the garment."

7.8   When the subject or direct object is placed before the verb, emphasis is being placed on that subject or direct object.

הָאָב שָׁלַח אֶת־הַסּוּס

"The father (not the mother) sent the horse."

אֶת־הַסּוּס שָׁלַח הָאָב

"The father sent the horse (not the garment)."

Negative Sentences

7.9   Sentences such as the examples in this chapter are made negative by the word לֹא. Any element of the sentence may be negated, and לֹא will be placed immediately before the negated element.

לֹא שָׁלַח הָאָב אֶת־הַסּוּס

"The father did not **send** the horse (he **kept** the horse)."

לֹא הָאָב שָׁלַח אֶת־הַסּוּס

"The **father** did not send the horse (the **mother** did)."

לֹא אֶת־הַסּוּס שָׁלַח הָאָב

"The father did not send the **horse** (he sent the **garment**)."

7.10   Though the English translation is the same in each case, the Hebrew sentences are logically different, as can be seen from the element of contrast within the parentheses.

Vocabulary

name, reputation	שֵׁם	404	sacrifice	זֶבַח (זֶבַח)	496
seek, inquire	דָּרַשׁ	74	heart, mind	לֵב / לֵבָב	390
sacrifice, slaughter	זָבַח	77	altar	מִזְבֵּחַ	426
know, care about	יָדַע	7	judgment, decision	מִשְׁפָּט	429
sit, dwell, inhabit	יָשַׁב	10	people	עַם	398

Notes:

○ The plurals of לֵב and לֵבָב are לִבּוֹת and לְבָבוֹת respectively.

○ For *patach* (◻) under the *chet* (ח) in מִזְבֵּחַ, see p. 17 n. 3.

○ The plural of מִזְבֵּחַ (ms) is מִזְבְּחוֹת.

Practice

Focusing On New Material

A. Focus on the subject. Translate the following Hebrew sentences.

	1.	זָכַר
1. He remembered.	2.	זָכַר הָאִישׁ
2. The man remembered.	3.	אֲנִי זָכַרְתִּי
3. I remembered.	4.	זָכְרָה
4. She remembered.	5.	זָכְרָה הָאִשָּׁה
5. The woman remembered.	6.	זְכַרְתֶּם
6. You (mp) remembered.	7.	זָכְרוּ הָאֲנָשִׁים
7. The men remembered.	8.	זָכְרוּ הַנָּשִׁים
8. The women remembered.	9.	בָּטַח הַבֵּן
9. The son trusted.	10.	בָּטְחָה הַבַּת
10. The daughter trusted.	11.	אַתָּה בָּטַחְתָּ
11. You (ms) trusted.	12.	אַתֵּן בְּטַחְתֶּן
12. You (fp) trusted.	13.	בָּטַחְנוּ
13. We trusted.	14.	הָלַךְ הַנָּבִיא

14. The prophet walked.	15.	הֵם הָלְכוּ
15. They walked.		

B. Focus on the direct object. Translate the following Hebrew sentences, paying attention to the indefinite direct object and the definite direct object.

	1.	לָקַח סוּס
1. He took a horse.	2.	לָקַח אֶת הַסּוּס
2. He took the horse.	3.	לָקַח אֶת־הַסּוּס
3. He took the horse.	4.	שָׁלַח אֶת־הַנַּעַר
4. He sent the boy.	5.	שָׁלַח אֶת־הַכֹּהֵן
5. He sent the priest.	6.	שָׁמַע דָּבָר
6. He heard a word.	7.	שָׁמַע אֶת הַדָּבָר
7. He heard the word.	8.	שָׁמַע אֶת־הַמֶּלֶךְ
8. He heard the king.		

C. Focus on word order. Translate the following Hebrew sentences, paying attention to the element in the sentence being emphasized.

	1.	שָׁלַח הַמֶּלֶךְ אֶת־הַנָּבִיא
1. The king sent the prophet.	2.	הַמֶּלֶךְ שָׁלַח אֶת־הַנָּבִיא
2. The king (not the priest) sent the prophet.	3.	אֶת־הַנָּבִיא שָׁלַח הַמֶּלֶךְ
3. The king sent the prophet (not the priest).	4.	אֲנִי שָׁמַרְתִּי אֶת־הָאָרֶץ
4. I (not anyone else) guarded the land.	5.	אֶת־הָאָרֶץ שָׁמַרְנוּ
5. We guarded the land (not the city).	6.	שְׁמַרְתֶּם אֶת הָעִיר
6. You (*mp*) guarded the city.	7.	הַכֹּהֵן שָׁפַט אֶת־הַמִּשְׁפָּחָה
7. The priest (not the king) judged the family.	8.	אֶת־הַמִּשְׁפָּחָה שָׁפַט הַכֹּהֵן
8. The priest judged the family (not the nation).		

D. Focus on the negative. Translate the following Hebrew sentences, paying attention to the element that is negated.

	1.	נָתַן הַנַּעַר אֶת־הַבֶּגֶד
1. The boy gave the garment.	2.	לֹא נָתַן הַנַּעַר אֶת־הַבֶּגֶד
2. The boy did not give the garment (he kept it).	3.	לֹא הַנַּעַר נָתַן אֶת־הַבֶּגֶד
3. The boy did not give the garment (the girl did).	4.	לֹא אֶת־הַבֶּגֶד נָתַן הַנַּעַר
4. The boy did not give the garment (he gave the shoes).		

Reviewing Previous Lessons

E. Focus on parsing. Parse the following Hebrew verbs.

	Verb	Pattern	Conj.	Person	Gender	Number	Root
1.	נָתְנָה						
2.	כָּתְבוּ						
3.	שְׁמַרְתֶּם						
4.	שָׁפַטְנוּ						
5.	אָכַלְתָּ						
6.	זָכַרְתִּי						
7.	כָּבֵד						

F. Focus on the class of the vowels. Review the vertical columns on the chart on p. 8 before doing this exercise.

1. Circle the "a" vowels: ◌ֱ ◌ַ וֹ ◌ָ ◌ֵ ◌ִי ◌ֵ ◌ֹ וּ ◌ֲ
2. Circle the "i" vowels: ◌ִי ◌ֵ ◌ַ ◌ֶ ◌ַ וּ ◌ֵ ◌ֵ ◌ֶ ◌ְ
3. Circle the "u" vowels: ◌ְ ◌ֻ וֹ ◌ֹ ◌ֻ ◌ֻ ◌ֻ ◌ַ ◌ֶ

G. Focus on the length of the vowels. Review the horizontal rows on the chart on p. 8 before doing this exercise.

1. Circle the long vowels: ◌ֵ ◌ָ וּ ◌ֵ ◌ֶ ◌ִי ◌ֶ ◌ֹ וֹ ◌ָ
2. Circle the medium vowels: ◌ַ ◌ֲ ◌ֹ ◌ֹ ◌ֻ וֹ ◌ֶ ◌ֵ ◌ֻ ◌ְ

3. Circle the short vowels: ◌ָ ◌ֶ ◌ֹ ◌ֻ ◌ַ ◌ֳ ◌ֲ ◌ֱ ◌ֵ

4. Circle the very short vowels: ◌ָ ◌ֲ ◌ֳ ◌ֱ ◌ְ ◌ַ ◌ֵ ◌ִ

Putting It All Together

H. Translate the following Hebrew sentences.

	1.	זָכַר הַמֶּלֶךְ אֶת־הַמַּלְכוּת
1. The king remembered the kingdom.	2.	לָקַחְתִּי נַעַר
2. I took a boy.	3.	הָלְכָה הָאֵם
3. The mother walked.	4.	שָׁלְחוּ הָאֵלִים אֶת הַנָּבִיא
4. The gods sent the prophet.	5.	שָׁמַע כֹּהֵן דָּבָר
5. A priest heard a word.	6.	לְקַחְתֶּם אֶת־הַסּוּסוֹת
6. You (*mp*) took the mares.		

Reading Your Hebrew Bible

I. The following are from Genesis 1:1, 4, 27.

1.   בְּרֵאשִׁית בָּרָא אֱלֹהִים אֵת הַשָּׁמַיִם וְאֵת הָאָרֶץ

4.   וַיַּרְא אֱלֹהִים אֶת־הָאוֹר כִּי־טוֹב

27.   וַיִּבְרָא אֱלֹהִים אֶת־הָאָדָם בְּצַלְמוֹ

1. Read the texts out loud, focusing on pronunciation.

2. Read the texts out loud and underline all definite direct objects.

3. Read the text out loud and circle all of the vocabulary learned to date.

THE NOUN: VOWEL CHANGES

More about Syllables

8.1   In Lesson 3, you learned four characteristics of Hebrew syllables:

➤ A syllable may not begin with a vowel.

➤ There are open syllables, for example, שָׁ, made up of a consonant + a vowel.

➤ There are closed syllables, for example, לַח, made up of a consonant + a vowel + a consonant.

➤ The last syllable is usually the accented syllable.

8.2   Syllables can also be defined in relation to the accent:

➤ A "tonic" syllable is accented.

➤ A "pretonic" syllable is one syllable before the accent.

➤ A "propretonic" syllable is two syllables before the accent.

Tonic	Pretonic	Propretonic	
רִים	בָ	דְּ	דְּבָרִים

More about Vowels

Syllables in Which Various Vowels Occur

8.3   **Long vowels** occur in

➤ an open syllable, for example, *cholem-vav* (וֹ) in עוֹלָם

➤ a closed accented syllable, for example, *cholem-vav* (וֹ) in אָחוֹת

8.4   **Medium vowels** occur in

➤ a pretonic open syllable, for example, the first *qamets* (ָ) in דָּבָר

➤ a closed accented syllable, for example, the second (ָ) in דָּבָר

42

8.5   **Short vowels** occur in

➤ open accented syllables, for example, the first *patach* (◌ַ) in נַעַר (נַֽעַר)

➤ closed syllables, for example, the second *patach* (◌ַ) in נַעַר

> *A closed unaccented syllable usually has a short vowel.*

8.6   **Very short vowels** occur in

➤ open propretonic syllables in nouns and verbs, for example, דְּבָרִים and קְטַלְתֶּם

➤ open pretonic syllables in verbs, for example, קְטְלָה

Vowels That Do Not Reduce to Sheva

8.7   There are two kinds of vowels that will not reduce to *sheva*:

➤ long vowels

➤ vowels in closed syllables

Vowels That Reduce to Sheva

8.8   In nouns

➤ The vowels *qamets* (◌ָ) and *tsere* (◌ֵ) in open propretonic syllables:

דְּבָרִים	דָּבָר
לְבָבוֹת	לֵבָב

➤ The vowel *tsere* (◌ֵ) in an open pretonic syllable, if no reduction occurs in the propretonic syllable:

זוֹכְרִים	זוֹכֵר

> *Cholem-vav* (וֹ), *being long, cannot reduce.*

מִזְבְּחוֹת	מִזְבֵּחַ

> *Chireq* (◌ִ), *being in a closed syllable, cannot reduce.*

8.9   In verbs

➤ Short and medium vowels in the syllable before a vocalic suffix, that is, one that begins with a vowel:

קָטְלָה	קָטַל
כָּבְדוּ	כָּבֵד

➤ Medium vowels in an open propretonic syllable:

קְטַלְתֶּם	קָטַל

Putting the Rules to Work for Nouns

8.10   Various suffixes can be added to nouns. You have learned the suffixes for *mp* (ים ָ◌), *fs* (ה ָ◌), and *fp* (ות).

8.11   Because the various vowels can occur only in particular kinds of syllables and because the accent is usually on the last syllable, when a suffix is added to a noun, the preceding syllables may change in character—for example, from an open pretonic to an open propretonic syllable. As a result, adding a suffix may produce changes in the vowels.

8.12   You will be better equipped to read the Hebrew Bible if you understand some of the dynamics of vowel changes in nouns.

8.13   When a suffix is added to a noun, **first** there is an attempt to **reduce the vowel in the propretonic syllable to *sheva*.**

➤   Sometimes the vowel in the propretonic syllable will not reduce because it is a long vowel.

עוֹלָמִים   עוֹלָם

➤   Sometimes the vowel in the propretonic syllable will not reduce because it is in a closed syllable.

מִשְׁפָּטִים   מִשְׁפָּט

➤   If the vowel is *qamets* (ָ◌) or *tsere* (ֵ◌), it will reduce to *sheva* (ְ◌).

דְּבָרִים   דָּבָר

לְבָבוֹת   לֵבָב

8.14   If no vowel reduction can take place in the propretonic syllable, there is an attempt to **reduce the vowel in the pretonic syllable.**

➤   Only if this vowel is *tsere* (ֵ◌) will it reduce in this situation.

מִשְׁפָּטִים   מִשְׁפָּט

מִזְבְּחוֹת   מִזְבֵּחַ

Segolate Nouns

8.15   There is a special group of nouns in Hebrew called "segolate nouns." These nouns have several characteristics in common.

➤   The accent is on the next to the last syllable.

➤   The typical vowels are *segol* + *segol* (ֶ◌ ֶ◌) in the singular form; this is why they are called segolate nouns.

אֶרֶץ　(אֶרֶץ)

בֶּגֶד　(בֶּגֶד)

דֶּרֶךְ　(דֶּרֶךְ)

מֶלֶךְ　(מֶלֶךְ)

נֶפֶשׁ　(נֶפֶשׁ)

➤ The expected *segol* (◌ֶ) may be a *patach* (◌ַ) if the following consonant is a guttural.

זֶבַח　(זֶבַח)

נַעַר　(נַעַר)

> *Guttural Characteristic #2: gutturals prefer "a" class vowels. Because the guttural sounds were originally made in the throat and the "a" class vowels are made in the back of the mouth, it was easier to make a guttural sound if the preceding vowel was an "a" class vowel.*

8.16　The plural form of all "segolate nouns has the same vowel pattern: *sheva* (◌ְ) under the first consonant and *qamets* (◌ָ)

בְּגָדִים　　בֶּגֶד

דְּרָכִים　　דֶּרֶךְ

זְבָחִים　　זֶבַח

8.17　If the first consonant is a guttural, the *sheva* (◌ְ) will become *chatef-patach* (◌ֲ).

אֲרָצוֹת　　אֶרֶץ

> *Guttural Characteristic #3: gutturals rarely have vocal sheva under them, but prefer chatef-patach (◌ֲ) or, less frequently, chatef-segol (◌ֱ) or chatef-qamets (◌ֳ).*

Unpredictable Vowel Changes

8.18　In some nouns the vowel pattern of the plural is unpredictably different from the vowel pattern of the singular. These are best memorized as encountered. Such nouns learned thus far are:

נָשִׁים	אִשָּׁה	אֲנָשִׁים	אִישׁ
בָּנוֹת	בַּת	בָּנִים	בֵּן
עָרִים	עִיר	בָּתִּים	בַּיִת
		יָמִים	יוֹם

Vocabulary

before	לִפְנֵי	923	to, for the sake of	אֶל	883
from	מִן	931	in, at, with	בְּ	890
on, on account of	עַל	941	within	בְּתוֹךְ	899
with	עִם	943	like, as, according to	כְּ	908
under, beneath	תַּחַת (תַּחַת)	951	to, for	לְ	915

Note:

○ The final vowel in לִפְנֵי is pronounced the same as *tsere* (⃞), *ey* as in *hey*, is long, and is called *tsere-yod*.

Practice

Focusing on New Material

A. Focus on the accent. Circle the accented syllable.

5. הַבֵּן   4. מְלָכִים   3. מֶלֶךְ   2. יָשַׁב   1. אָדָם

10. נַעַר   9. עוֹלָם   8. זֶבַח   7. נֶפֶשׁ   6. כָּתְבוּ

B. Focus on the syllable. Circle the closed syllables and underline the open syllables.

5. עוֹלָם   4. מְלָכִים   3. מֶלֶךְ   2. מַלְכוּת   1. אָדָם

10. נַעַר   9. יוֹם   8. מִלְחָמָה   7. נֶפֶשׁ   6. מִשְׁפָּט

C. Focus on vowel changes in the plural. Match the plural form of the right column with the corresponding singular form in the left column.

דָּבָר	a.	_____ נְעָרִים	1.
לֵבָב	b.	_____ מְלָכִים	2.
נָבִיא	c.	_____ מִשְׁפָּטִים	3.
עוֹלָם	d.	_____ דְּבָרִים	4.
דֶּרֶךְ	e.	_____ זְבָחִים	5.

מֶלֶךְ	f.	6. לְבָבוֹת ___	
נֶפֶשׁ	g.	7. דְּרָכִים ___	
נַעַר	h.	8. נְבִיאִים ___	
מִשְׁפָּט	i.	9. אֲרָצוֹת ___	
זֶבַח	j.	10. עוֹלָמִים ___	
מִזְבֵּחַ	k.	11. נְפָשׁוֹת ___	
אֶרֶץ	l.	12. מִזְבְּחוֹת ___	

Reviewing Previous Lessons

D. Parse the following.

Verb	Pattern	Conj.	Person	Gender	Number	Root
1. כָּבֵד						
2. הָלַכְתִּי						
3. יָשַׁבְתָּ						
4. לְקַחְתֶּם						
5. שָׁמְעוּ						
6. שָׁמְעָה						
7. אָכַלְנוּ						

Putting It All Together

E. Translate the following.

	1.	יָשַׁב הַכֹּהֵן
1. The priest sat.	2.	כָּבֵד הַכֹּהֵן
2. The priest is heavy (stative-present)	3.	יָדַע אֶת־הַמִּשְׁפָּט
3. He knew the judgment.	4.	יָדְעוּ הָאֲנָשִׁים אֶת־הַמִּשְׁפָּטִים
4. The men knew the judgments.	5.	שָׁלַחְתִּי אֶת־הַנַּעַר
5. I sent the boy.	6.	שָׁלְחוּ הַנְּבִיאִים אֶת־הַנְּעָרִים
6. The prophets sent the boys.	7.	זָבְחוּ אֶת הַזְּבָחִים

7. They sacrificed the sacrifices.	8.	שָׁמַע הָאִישׁ דָּבָר
8. The man heard a word.	9.	שָׁמַעְנוּ אֶת־הַדְּבָרִים
9. We heard the words.	10.	זָכַרְתָּ אֶת הַיּוֹם
10. You remembered the day.	11.	זָכְרָה הָאִשָּׁה אֶת־הָעִיר
11. The woman remembered the city.	12.	לָקְחוּ הַמְּלָכִים עִיר
12. The kings seized a city.	13.	שָׁמְעָה הָאֵם אֶת־הַשֵּׁם
13. The mother heard the name.	14.	אֶת־הַמִּלְחָמוֹת שָׁמְעוּ הַמִּשְׁפָּחוֹת
14. The families heard the battles (not the animals).	15.	אֶת הַמַּלְכוּת יְדַעְתֶּם
15. You knew the kingdom.		

Reading Your Hebrew Bible

F. The following is 1 Kings 1:11.

וַיֹּאמֶר נָתָן אֶל בַּת שֶׁבַע אֵם שְׁלֹמֹה לֵאמֹר

הֲלוֹא שָׁמַעַתְּ כִּי מָלַךְ אֲדֹנִיָּהוּ בֶן חַגִּית

וַאֲדֹנֵינוּ דָוִד לֹא יָדָע

1. Read the text out loud and circle all vocabulary and verb forms learned to date.

2. Read the text out loud and underline the following names: Nathan, Bathsheba, and David.

3. If מֶלֶךְ means "king," what would מָלַךְ mean (in the middle of line two)?

4. Can you translate the last three words?

PREPOSITIONS AND VAV CONJUNCTION

Prepositions

9.1 A preposition is a word placed before a noun or pronoun to show the relation of the noun or pronoun to another part of the sentence, for example, "He walked *to* the city," or "He walked *on* the land."

9.2 Hebrew prepositions are used like English prepositions.

"He walked *to* the city."	הָלַךְ אֶל הָעִיר
"He walked *on* the land."	הָלַךְ עַל הָאָרֶץ

9.3 Hebrew has two kinds of prepositions: *independent* and *inseparable*.

Independent Prepositions

9.4 Independent prepositions are independent words, like English prepositions. The following are examples of independent prepositions.

"He sat *within* the house."	יָשַׁב בְּתוֹךְ הַבַּיִת
"He sat *before* the altar."	יָשַׁב לִפְנֵי הַמִּזְבֵּחַ
"He walked *from* the city."	הָלַךְ מִן הָעִיר
"He walked *with* the woman."	הָלַךְ עִם הָאִשָּׁה

9.5 The prepositions אֶל and עַל are almost always written with *maqqef*.

"He walked *to* the city."	הָלַךְ אֶל־הָעִיר
"He walked *on* the land."	הָלַךְ עַל־הָאָרֶץ

Inseparable Prepositions

9.6 Inseparable prepositions are not independent words but are joined to the word they govern. There are three inseparable prepositions in Hebrew: בְּ ("in," "at," "with"), כְּ ("like," "as," "according to"), and לְ ("to," "for").

9.7   The regular vowel of the inseparable preposition is *sheva* (֠).

"in a battle"	בְּמִלְחָמָה
"like a battle"	כְּמִלְחָמָה
"to a battle"	לְמִלְחָמָה

9.8   If a word begins with a *sheva* (֠), the vowel will be *chireq* (֠).

"with prophets"	בִּנְבִיאִים
"like prophets"	כִּנְבִיאִים
"to prophets"	לִנְבִיאִים

9.9   If a word begins with *chatef-patach* (֠), *chatef-segol* (֠), or *chatef-qamets* (֠), the vowel will be the corresponding short vowel.

"in lands"	בַּאֲרָצוֹת
"in truth"	בֶּאֱמֶת
"in sickness"	בָּחֳלִי

9.10   Sometimes, if a word begins with *chatef-segol* (֠) under an א, the vowel under the א will drop out and the vowel under the preposition will be *tsere* (֠).

"to God"	לֵאלֹהִים

9.11   When an inseparable preposition is added to a definite noun, the ה of the definite article is replaced by the consonantal element of the preposition.

"in the day"	בַּיּוֹם	הַיּוֹם
"like the mother"	כָּאֵם	הָאֵם
"to the hills"	לֶהָרִים	הֶהָרִים

The Preposition מִן

9.12   The preposition מִן is treated sometimes as independent and sometimes as inseparable.

➤   Before definite nouns, מִן is usually independent and joined with *maqqef*.

"from the city"	מִן־הָעִיר

➤   Before indefinite nouns, מִן is usually inseparable. The נ is *assimilated* to the following consonant, that is, the נ begins to sound like the following consonant, as in *irregular* from **inregular*, then the נ is written like the following consonant and is indicated with a strong *dagesh*.

"from a sacrifice"	מִזֶּבַח	<	מִזְזֶבַח	<	מִזְזֶבַח
"from a hand"	מִיָּד	<	מִיְיָד	<	מִןְיָד
"from a name"	מִשֵּׁם	<	מִשְׁשֵׁם	<	מִןְשֵׁם

> *The assimilation of נ occurs frequently in Hebrew. Occurrences in other contexts will be pointed out as they are encountered.*

➤ Before indefinite nouns beginning with a guttural or *resh*, the נ is dropped and not indicated by strong *dagesh*, since gutturals do not take *dagesh* (see Guttural Characteristic #1, p. 15). The expected *chireq* (◌) is lengthened to *tsere* (◌) to compensate for not doubling the following consonant (see "compensatory lengthening," p. 25).

"from a father"	מֵאָב	<	מִאָאָב	<	מִןְאָב
"from a mother"	מֵאֵם	<	מִאָאֵם	<	מִןְאֵם
"from a people"	מֵעַם	<	מִעֲעַם	<	מִןְעַם

Vav Conjunction

9.13   A "conjunction" is a word that joins two parts of a sentence. Hebrew, like English, has two kinds of conjunctions: *coordinating* and *subordinating*. Subordinating conjunctions will be learned in future lessons. The coordinating conjunction in Hebrew is *vav* (ו).

Form of Vav Conjunction

9.14   The *vav* conjunction is inseparable and usually written with a *sheva* (◌).

"and a heart"	וְלֵב
"and a soul"	וְנֶפֶשׁ
"and a people"	וְעַם

9.15   Before a word beginning with ב, מ, or פ, the form is וּ. (A *mnemonic* is *bump*.)

"and a house"	וּבַיִת
"and a judgment"	וּמִשְׁפָּט
"and an entrance"	וּפֶתַח

9.16   Before a word beginning with *chatef-patach* (⬚), *chatef-segol* (⬚), or
chatef-qamets (⬚), the vowel is the corresponding short vowel.

"and lands"	וַאֲרָצוֹת
"and truth"	וֶאֱמֶת
"and sickness"	וָחֳלִי

Use of Vav Conjunction

9.17   *Vav* is used to join various parts of a sentence. Here are a few examples.

➤   *Vav* can be used to join two subjects.

הָלְכוּ הָאִישׁ וְהָאִשָּׁה

"The man and the woman walked."

שָׁפְטוּ הַמֶּלֶךְ וְהַכֹּהֵן

"The king and the priest judged."

➤   *Vav* can be used to join two direct objects.

שָׁלַח אֶת־הַנָּבִיא וְאֶת־הַכֹּהֵן

"He sent the prophet and the priest."

שָׁמַר אֶת־הַנָּבִיא וְאֶת־הַכֹּהֵן

"He guarded the prophet and the priest."

➤   *Vav* can be used to join verbs, but this will be dealt with in a future
lesson.

Vocabulary

unclean, impure	טָמֵא	627	large, great	גָּדוֹל	415
straight, right	יָשָׁר	512	alive, living	חַי [1]	384
holy, sacred	קָדוֹשׁ	549	wise, skillful	חָכָם	500
much, great, many	רַב	439	clean, pure	טָהוֹר	626
guilty, wicked	רָשָׁע	483	good, pleasing	טוֹב	385

1. For the pronunciation of the sequence ⬚י , see the boxed note at the bottom of
p. 70.

Practice

Focusing on New Material

A. Focus on prepositions. Translate the following prepositional phrases.

4. לִפְנֵי מִזְבֵּחַ	3. עַל־מִזְבֵּחַ	2. בְּתוֹךְ מִזְבֵּחַ	1. אֶל־מִזְבֵּחַ
8. כַּמִּזְבֵּחַ	7. כְּמִזְבֵּחַ	6. עִם מִזְבֵּחַ	5. תַּחַת מִזְבֵּחַ
12. בְּמִזְבֵּחַ	11. בַּמִּזְבֵּחַ	10. לַמִּזְבֵּחַ	9. לְמִזְבֵּחַ
16. בְּעִיר	15. מֵעִיר	14. מִמִּזְבֵּחַ	13. מִן־הַמִּזְבֵּחַ
20. כָּאָרֶץ	19. כְּאָרֶץ	18. לָעִיר	17. לְעִיר

B. Focus on *vav* conjunction. Translate the following.

4. לֵב וְנֶפֶשׁ	3. כֹּהֵן וְנָבִיא	2. מִזְבֵּחַ וְזֶבַח	1. אַתָּה וְהוּא
8. הֵם וַאֲנַחְנוּ	7. בֵּן וּבַת	6. כֹּהֵן וּמֶלֶךְ	5. עִיר וּבַיִת

C. Focus on prepositions and *vav* conjunction. Translate the following.

	1.	עַל־הַדֶּרֶךְ וְאֶל־הָעִיר
1. On the road and to the city.	2.	עִם הַנָּבִיא וְלִפְנֵי הַמֶּלֶךְ
2. With the prophet and before the king.	3.	בְּתוֹךְ הַמַּלְכוּת וְלַמֶּלֶךְ
3. Within the kingdom and to/for the king.	4.	מֵעִיר וּבַיִת
4. From a city and a house.	5.	בְּבֵן וּבְבַת
5. With a son and with a daughter.	6.	בַּבֵּן וּבַבַּת
6. With the son and with the daughter.	7.	לְאָדָם וְלָאֵל
7. To the man and to the god.	8.	כְּאִישׁ וְכָאִשָּׁה
8. Like a man and like the woman.		

Reviewing Previous Lessons

D. Focus on gender. Read the following Hebrew words; circle the masculine words and underline the feminine words.

1. סוּס סוּסָה סוּסִים סוּסוֹת בֶּגֶד אָחוֹת מִלְחָמָה מִשְׁפָּחָה מִשְׁפָּט

2. אֵם אֲרָצוֹת אֶרֶץ זֶבַח נַעַר נְפָשׁוֹת נֶפֶשׁ אִשָּׁה נָשִׁים בַּיִת

E. Focus on number. Read the following Hebrew words; circle the singular words and underline the plural words.

1. סוּס סוּסָה סוּסִים סוּסוֹת בְּגָדִים אָחוֹת מִלְחָמוֹת אָבוֹת עוֹלָם

2. אַתֶּם אַתָּה אַתְּ הֵם הֵנָּה מַלְכוּת מִשְׁפָּטִים כֹּהֵן יוֹם אֲרָצוֹת שָׁם

F. Parse the following.

	Verb	Pattern	Conj.	Person	Gender	Number	Root
1.	זָבְחוּ						
2.	שְׁפַטְנוּ						
3.	הָלַכְתָּ						
4.	כָּבַדְתִּי						
5.	זָכְרָה						
6.	כְּתַבְתֶּם						

Putting It All Together

G. Translate the following.

		1.	הָלַכְתִּי עִם הַכֹּהֵן אֶל־הַמִּזְבֵּחַ
1. I walked with the priest to the altar.		2.	נָתְנָה הָאֵם אֶת־הַבֶּגֶד לַבַּת
2. The mother gave the garment to the daughter.		3.	שָׁמְעוּ אֶת־הַמֶּלֶךְ וְאֶת־הַנָּבִיא
3. They heard the king and the prophet.		4.	שָׁמְעוּ הַמֶּלֶךְ וְהַנָּבִיא אֶת־הַדְּבָרִים
4. The king and the prophet heard the words.		5.	שְׁלַחְתֶּם אֶת־הַכֹּהֵן וְאֶת־הַזֶּבַח לַמִּלְחָמָה

5. You (*mp*) sent the priest and the sacrifice to the battle.	6. יְשַׁבְנוּ עִם הַמִּשְׁפָּחָה בָּאָרֶץ וּבָעִיר
6. We dwelled with the family in the land and in the city.	7. שָׁמְרוּ הָאָב וְהָאֵם אֶת־הַבֵּן וְאֶת־הַבַּת עַל־הַדֶּרֶךְ
7. The father and the mother guarded the son and the daughter on the journey.	8. לֹא לָקַח הָעָם אֶת־הַמַּלְכוּת לֵאלֹהִים
8. The people did not seize the kingdom for God.	

Reading Your Hebrew Bible

H. Translate the following verses from the Hebrew Bible.

Joshua 2:5	לֹא יָדַעְתִּי אָנָה (where) הָלְכוּ הָאֲנָשִׁים	1.
Judges 21:22	לֹא לָקַחְנוּ אִישׁ	2.
1 Samuel 4:18	וְהוּא שָׁפַט אֶת־יִשְׂרָאֵל (Israel)	3.
Jeremiah 34:17	אַתֶּם לֹא־שְׁמַעְתֶּם	4.

10

THE ADJECTIVE

Adjectives in Hebrew

10.1 An adjective is a word that describes a noun, for example, the *good* boy and the *nice* girl. Hebrew has relatively few adjectives.

Form of Adjectives

10.2 Adjectives are marked for gender and number, just like nouns. The following chart should be memorized.

	Plural	Singular
Masculine	טוֹבִים	טוֹב
Feminine	טוֹבוֹת	טוֹבָה

10.3 As with nouns, when gender and number endings are added to adjectives, the nature of the syllables may change, resulting in changes in the vowels. The same rules learned in Lesson 8 for vowel changes in the noun apply to adjectives. Here are some examples.

➤ Sometimes there will be no change.

טוֹבִים   טוֹב

Cholem-vav (וֹ), being long, cannot reduce.

➤ The vowel qamets (ָ) will reduce to sheva (ְ) in an open propretonic syllable.

גְּדוֹלִים   גָּדוֹל

טְמֵאָה   טָמֵא

יְשָׁרוֹת   יָשָׁר

חֲכָמִים   חָכָם

Chet (ח), being a guttural, takes chatef-patach (ֲ) instead of sheva (ְ) (see Guttural Characteristic #3, p. 45).

Geminate Roots

10.4   Geminate roots are those in which the second and third consonants are identical, for example, לבב or רבב. The duplicate consonants will be dealt with in one of two ways in Hebrew: *gemination* or *reduplication*.

➤   In gemination only one consonant is written when there is no ending, for example, לֵב ("heart"); but when an ending is added, two consonants are written, indicated by a strong *dagesh*, for example, לִבּוֹת ("hearts").

> *The vowel changes from tsere (◌ֵ) to chireq (◌ִ), because a closed unaccented syllable usually has a short vowel (see "Short vowels," p. 43).*

➤   In reduplication, both consonants are written and a vowel is placed in between, for example, לֵבָב. The vowel changes follow the typical rules, for example, לְבָבוֹת.

> *The vowel tsere (◌ֵ) reduces to sheva in an open propretonic syllable (see "Vowels That Reduce to Sheva," p. 43).*

10.5   The other nouns from geminate roots learned to this point are:

"mother(s)"	אִמּוֹת	אֵם
"people(s)"	עַמִּים	עַם

> Geminate nouns and adjectives are often recognizable in the ms form by the presence of a patach (◌ַ) under the first of two consonants, for example, עַם, חַי, and רַב.

Adjectives from Geminate Roots

10.6   Adjectives from geminate roots manifest gemination, not reduplication.

רַבּוֹת	רַבָּה	רַבִּים	רַב
חַיּוֹת	חַיָּה	חַיִּים	חַי

Use of Adjectives

10.7   Adjectives have three uses in Hebrew: *attributive*, *predicative*, and *substantive*.

10.8   An attributive adjective describes a noun, for example, the *good* boy.

➤   An attributive adjective must agree in gender, number, and definiteness, and follow the noun it describes.

"a good horse"	סוּס טוֹב
"the good horse"	הַסּוּס הַטּוֹב

"a good mare"	סוּסָה טוֹבָה
"the good mare"	הַסּוּסָה הַטּוֹבָה
"good horses"	סוּסִים טוֹבִים
"the good horses"	הַסּוּסִים הַטּוֹבִים
"good mares"	סוּסוֹת טוֹבוֹת
"the good mares"	הַסּוּסוֹת הַטּוֹבוֹת

> *An adjective will always agree with the true gender—not the apparent gender—of a noun. The noun* אֶרֶץ *looks ms but is actually fs, so "a good land" is* אֶרֶץ טוֹבָה. *The mp form of* אָב *is* אָבוֹת, *so "good fathers" is* אָבוֹת טוֹבִים.

10.9 A predicate adjective serves as the predicate (the part of the sentence telling something about the subject) of a sentence, for example, the boy *is good.* As when an adjective is the predicate, a form of "to be" is supplied in an English translation.

➤   A predicate adjective must agree in gender and number with the subject but will not have the definite article and will tend to come before the noun it describes.

"The horse is good."	טוֹב הַסּוּס
"The mare is good."	טוֹבָה הַסּוּסָה
"The horses are good."	טוֹבִים הַסּוּסִים
"The mares are good."	טוֹבוֹת הַסּוּסוֹת

10.10 A substantive adjective is used as a noun. Context will indicate substantive use of this sort.

"a good man"	טוֹב
"a good woman"	טוֹבָה
"the good men"	הַטּוֹבִים
"the good women"	הַטּוֹבוֹת

Adjectives as Comparatives

10.11 To form a comparison in English, we add *-er* to an adjective, for example, wise/wis*er*. Hebrew expresses the comparative by using an adjective + noun/pronoun + מִן + noun/pronoun.

חָכָם הַמֶּלֶךְ מִן־הַכֹּהֵן
"The king is wiser than the priest."

גְּדוֹלָה אֵם מִבַּת

"A mother is bigger than a daughter."

Adjectives and Vav Conjunction

10.12 Adjectives may be joined by *vav* conjunction to describe a single noun. The same rules of agreement apply.

נָבִיא גָּדוֹל וְחָכָם

"a great and wise prophet"

הָעַמִּים הַטְּמֵאִים וְהָרְשָׁעִים

"the unclean and guilty peoples"

טָהוֹר וְקָדוֹשׁ הַכֹּהֵן

"The priest is clean and holy."

Vocabulary

water, waters	מַיִם (מֵיִם)	392	other, another	אַחֵר	489
sky, heaven	שָׁמַיִם (שְׁמֵיִם)	444	covenant	בְּרִית	457
cut	כָּרַת	44	old, elder	זָקֵן	497
rule, be king	מָלַךְ	47	firm, strong	חָזָק	615
lie down	שָׁכַב	60	bread, food	לֶחֶם (לֶחֶם)	425

Note:

○ The expression כָּרַת בְּרִית means "make a covenant." At times, a *covenant* was made by *cutting* animals in two and having one of the parties walk between the pieces as a part of an oath (see Gen 15:9-21 and Jer 34:18-20).

Practice

Focusing on New Material

A. Focus on attributive adjectives. Translate the following phrases.

4. נְפָשׁוֹת חַיּוֹת	3. מִשְׁפָּחָה טוֹבָה	2. נְעָרִים רַבִּים	1. מֶלֶךְ גָּדוֹל
8. אֵם חֲכָמָה	7. הָאָרֶץ הַטְּהוֹרָה	6. הַמִּלְחָמוֹת הָרַבּוֹת	5. הַדֶּרֶךְ הַיָּשָׁר
12. הֶעָרִים הַטּוֹבוֹת	11. לֵב טָהוֹר	10. הַכֹּהֲנִים הַקְּדוֹשִׁים	9. מִשְׁפָּט רָשָׁע

B. Focus on predicative adjectives. Translate the following sentences.

4. קְדוֹשִׁים הַזְּבָחִים	3. רַבּוֹת הַנָּשִׁים	2. חֲכָמָה הַבַּת	1. טָמֵא הַמִּזְבֵּחַ
8. גָּדוֹל הַבַּיִת	7. חַי הַדָּבָר	6. טוֹבִים הַיָּמִים	5. הַנְּעָרִים רְשָׁעִים

C. Focus on the difference between attributive and predicate adjectives. Read the following phrases and sentences and fill in the blanks for use of adjective (*a* for attributive and *p* for predicative) and for gender and number.

Use	Gender	Number		
a	f	s	1.	הָאִשָּׁה הַטּוֹבָה
			2.	יָשָׁר הָאָדָם
			3.	הַמִּזְבֵּחַ הַטָּהוֹר
			4.	הַבַּת הַטּוֹבָה
			5.	טְמֵאִים הָאֵלִים
			6.	הָאֱלֹהִים הַחַיִּים
			7.	גְּדוֹלִים הַבְּגָדִים
			8.	רְשָׁעָה הַמַּלְכוּת
			9.	לֵב חָכָם
			10.	הָאֲרָצוֹת הָרַבּוֹת

Reviewing Previous Lessons

D. Focus on vowel changes in the plural. Match the plural form of the right column with the corresponding singular form in the left column.

אִשָּׁה	.a	____	בְּגָדִים	1.
לֵבָב	.b	____	אֵלִים	2.
בֵּן	.c	____	עַמִּים	3.
בֶּגֶד	.d	____	לִבּוֹת	4.
מִזְבֵּחַ	.e	____	לְבָבוֹת	5.
נָבִיא	.f	____	אֲנָשִׁים	6.
עִיר	.g	____	בָּנִים	7.
אֵל	.h	____	נְבִיאִים	8.
לֵב	.i	____	מִזְבְּחוֹת	9.
אֵם	.j	____	עָרִים	10.
עַם	.k	____	אִמּוֹת	11.
אִישׁ	.l	____	נָשִׁים	12.

E. Parse the following.

	Verb	Pattern	Conj.	Person	Gender	Number	Root
1.	קְטַלְתֶּם						
2.	יָשַׁבְתִּי						
3.	לָקַחְתְּ						
4.	יָדְעָה						
5.	הָלְכוּ						
6.	זָכַרְנוּ						
7.	דָּרַשְׁתָּ						
8.	כָּבֵד						

Putting It All Together

F. Translate the following.

	1. הָלְכוּ הָאִישׁ וְהָאִשָּׁה עַל־הַדֶּרֶךְ
1. The man and the woman walked on the road.	2. שָׁלַח הַמֶּלֶךְ הַגָּדוֹל אֶת־הַנָּבִיא הַקָּדוֹשׁ אֶל־הָעִיר הָרְשָׁעָה
2. The great king sent the holy prophet to the wicked city.	3. נָתַן הַכֹּהֵן אֶת־הַזְּבָחִים הַטְּהוֹרִים לִפְנֵי הַמִּזְבֵּחַ
3. The priest put the clean sacrifices before the altar.	4. חָכָם וְקָדוֹשׁ אַתָּה כֵּאלֹהִים
4. You are wise and holy like God.	5. יָשְׁבָה הַמִּשְׁפָּחָה בָּעִיר הַגְּדוֹלָה וּבַבַּיִת הַגָּדוֹל
5. The family lived in the large city and in the large house.	6. לָקַחְתָּ אֶת־הַבֵּן וְאֶת־הַבַּת מִן־הַמִּלְחָמָה
6. You took the son and the daughter from the battle.	7. טוֹב לֵב טָהוֹר מִלֵּב טָמֵא
7. A pure heart is better than an impure heart.	8. שָׁמַעְנוּ דְּבָרִים יְשָׁרִים מֵאָב
8. We heard right words from a father.	

Reading Your Hebrew Bible

G. Translate the following lines from the Hebrew Bible.

Deuteronomy 2:10	עַם גָּדוֹל וָרָב	1.
Joshua 24:19	אֱלֹהִים קְדֹשִׁים הוּא	2.
Exodus 18:17	לֹא־טוֹב הַדָּבָר	3.
Jeremiah 10:10	הוּא אֱלֹהִים חַיִּים	4.

11

THE VERB: QAL IMPERFECT

Form of the Qal Imperfect

11.1 The base form of the qal imperfect is קְטֹל. The particular forms are made by adding prefixes and suffixes to this base. The prefixes and suffixes are printed in color in order to highlight them. The prefixes are related to the personal pronouns, except in the 3rd person forms.

		Verb	Pronoun	
יִקְטֹל		יִקְטֹל		3ms
תִּקְטֹל		תִּקְטֹל		3fs
תִּקְטֹל		תִּקְטֹל	אַתָּה	2ms
תִּקְטְלִי		תִּקְטְלִי	אַתְּ	2fs
אֶקְטֹל		אֶקְטֹל	אֲנִי / אָנֹכִי	1cs
יִקְטְלוּ		יִקְטְלוּ		3mp
תִּקְטֹלְנָה		תִּקְטֹלְנָה		3fp
תִּקְטְלוּ		תִּקְטְלוּ	אַתֶּם	2mp
תִּקְטֹלְנָה		תִּקְטֹלְנָה	אַתֵּן	2fp
נִקְטֹל		נִקְטֹל	אֲנַחְנוּ	1cp

11.2 In the 2*fs*, 3*mp*, and 2*mp* forms, the theme vowel, *cholem* (◌ֹ) in this case, reduces to *sheva* (◌ְ) before the vocalic suffix (see "In verbs," p. 43).

11.3 The accent is on the next to the last syllable in the 3*fp* and 2*fp* forms: תִּקְטֹלְנָה. Memorize these forms with the accent.

11.4 The theme vowel of action verbs typically is *cholem* (◌ֹ), for example, יִשְׁמֹר ("he will guard"). The theme vowel of stative verbs typically is *patach* (◌ַ), for example, יִכְבַּד ("he will be heavy"). This distinction is not maintained consistently. For example, action verbs with a guttural

63

as the third root letter will often have *patach* (☐) as the theme vowel, for example, יִשְׁלַח ("he will send") (see Guttural Characteristic #2, p. 45).

> The imperfect conjugation will be abbreviated impf.

Use of the Qal Imperfect

11.5 The imperfect conjugation is used in a variety of ways. Only two will be introduced at this point: "future imperfect" and "present progressive imperfect."

➤ The future imperfect is for expressing a **future situation**, best translated into English with a future tense.

"He will seek."	יִדְרֹשׁ
"He will write."	יִכְתֹּב
"He will rule."	יִמְלֹךְ

➤ The present progressive imperfect is for expressing an **ongoing situation in the present**, best translated into English with a present progressive tense.

"He is seeking."	יִדְרֹשׁ
"He is writing."	יִכְתֹּב
"He is ruling."	יִמְלֹךְ

11.6 Because the stative perfect expresses the present, the stative imperfect typically expresses the future, not the present.

11.7 The context will determine whether the use of an imperfect is future or present progressive. For the exercises, use the future.

Vocabulary

teaching, law	תּוֹרָה	486	tent, dwelling	אֹהֶל (אֱהֶל)	407
say	אָמַר	2	book, document	סֵפֶר (סֶפֶר)	534
go across, transgress	עָבַר	15	holiness	קֹדֶשׁ (קֹדֶשׁ)	401
stand	עָמַד	17	voice, sound	קוֹל	400
visit, take care of	פָּקַד	57	year	שָׁנָה	405

Practice

Focusing on New Material

A. Focus on the form of the imperfect. Parse the following imperfect verbs.

	Verb	Pattern	Conj.	Person	Gender	Number	Root
1.	יִקְטֹל						
2.	יִכְתְּבוּ						
3.	אֶשְׁפֹּט						
4.	תִּשְׁלַח						
5.	תִּשְׁמְרוּ						
6.	תִּשְׁמְעִי						
7.	נִבְטַח						
8.	תִּקְטֹלְנָה						

B. Focus on the use of the imperfect. Translate the following imperfect forms as future imperfects.

5. תִּבְטַח   4. נִשְׁפֹּט   3. תִּשְׁמְרוּ   2. אֶמְלֹךְ   1. יִזְכֹּר

10. יִכְתְּבוּ   9. יִכְרֹת   8. תִּשְׁמַעְנָה   7. יִשְׁכְּבוּ   6. תִּדְרְשִׁי

15. תִּשְׁמַע   14. יִשְׁמְרוּ   13. אֶבְטַח   12. נִמְלֹךְ   11. יִזְבַּח

C. Translate the following.

	1.	יִשְׁפֹּט הַנָּבִיא אֶת־הָעִיר
1. The prophet will judge the city.	2.	יִשְׁפְּטוּ הַנְּבִיאִים אֶת־הֶעָרִים
2. The prophets will judge the cities.	3.	אֶדְרֹשׁ אֶת־הָאֱלֹהִים
3. I will seek God.	4.	תִּשְׁמַע דְּבָרִים
4. She/you (*ms*) will hear words.	5.	נִשְׁמַע אֶת־הַזְּקֵנִים

5. We will listen to the elders.	6.	יִשְׁלַח הָאִישׁ אֶת־הַנַּעַר אֶל־הַכֹּהֵן
6. The man will send the boy to the priest.	7.	תִּמְלֹךְ עַל־הַמַּלְכוּת לְעוֹלָם
7. She/You (ms) will reign over the kingdom forever.	8.	יִבְטְחוּ הָאֲנָשִׁים בֵּאלֹהִים לְעוֹלָם
8. The men will trust in God forever.		

Reviewing Previous Lessons

D. Parse the following.

	Verb	Pattern	Conj.	Person	Gender	Number	Root
1.	כָּרְתוּ						
2.	שָׁכַבְתִּי						
3.	מָלַכְתָּ						
4.	זָבַחְנוּ						
5.	יְדַעְתֶּם						
6.	יָשַׁבְתָּ						
7.	דָּרְשָׁה						
8.	כָּבֵד						
9.	בְּטַחְתֶּן						

E. Focus on the syllable. Underline the closed syllables and circle the open propretonic syllables.

1. גָּדוֹל	2. מַלְכוּת	3. קְדוֹשָׁה	4. מְלָכִים	5. עוֹלָם
6. חֲכָמִים	7. יְשָׁרוֹת	8. רְשָׁעָה	9. טוֹבִים	10. נַעַר

Putting It All Together

F. Translate the following.

	1.	שָׁפַט אֱלֹהִים אֶת־הָעַמִּים הָרְשָׁעִים
1. God judged the wicked peoples.	2.	יִשְׁפֹּט הָאֱלֹהִים הַחַיִּים אֶת־הָעַמִּים הָרְשָׁעִים
2. The living God will judge the wicked peoples.	3.	תִּשְׁלַח הָאֵם אֶת־הַבַּת עִם־הַבֵּן
3. The mother will send the daughter with the son.	4.	נִזְכֹּר אֶת־הָאָב הֶחָכָם לְעוֹלָם
4. We will remember the wise father forever.	5.	הָלְכוּ הָאֲנָשִׁים וְהַנְּעָרִים אֶל־הַמִּלְחָמָה הַגְּדוֹלָה
5. The men and the boys went to the great battle.	6.	יֵשְׁבָה הַמִּשְׁפָּחָה בַּבַּיִת
6. The family lived in the house.	7.	טוֹב הַזֶּבַח הַטָּהוֹר מִן־הַזֶּבַח הַטָּמֵא
7. The clean sacrifice is better than the unclean sacrifice.	8.	יִשְׁכְּבוּ הַכֹּהֲנִים וְהַנְּבִיאִים לִפְנֵי הַמִּזְבֵּחַ
8. The priests and the prophets will lie down in front of the altar.		

Reading Your Hebrew Bible

G. Translate the following lines from the Hebrew Bible.

Psalm 146:10   .1 יִמְלֹךְ יְהוָה לְעוֹלָם

Ecclesiastes 3:17   .2 וְאֶת־הָרָשָׁע יִשְׁפֹּט

Deuteronomy 17:1   .3 לֹא תִזְבַּח לַיהוָה

CONSTRUCT RELATIONSHIP: SINGULAR

Construct and Absolute States

12.1 Hebrew nouns occur in one of two states: *construct* and *absolute*.

➤ The *absolute* state is the "regular" form of the noun, the form learned in the vocabulary.

➤ The *construct* state is the form of the noun when it is in *construc*tion with another noun.

Use of the Construct State

12.2 Hebrew has no word equivalent to English "of." "Of" is expressed in Hebrew by placing a noun in the construct state in front of a noun in the absolute state. The construct relationship can often be recognized by the presence of a *maqqef* between the nouns.

"the horse *of* the king"	סוּס־הַמֶּלֶךְ
"the soul *of* the prophet"	נֶפֶשׁ־הַנָּבִיא

12.3 A noun in the construct state *never* has the definite article.

➤ If the last noun is definite, the noun in construct is also definite.

"*the* horse of *the* king"	סוּס־הַמֶּלֶךְ
"*the* soul of *the* prophet"	נֶפֶשׁ־הַנָּבִיא

> *Personal names are definite, so* יוֹם־יְהוָה *is translated "the day of the* Lord*."*

➤ If the last noun is not definite, the noun in construct is not definite.

"*a* horse of *a* king"	סוּס־מֶלֶךְ
"*a* soul of *a* prophet"	נֶפֶשׁ־נָבִיא

> *The construct relationship cannot be used to say "the horse of a king."*
> *Instead, the preposition* לְ *is used, for example,* הַסּוּס לְמֶלֶךְ, *"the horse*
> *belonging to a king" > "the horse of a king." "The soul of a prophet" would*
> *be* הַנֶּפֶשׁ לְנָבִיא.

12.4   The English word "of" expresses a variety of relationships: for example,
"the book of the student" = "the book *belonging to* the student"; "the
throne of gold" = "the throne *made out of* gold"; "the mountain of holiness" = "the holy mountain"; "the love of the teacher" = either "the love
the teacher has for students" or "the love students have for the teacher." **The construct relationship also expresses a variety of relationships.** Two will be learned at this point: *possessive* and *adjectival.*

➤   Most frequently, **the construct relationship expresses possession**.

סוּס הַמֶּלֶךְ

"the horse of the king" = "the horse *belonging to* the king"

סֵפֶר־הַכֹּהֵן

"the book of the priest" = "the book *belonging to* the priest"

➤   *Possession* is used rather loosely.

"the daughter of the mother"   בַּת־הָאֵם

➤   Typically, such expressions are translated with apostrophe + *s*.

בַּת הָאֵם

"the daughter of the mother" = "the mother's daughter"

סֵפֶר הַכֹּהֵן

"the book of the priest" = "the priest's book"

➤   Sometimes, **the construct relationship is adjectival**.

בֶּגֶד הַקֹּדֶשׁ

"the garment of the holiness" = "the holy garment"

שֵׁם־עוֹלָם

"a name of eternity" = "an eternal name"

Form of the Singular Construct State

Masculine Singular

12.5   Sometimes the construct state has the same form as the absolute state.

➤ In one-syllable nouns with a long vowel.

"the king's horse"	סוּס הַמֶּלֶךְ
"the family's city"	עִיר־הַמִּשְׁפָּחָה
"the day of the sacrifice"	יוֹם הַזֶּבַח

➤ In one-syllable nouns with a short vowel.

"the people of the land"	עַם־הָאָרֶץ
"the people of God"	עַם הָאֱלֹהִים

➤ In segolate nouns.

"the city's king"	מֶלֶךְ הָעִיר
"the holy way"	דֶּרֶךְ־הַקֹּדֶשׁ
"the woman's garment"	בֶּגֶד הָאִשָּׁה

12.6 Sometimes the vowels change. Two nouns in construct are treated as one word, in terms of accent, with the accent on the second noun. Since there will often be no accent on the noun in construct, the vowels will change according to the rules learned previously.

➤ A medium vowel will often reduce to a short vowel in a final closed syllable, because the syllable is now closed and unaccented (see "Short vowels," p. 43).

"the king's son"	בֶּן־הַמֶּלֶךְ	בֵּן
"the king's decision"	מִשְׁפַּט הַמֶּלֶךְ	מִשְׁפָּט
"the antiquity of the king"	עוֹלַם־הַמֶּלֶךְ	עוֹלָם

➤ In addition, a medium vowel will reduce to *sheva* (◌ְ) in the first of two syllables, if the syllable is open.

"the king's word"	דְּבַר הַמֶּלֶךְ	דָּבָר
"the king's heart"	לְבַב־הַמֶּלֶךְ	לֵבָב

➤ Nouns vocalized like בַּיִת (בַּיִת) have the construct form בֵּית.

> *The sequence ◌ַי (pronounced "eye") is neither a vowel + consonant nor a vowel with the yod (י) functioning as a vowel letter, as in ◌ִי (chireq-yod), but is a "diphthong." A diphthong may only occur in an accented syllable. Since the construct form has no accent, the diphthong ◌ַי changes to the vowel ◌ֵי (tsere-yod [see Vocabulary Note, p. 46]).*

Feminine Singular

12.7   Feminine singular nouns ending in הָ often form the construct by replacing the הָ with תַ, accompanied by appropriate vowel changes.

"the law of the LORD"   תּוֹרַת יְהֹוָה   תּוֹרָה

"the year of the battle"   שְׁנַת הַמִּלְחָמָה   שָׁנָה

12.8   Feminine singular nouns beginning with a מ prefix and ending with הָ often form the construct with segolization.

"the battle of the day"   מִלְחֶמֶת הַיּוֹם   מִלְחָמָה

"the father's family"   מִשְׁפַּחַת הָאָב   מִשְׁפָּחָה

> *The change to patach (ַ) is because of the guttural (see Guttural Characteristic #2, p. 45).*

Vocabulary

slave, servant	עֶבֶד (עֲבֶד)	395	lord, master	אָדוֹן	370
redeem, claim	גָּאַל	70	gold	זָהָב	418
be strong, courageous	חָזַק	33	all, every, whole	כֹּל	389
fall	נָפַל	52	money, silver	כֶּסֶף (כֶּסֶף)	424
serve, work, worship	עָבַד	55	place	מָקוֹם	428

Practice

Focusing on New Material

A. Focus on the form of the construct. Circle the words that are in a construct form that differs from the absolute form.

1. סוּס   עַם   נֶפֶשׁ   דְּבַר   בֵּן   סֵפֶר   נְבִיא   עִיר   תּוֹרַת   סוּסַת

2. קוֹל   לְבַב   קֹדֶשׁ   מִשְׁפַּט   מִלְחֶמֶת   יַד   בֵּית   מַלְכוּת   שֵׁם

B. Focus on the form of the construct. Match the construct form of the right-hand column with the corresponding absolute form of the left-hand column.

מִשְׁפָּחָה	a.	____	דְּבַר	1.
לֵב	b.	____	שְׁנַת	2.
שָׁנָה	c.	____	לְכַב	3.
יָד	d.	____	נְבִיא	4.
מִשְׁפָּט	e.	____	לֵב	5.
נָבִיא	f.	____	מִשְׁפַּחַת	6.
דָּבָר	g.	____	בֶּן	7.
תּוֹרָה	h.	____	מִשְׁפַּט	8.
לְבָב	i.	____	יַד	9.
בֵּן	j.	____	תּוֹרַת	10.

C. Focus on the use of the construct. Translate the following phrases and indicate whether the use is possession (*p*) or adjectival (*a*).

		1.	לְבַב הַנָּבִיא
the heart of the prophet	p	2.	תּוֹרַת הַמֶּלֶךְ
the law of the king	p	3.	בֶּגֶד־קֹדֶשׁ
a holy garment	a	4.	דְּבַר הַנָּבִיא
the word of the prophet	p	5.	נְבִיא הָאָרֶץ
the prophet of the land	p	6.	זֶבַח־הַיּוֹם
the daily sacrifice	a	7.	יַד הַנַּעַר
the hand of the boy	p	8.	מִשְׁפַּחַת הָאֵם
the family of the mother	p	9.	מִלְחֶמֶת־יְהוָה
the battle of the Lord	p	10.	אִישׁ הָאֱלֹהִים
the man of God	p		

Reviewing Previous Lessons

D. Focus on the difference between attributive and predicate adjectives. Read the following phrases and sentences and fill in the blanks for use of adjective (*a* for attributive and *p* for predicative) and for gender and number.

Use	Gender	Number		
			1.	הַכֹּהֲנִים הַקְּדוֹשִׁים
			2.	קְדוֹשִׁים הַכֹּהֲנִים
			3.	יָשָׁר הַדֶּרֶךְ
			4.	הַמִּזְבֵּחַ הַטָּמֵא
			5.	זְקֵנוֹת הַתּוֹרוֹת
			6.	הָאֵם הַזְּקֵנָה
			7.	הֶעָרִים הַגְּדוֹלוֹת
			8.	טוֹבָה הָאָרֶץ
			9.	הָאָבוֹת הַחֲכָמִים
			10.	רְשָׁעָה הַמִּשְׁפָּחָה

E. Parse the following.

	Verb	Pattern	Conj.	Person	Gender	Number	Root
1.	אֶפְקֹד						
2.	זָכַרְנוּ						
3.	נִדְרַשׁ						
4.	תִּכְתֹּבְנָה						
5.	עָמְדָה						
6.	שָׁמְעוּ						
7.	תִּכְרֹת						
8.	שְׁפַטְתֶּם						
9.	מָלַכְתְּ						

Putting It All Together

F. Translate the following.

	1. שָׁלַח הַמֶּלֶךְ אֶת־סֵפֶר־הַנָּבִיא לַכֹּהֵן
1. The king sent the prophet's book to the priest.	2. יִכְתֹּב נְבִיא הַמֶּלֶךְ סְפָרִים בְּבֵית הַמֶּלֶךְ
2. The king's prophet will write books in the king's palace.	3. יִשְׁמְעוּ הָעַמִּים הָרְשָׁעִים אֶת קוֹל־יְהוָה בְּיוֹם־יְהוָה
3. The wicked peoples will hear the voice of the LORD in the day of the LORD.	4. עָמַדְנוּ בְּתוֹךְ הָאֲנָשִׁים הַחֲכָמִים וְהַנָּשִׁים הַטּוֹבוֹת
4. We stood in the midst of the wise men and the good women.	5. תִּזְכֹּר אַתָּה אֶת־שֵׁם־הַבֵּן לְעוֹלָם
5. You will remember the son's name forever.	6. חָכְמָה הָאִשָּׁה הַזְּקֵנָה מִן־הַנַּעַר
6. The old woman is wiser than the boy.	7. אֶדְרֹשׁ אֶת־יְהוָה בְּלֵב טָהוֹר וְטוֹב
7. I will seek the LORD with a pure and good heart.	8. יְשַׁבְתֶּם תַּחַת הַשָּׁמַיִם עַל דֶּרֶךְ הַקֹּדֶשׁ
8. You (*mp*) sat under the sky on the holy road.	

Reading Your Hebrew Bible

G. Translate the following lines from the Hebrew Bible.

Genesis 21:17	1. שָׁמַע אֱלֹהִים אֶל־קוֹל הַנַּעַר	
Joshua 7:15	2. עָבַר בְּרִית יְהוָה	
Proverbs 21:1	3. לֶב־מֶלֶךְ בְּיַד יְהוָה	
2 Chronicles 30:16	4. כְּתוֹרַת מֹשֶׁה (Moses) אִישׁ־הָאֱלֹהִים	

13

CONSTRUCT RELATIONSHIP: PLURAL

Form of the Plural Construct State

Masculine Plural

13.1   The absolute plural ending ־ִים is changed to ־ֵי in the masculine plural construct.

"God of"	אֱלֹהֵי	אֱלֹהִים
"horses of"	סוּסֵי	סוּסִים
"people of"	עַמֵּי	עַמִּים

13.2   Because the accent shifts, appropriate vowel changes take place.

➤   Medium vowels in open syllables usually reduce to *sheva* (ְ).

"sons of"	בְּנֵי	בֵּן
"judgments of"	מִשְׁפְּטֵי	מִשְׁפָּט
"prophets of"	נְבִיאֵי	נָבִיא

➤   If the vowel reduction to *sheva* (ְ) results in two successive vocal *sheva*s, the first becomes *chireq* (ִ) or *patach* (ַ).

"words of"	דִּבְרֵי	דְּבְרֵי	דְּבָרִים
"elders of"	זִקְנֵי	זְקְנֵי	זְקֵנִים
"kings of"	מַלְכֵי	מְלְכֵי	מְלָכִים
"men of"	אַנְשֵׁי	אֲנְשֵׁי	אֲנָשִׁים

Feminine Plural

13.3   The plural construct ending is the same as the plural absolute ending, namely, וֹת.

"mares of"	סוּסוֹת־
"voices of"	קוֹלוֹת־
"laws of"	תּוֹרוֹת־

13.4   Because the accent shifts, appropriate vowel changes take place.

➤   Medium vowels in open syllables usually reduce to *sheva* (◻).

"families of"	מִשְׁפְּחוֹת	מִשְׁפָּחוֹת
"battles of"	מִלְחֲמוֹת	מִלְחָמוֹת

➤   If the vowel reduction to *sheva* (◻) results in two successive vocal *shevas*, the first usually becomes *patach* (◻).

"lands of"	אַרְצוֹת	אֲרָצוֹת	אֲרָצוֹת
"souls of"	נַפְשׁוֹת	נְפָשׁוֹת	נְפָשׁוֹת

Construct Chains

13.5   Two words in a construct relationship are called a "construct chain." It is possible to have more than two words in a construct chain. Only the last word may have the definite article.

דִּבְרֵי נְבִיאֵי הַמֶּלֶךְ

"the words of the prophets of the king"

בְּנֵי מִשְׁפְּחוֹת הָעִיר

"the sons of the families of the city"

Agreement and the Construct State

Agreement and Verbs

13.6   When a construct chain is the subject of a sentence, the verb agrees with the noun in the construct state, because it is the primary noun, the others being qualifiers.

"The son of the king reigned."	מָלַךְ בֶּן־הַמֶּלֶךְ
"The daughter of the king reigned."	מָלְכָה בַּת־הַמֶּלֶךְ
"The sons of the king reigned."	מָלְכוּ בְּנֵי־הַמֶּלֶךְ

Agreement and Adjectives

13.7   Any part of a construct chain can be modified by an adjective. The adjective agrees with the part of the chain that it modifies. If the adjective is attributive, it follows the entire chain.

"the words of the good king"	דִּבְרֵי הַמֶּלֶךְ הַטּוֹב
"the good words of the king"	דִּבְרֵי הַמֶּלֶךְ הַטּוֹבִים
"The words of the king are good."	טוֹבִים דִּבְרֵי הַמֶּלֶךְ

"All," "Every," and "the Whole" (כֹּל)

13.8   The construct form of כֹּל is כָּל־ (*qamets-chatuf*).

➤   In construction with a definite plural noun, כָּל־ is best translated "all of."

"all of the words"	כָּל־הַדְּבָרִים
"all of the kings"	כָּל־הַמְּלָכִים

➤   In construction with an indefinite singular noun, כָּל־ is best translated "every."

"every house"	כָּל־בַּיִת
"every city"	כָּל־עִיר

➤   In construction with a definite singular noun, כָּל־ is best translated "the whole."

"the whole house"	כָּל־הַבַּיִת
"the whole city"	כָּל־הָעִיר

Vocabulary

create	בָּרָא	132	morning	בֹּקֶר (בֹּקֶר)	456
sin	חָטָא	34	new moon, month	חֹדֶשׁ (חֹדֶשׁ)	419
find	מָצָא	48	night *m*	לַיְלָה (לַיְלָה)	466
lift, carry, forgive	נָשָׂא	13	evening	עֶרֶב (עֶרֶב)	540
call, read aloud	קָרָא	21	time	עֵת	436

Practice

Focusing on New Material

A. Focus on the form of the construct. Circle the words that are in construct form that is different from the absolute form.

1. סוּסִים עַמֵּי נַפְשׁוֹת דְּבָרִים בְּנֵי סְפְרֵי נְבִיאִים מִשְׁפָּחוֹת

2. קוֹלוֹת לְבָבוֹת דַּרְכֵי זִקְנֵי מִלְחֲמוֹת סוּסוֹת בְּגָדִים מִזְבְּחוֹת

B. Focus on the form of the construct. Match the construct form in the right column with the corresponding absolute form in the left column.

Left		Right	
מָקוֹם	.a	_____ דִּבְרֵי	.1
מִשְׁפָּחָה	.b	_____ מַלְכֵי	.2
זֶבַח	.c	_____ יְדוֹת	.3
דֶּרֶךְ	.d	_____ מְקוֹמוֹת	.4
יָד	.e	_____ זִבְחֵי	.5
דָּבָר	.f	_____ מִשְׁפָּחוֹת	.6
מִלְחָמָה	.g	_____ עַמֵּי	.7
מֶלֶךְ	.h	_____ דַּרְכֵי	.8
עַם	.i	_____ מִלְחָמוֹת	.9

C. Focus on agreement between adjectives and construct chains. Translate the following phrases, paying attention to the correct noun modified by the adjective.

	1.	שְׁנַת הַמִּלְחָמוֹת הַטּוֹבָה
1. the good year of the battles	2.	שְׁנַת הַמִּלְחָמוֹת הַטּוֹבוֹת
2. the year of the good battles	3.	בְּנֵי־הַמֶּלֶךְ הַגָּדוֹל
3. the sons of the great king	4.	בְּנֵי־הַמֶּלֶךְ הַגְּדוֹלִים
4. the great sons of the king	5.	מִשְׁפַּחַת הַנְּבִיאִים הַחֲכָמָה
5. the wise family of the prophets	6.	מִשְׁפַּחַת הַנְּבִיאִים הַחֲכָמִים
6. the family of the wise prophets	7.	עֶבֶד־הָאֵם הֶחָזָק
7. the strong servant of the mother	8.	סֵפֶר־הַכֹּהֵן הַקָּדוֹשׁ
8. the holy book of the priest or the book of the holy priest (context will clarify)	9.	זְהַב הָעִיר הַטָּהוֹר
9. the pure gold of the city (Remember: עִיר is feminine.)	10.	דִּבְרֵי תּוֹרַת יְהוָה הַטּוֹבִים
10. the good words of the law of the LORD		

D. Focus on the use of כֹּל. Translate the following phrases, paying attention to the varying uses of כֹּל.

	1.	כָּל־הַדְּרָכִים
1. all of the roads	2.	כָּל־הַדֶּרֶךְ
2. the whole road	3.	כָּל־דֶּרֶךְ
3. every road	4.	כָּל־הַמִּזְבֵּחַ
4. the whole altar	5.	כָּל־הָאֵלִים
5. all of the gods	6.	כָּל־בַּיִת
6. every house		

Reviewing Previous Lessons

E. Parse the following.

	Verb	Pattern	Conj.	Person	Gender	Number	Root
1.	גָּאַלְתִּי						
2.	יִפְקְדוּ						
3.	אָמְרוּ						
4.	נִשְׁכַּב						
5.	מָלַכְנוּ						
6.	יְדַעְתֶּם						
7.	אֶזְבַּח						
8.	תִּבְטְחִי						
9.	תִּכְתְּבוּ						
10.	שָׁמְרָה						

F. Focus on the inseparable prepositions. Circle the words that have an inseparable preposition with the definite article.

1. כְּסוּסִים כַּסוּסִים בַּדְּבָרִים לְבָנִים בַּסְּפָרִים לַנָּבִיא כְּמִשְׁפָּחָה

2. בְּקוֹל לַלֵּבָב בַּדֶּרֶךְ לִזְקֵנִים כְּמִלְחָמוֹת כַּסּוּסוֹת בִּבְגָדִים לַמִּזְבְּחוֹת

Putting It All Together

G. Translate the following.

	1.	נָתַן נְבִיא יְהוָה אֶת־הַתּוֹרָה לָעָם
1. The prophet of the LORD gave the law to the people.	2.	יִדְרְשׁוּ אֶת־סֵפֶר־הַבְּרִית בְּבֵית יְהוָה
2. They will seek the book of the Covenant in the house of the LORD.	3.	הָלְכוּ אַנְשֵׁי הָעִיר הַחֲזָקִים לְמִלְחָמָה גְדוֹלָה
3. The strong men of the city went to a great battle.	4.	נִשְׁלַח כֶּסֶף וְזָהָב אֶל־בְּנֵי־הָאָב הַטּוֹבִים
4. We will send silver and gold to the father's good sons.	5.	הָאֵם וְהַבַּת יָשְׁבוּ תַּחַת הַשָּׁמַיִם
5. The mother and the daughter sat under the sky.	6.	לֹא תִזְבְּחוּ אֶת־זִבְחֵי יְהוָה הַטְּהוֹרִים עַל־מִזְבֵּחַ טָמֵא
6. You (*mp*) will not offer the LORD's clean sacrifices on an unclean altar.	7.	בִּמְקוֹם־קֹדֶשׁ עָמַדְתָּ לִפְנֵי הָאֱלֹהִים
7. You stood before God in a holy place.	8.	טוֹב שֵׁם טוֹב מִכֶּסֶף רַב
8. A good name is better than much money.		

Reading Your Hebrew Bible

H. Translate the following from the Hebrew Bible.

Numbers 11:16   1. הֵם זִקְנֵי הָעָם

Deuteronomy 13:4   2. לֹא תִשְׁמַע אֶל־דִּבְרֵי הַנָּבִיא

Psalm 18:22   3. שָׁמַרְתִּי דַּרְכֵי יְהוָה

Leviticus 16:4   4. בִּגְדֵי־קֹדֶשׁ הֵם

14

QAL PERFECT AND IMPERFECT: WEAK ROOTS

Weak Roots

14.1   Hebrew has two kinds of roots: "strong" and "weak."

➤   Strong roots are "regular." They follow the standard paradigm (קְטֹל)
exactly.

מְלַכְתֶּם   זְכַרְתֶּם   קְטַלְתֶּם

➤   Weak roots are "irregular." They vary from the standard paradigm
(קְטֹל) in one way or another.

14.2   The "weakness" in weak roots is designated in two ways: the location of
the weakness and the nature of the weakness.

➤   If the weakness is located in the first, second, or third letter, the Roman numerals I, II, or III are used, respectively, to identify the *location*
of the weakness.

➤   The weakness is also identified according to the specific nature of the
weakness. For example, roots with gutturals are weak, because gutturals have characteristics that cause the verbal forms of these roots
to vary from the standard paradigm.

Examples:

עָבַד is a I Guttural verb.

גָּאַל is a II Guttural verb.

בָּטַח is a III Guttural verb.

14.3   In this lesson, I Guttural verbs and III Alef verbs are introduced.

I Guttural Verbs: Qal Perfect and Imperfect

14.4   I Guttural verbs vary from the standard paradigm mainly in one way:
where the standard paradigm has a *sheva* (ְ), I Guttural verbs have
a *chatef-patach* (ֲ) or a *chatef-segol* (ֱ).

Qal Perfect

14.5   The qal pf follows the standard paradigm except in the 2*mp* and 2*fp* forms, where the *sheva* (◌ְ) is replaced by *chatef-patach* (◌ֲ).

	I Guttural	Strong	
עֲמַדְתֶּם	עֲמַדְתֶּם	קְטַלְתֶּם	2mp
עֲמַדְתֶּן	עֲמַדְתֶּן	קְטַלְתֶּן	2fp

Qal Imperfect

14.6   The qal impf varies from the standard paradigm in three ways: (1) *sheva* (◌ְ) under the first root letter is replaced by *chatef-patach* (◌ֲ) or *chatef-segol* (◌ֱ), (2) the vowel under the prefix will be the corresponding short vowel (*patach* [◌ַ] or *segol* [◌ֶ]), and (3) in the 2*fs*, 3*mp* and 2*mp* the first *sheva* (◌ְ) becomes *patach* (◌ַ).

	I Guttural	Strong	
יַעֲמֹד	יַעֲמֹד	יִקְטֹל	3ms
תַּעֲמֹד	תַּעֲמֹד	תִּקְטֹל	3fs
תַּעֲמֹד	תַּעֲמֹד	תִּקְטֹל	2ms
תַּעַמְדִי	תַּעַמְדִי	תִּקְטְלִי	2fs
אֶעֱמֹד	אֶעֱמֹד	אֶקְטֹל	1cs
יַעַמְדוּ	יַעַמְדוּ	יִקְטְלוּ	3mp
תַּעֲמֹדְנָה	תַּעֲמֹדְנָה	תִּקְטֹלְנָה	3fp
תַּעַמְדוּ	תַּעַמְדוּ	תִּקְטְלוּ	2mp
תַּעֲמֹדְנָה	תַּעֲמֹדְנָה	תִּקְטֹלְנָה	2fp
נַעֲמֹד	נַעֲמֹד	נִקְטֹל	1cp

> *Verbs with patach (◌ַ) as the theme vowel are vocalized like* יֶחֱזַק.

III Alef (א) Verbs: Qal Perfect and Imperfect

14.7   III Alef verbs vary from the standard paradigm because *alef* is silent when it closes a syllable.

Qal Perfect

14.8   In forms where *alef* would close a syllable, the *alef* is silent, so (1) there is no *sheva* (⬚) written under the *alef* and (2) compensatory lengthening (see p. 25) takes place: the expected short *patach* (⬚) is lengthened to medium *qamets* (⬚). And because the *tav* (ת) of the suffixes is now preceded by a vowel, the *alef* being silent, the weak *dagesh* is lost (see "Letters with Two Pronunciations," p. 4).

		III Alef	Strong	
מָצָא		מָצָא	קָטַל	3ms
מָצְאָה		מָצְאָה	קָטְלָה	3fs
מָצָאתָ		מָצָאתָ	קָטַלְתָּ	2ms
מָצָאת		מָצָאת	קָטַלְתְּ	2fs
מָצָאתִי		מָצָאתִי	קָטַלְתִּי	1cs

מָצְאוּ		מָצְאוּ	קָטְלוּ	3cp
מְצָאתֶם		מְצָאתֶם	קְטַלְתֶּם	2mp
מְצָאתֶן		מְצָאתֶן	קְטַלְתֶּן	2fp
מָצָאנוּ		מָצָאנוּ	קָטַלְנוּ	1cp

Qal Imperfect

14.9   Because *alef* is a guttural, the theme vowel is an "a" class vowel (as in יִשְׁלַח), not the "u"-class vowel *cholem* (⬚). In forms where *alef* would close a syllable, the *alef* is silent, so compensatory lengthening takes place: the expected short *patach* (⬚) is lengthened to medium *qamets* (⬚), except in the 3*fp* and 2*fp*, which have a *segol* (⬚).

		III Alef	III Guttural	
יִמְצָא		יִמְצָא	יִשְׁלַח	3ms
תִּמְצָא		תִּמְצָא	תִּשְׁלַח	3fs
תִּמְצָא		תִּמְצָא	תִּשְׁלַח	2ms
תִּמְצְאִי		תִּמְצְאִי	תִּשְׁלְחִי	2fs
אֶמְצָא		אֶמְצָא	אֶשְׁלַח	1cs

	III Alef	III Guttural	
יִמְצְאוּ	יִמְצְאוּ	יִשְׁלְחוּ	*3mp*
תִּמְצֶאנָה	תִּמְצֶאנָה	תִּשְׁלַחְנָה	*3fp*
תִּמְצְאוּ	תִּמְצְאוּ	תִּשְׁלְחוּ	*2mp*
תִּמְצֶאנָה	תִּמְצֶאנָה	תִּשְׁלַחְנָה	*2fp*
נִמְצָא	נִמְצָא	נִשְׁלַח	*1cp*

Vocabulary

touch, hurt	נָגַע	92	cry	בָּכָה	69
approach	נָגַשׁ	93	build, fortify	בָּנָה	29
start out	נָסַע	95	reveal, go away	גָּלָה	73
make, do	עָשָׂה	18	see, see a vision	חָזָה	142
see, know	רָאָה	22	cease, finish	כָּלָה	43

Practice

Focusing on New Material

A. Focus on weak roots. Before doing this exercise, go back and review the paradigms in Lessons 6 and 11. Underline the verbs below that vary from the standard paradigm and circle the point(s) at which the variance occurs.

1. עֲבַרְתֶּם חֲזַקְתֶּם עָבְדָה גָּאֲלָה נָשְׂאָה מָצָא עֲמַדְתֶּם מָצָאתִי

2. יַעֲבֹר יִגְאֲלוּ תַּעֲמֹדוּ תִּקְרָא יִבְרָא נַעֲבֹד תִּמְצָאִי

3. נָשְׂאוּ אֶמֹד גָּאֲלוּ מְצָאתֶם תַּעֲבְדִי חָזְקָה חֲזַקְתֶּם

B. Focus on weak roots. Parse the following.

	Verb	Pattern	Conj.	Person	Gender	Number	Root
1.	חָטָא						
2.	עֲבַרְתֶּם						

3.	נַעֲמֹד					
4.	תִּמְצָא					
5.	חֲטָאתֶם					
6.	יַעֲבְדוּ					
7.	גָּאֲלָה					
8.	אֲמַרְתֶּם					

Reviewing Previous Lessons

C. Focus on the construct state. Translate the following construct forms.

שָׁנוֹת .4		מַלְכֵי .3		מִשְׁפַּט .2		נְבִיא .1	
בֶּן .8		מִשְׁפַּחַת .7		תּוֹרַת .6		דְּבַר .5	
זְהַב .12		מִשְׁפְּחוֹת .11		זִבְחֵי .10		דַּרְכֵי .9	
נַפְשׁוֹת .16		עַבְדֵי .15		מִלְחֲמוֹת .14		סוּסַת .13	

D. Focus on the form of the construct. Match the construct form of the right column with the corresponding absolute singular form of the left column.

סוּסָה .a	____	תּוֹרַת .1	
מִשְׁפָּחָה .b	____	יְדוֹת .2	
יָשָׁר .c	____	כַּסְפֵּי .3	
כֶּסֶף .d	____	מִשְׁפְּחוֹת .4	
תּוֹרָה .e	____	אַנְשֵׁי .5	
מִלְחָמָה .f	____	יִשְׁרֵי .6	
אִישׁ .g	____	עַמִּי .7	
זָקֵן .h	____	מִלְחֶמֶת .8	
עַם .i	____	סוּסַת .9	
יָד .j	____	זִקְנֵי .10	

E. Parse the following.

	Verb	Pattern	Conj.	Person	Gender	Number	Root
1.	יִזְבַּח						
2.	שָׁלְחוּ						
3.	נָשָׂאנוּ						
4.	יַעַבְדוּ						
5.	הֲלַכְתֶּם						
6.	מָלַכְתָּ						
7.	נִשְׁפֹּט						
8.	אֶעֱמֹד						
9.	תִּמְצָא						
10.	תִּקְטֹלְנָה						

Putting It All Together

F. Translate the following.

	1. גָּאֲלוּ אַנְשֵׁי הָעִיר אֶת הָעָם

1. The men of the city redeemed the people.	2.	יִקְרָא הַכֹּהֵן אֶת־סֵפֶר־הַבְּרִית לִבְנֵי הַמֶּלֶךְ הָרְשָׁעִים
2. The priest will read the Book of the Covenant to the king's wicked sons.	3.	מָצָאתָ אֶת הַזָּהָב הַטָּהוֹר בְּבֵית הָאִשָּׁה הַטּוֹבָה
3. You (*ms*) found the pure gold in the good woman's house.	4.	יַעַמְדוּ הַנְּבִיאִים לִפְנֵי־יְהוָה בַּבֹּקֶר וּבָעֶרֶב
4. The prophets will stand before the LORD in the morning and in the evening.	5.	יַעַבְדוּ עַמֵּי הָאָרֶץ אֶת הָאֱלֹהִים בְּכָל־מָקוֹם
5. The peoples of the earth will serve God in every place.	6.	יָדַעְתִּי אֶת־עַבְדֵי־הַנָּשִׁים הַחֲכָמוֹת
6. I knew the servants of the wise women.	7.	זָקֵן הָאִישׁ מִן־הַנַּעַר
7. The man is older than the boy.	8.	נְשָׂאתֶם אַתֶּם מַיִם לָאֹהֶל הַגָּדוֹל
8. You (*mp*) carried water to the big tent.		

Reading Your Hebrew Bible

G. Translate the following from the Hebrew Bible.

1. הֵמָּה יַעַמְדוּ לְמִשְׁפָּט   Ezekiel 44:24

2. לֹא אָכַל . . . כָּל־הַיּוֹם וְכָל־הַלַּיְלָה   1 Samuel 28:20

3. בָּרָא אֱלֹהִים אֵת הַשָּׁמַיִם וְאֵת הָאָרֶץ   Genesis 1:1

QAL PERFECT AND IMPERFECT: I NUN AND III HEY

I Nun (נ) Verbs: Perfect and Imperfect

15.1 I Nun verbs vary from the standard paradigm, because when the *nun* of the root is followed by a non-guttural consonant, the *nun* assimilates to that consonant (see "assimilated," p. 50).

Qal Perfect

15.2 Because the *nun* is never followed by a consonant in the *qal pf*, these forms are regular, for example, נָפַל and נְפַלְתֶּם.

Qal Imperfect

15.3 In all forms, the *nun* is followed by a consonant; as a result, the *nun* is assimilated to that consonant and is indicated by strong *dagesh*, for example: יִפֹּל < יִנְפֹּל < יִנְפֹּל.

I Nun	Strong	
יִפֹּל	יִקְטֹל	*3ms*
תִּפֹּל	תִּקְטֹל	*3fs*
תִּפֹּל	תִּקְטֹל	*2ms*
תִּפְּלִי	תִּקְטְלִי	*2fs*
אֶפֹּל	אֶקְטֹל	*1cs*
יִפְּלוּ	יִקְטְלוּ	*3mp*
תִּפֹּלְנָה	תִּקְטֹלְנָה	*3fp*
תִּפְּלוּ	תִּקְטְלוּ	*2mp*
תִּפֹּלְנָה	תִּקְטֹלְנָה	*2fp*
נִפֹּל	נִקְטֹל	*1cp*

Qal Imperfect of לקח

15.4   The verb לקח acts as if it were a I Nun verb in the *impf.* Because the final consonant is a guttural, the theme vowel is *patach* (◌ַ).

לקח	Strong	
יִקַּח	יִקְטֹל	*3ms*
תִּקַּח	תִּקְטֹל	*3fs*
תִּקַּח	תִּקְטֹל	*2ms*
תִּקְחִי	תִּקְטְלִי	*2fs*
אֶקַּח	אֶקְטֹל	*1cs*

יִקְחוּ	יִקְטְלוּ	*3mp*
תִּקַּחְנָה	תִּקְטֹלְנָה	*3fp*
תִּקְחוּ	תִּקְטְלוּ	*2mp*
תִּקַּחְנָה	תִּקְטֹלְנָה	*2fp*
נִקַּח	נִקְטֹל	*1cp*

III Hey (ה) Verbs: Perfect and Imperfect

15.5   III Hey verbs vary from the standard paradigm, because the final *hey* (ה) is not a consonant but a vowel letter. Most of the III Hey roots originally ended with a consonantal *yod* (י), which dropped off at a certain point in time, leaving only a vowel, now indicated by the final *hey* (ה). Vestiges of the original *yod* appear in certain forms of the verb.

Qal Perfect

15.6   The 3*ms* has הָ◌ as the ending; hence the name III Hey. Most forms have ◌ִי after the second root letter; the *yod* is a vestige of a time when most of these verbs ended with consonantal *yod*; since the *tav* (ת) of the suffix is preceded by a vowel, the weak *dagesh* is lost (see "Letters with Two Pronunciations," p. 4). The 3*fs* has two feminine endings: (1) ת and (2) הָ◌.

III Hey	Strong	
גָּלָה	קָטַל	3ms
גָּלְתָה	קָטְלָה	3fs
גָּלִיתָ	קָטַלְתָּ	2ms
גָּלִית	קָטַלְתְּ	2fs
גָּלִיתִי	קָטַלְתִּי	1cs

III Hey	Strong	
גָּלוּ	קָטְלוּ	3cp
גְּלִיתֶם	קְטַלְתֶּם	2mp
גְּלִיתֶן	קְטַלְתֶּן	2fp
גָּלִינוּ	קָטַלְנוּ	1cp

Qal Imperfect

15.7   The ending הָ□ is found on half of the forms. The 2*fs*, 3*mp*, and 2*mp*
attach the vocalic suffix to the second/final root letter. The 3*fp* and 2*fp*
have ֶי□ after the second/final root letter and before the נָה suffix.

III Hey	Strong	
יִגְלֶה	יִקְטֹל	3ms
תִּגְלֶה	תִּקְטֹל	3fs
תִּגְלֶה	תִּקְטֹל	2ms
תִּגְלִי	תִּקְטְלִי	2fs
אֶגְלֶה	אֶקְטֹל	1cs

III Hey	Strong	
יִגְלוּ	יִקְטְלוּ	3mp
תִּגְלֶינָה	תִּקְטֹלְנָה	3fp
תִּגְלוּ	תִּקְטְלוּ	2mp
תִּגְלֶינָה	תִּקְטֹלְנָה	2fp
נִגְלֶה	נִקְטֹל	1cp

Doubly Weak Verbs

15.8 Numerous roots have two weaknesses. The forms show the characteristics of each weak paradigm. An example is עשׂה, which is I Guttural and III Hey.

15.9 The *pf* displays the characteristics of the III Hey verbs in all forms and the characteristics of the I Guttural verbs in the 2mp, which is the only doubly weak form in this case.

III Hey		Doubly Weak		I Guttural	
גְּלִיתֶם	→	עֲשִׂיתֶם	←	עֲמַדְתֶּם	*2mp*

15.10 The *impf* displays the characteristics of both the III Hey and the I Guttural verbs in all forms.

III Hey		Doubly Weak		I Guttural	
יִגְלֶה	→	יַעֲשֶׂה	←	יַעֲמֹד	*3ms*

Vocabulary

mouth	פֶּה	437	ear *f*	אֹזֶן (אֹזֶן)	490
face	פָּנִים	399	nose, anger	אַף	453
head	רֹאשׁ	402	arm *f*	זְרוֹעַ	611
beginning	רֵאשִׁית	695	shoulder *f*	כָּתֵף	636
foot *f*	רֶגֶל (רֶגֶל)	481	eye *m* and *f*	עַיִן (עַיִן)	396

Notes:

❍ Most body parts that occur in pairs are feminine, in spite of their masculine appearance (see "Irregular Singular Nouns," p. 19).

❍ The noun פָּנִים is plural in form but singular or plural in sense, "(one) face" or "faces." The preposition לִפְנֵי ("before") is made up of the preposition לְ and the *mp* construct of פָּנִים, "to the face of" > "before."

❍ The *alef* (א) in רֹאשׁ and רֵאשִׁית is silent. Silent *alef* can always be identified, because there is neither a vowel nor a *sheva* (◌ְ) written with it.

Practice

Focusing on New Material

A. Focus on weak roots. Before doing this exercise, go back and review the paradigms in Lessons 6 and 11. Underline the verbs that vary from the standard paradigm and circle the point(s) at which the variation occurs.

1. בָּכָה　גָּלִיתָ　נָפַלְנוּ　עָשׂוּ　שָׁלַחְתִּי　חֲזִיתֶם　נָגַע

2. יִפֹּל　יִשְׁפְּטוּ　יִבְנֶה　תִּגְּשׁוּ　נִסַּע　תִּמְלְכִי　תִּכְלִי

3. בָּכְתָה　תִּפֹּלְנָה　יִבְנוּ　עֲשִׂיתֶם　נָסְעָה　תִּכְלֶה

B. Focus on weak roots. Parse the following.

	Verb	Pattern	Conj.	Person	Gender	Number	Root
1.	יִפֹּל						
2.	כָּלְתָה						
3.	תַּעֲשֶׂה						
4.	נִגַּשׁ						
5.	חֲזִיתֶם						
6.	בָּנִינוּ						
7.	תִּגְּעִי						
8.	רָאִיתָ						

Reviewing Previous Lessons

C. Focus on the construct state. Translate the following construct forms.

4. נַפְשׁוֹת	3. זִבְחֵי	2. סוּסַת	1. מְקוֹם
8. תּוֹרַת	7. דְּבַר	6. מִלְחֶמֶת	5. כַּסְפֵּי
12. סִפְרֵי	11. מִשְׁפְּחוֹת	10. מִשְׁפַּחַת	9. זְהַב
16. אַנְשֵׁי	15. מִשְׁפְּטֵי	14. דַּרְכֵי	13. יַד

D. Focus on the form of the construct. Match the construct form of the right column with the corresponding absolute singular form of the left column.

זָהָב	.a	____	נְבִיא .1
מִשְׁפָּט	.b	____	דִּבְרֵי .2
סוּסָה	.c	____	תּוֹרַת .3
דָּבָר	.d	____	נַפְשׁוֹת .4
נֶפֶשׁ	.e	____	אַנְשֵׁי .5
רַב	.f	____	מִשְׁפַּט .6
שָׁנָה	.g	____	רַבֵּי .7
נָבִיא	.h	____	סוּסַת .8
אִישׁ	.i	____	זְהַב .9
תּוֹרָה	.j	____	שְׁנַת .10

E. Parse the following.

Verb	Pattern	Conj.	Person	Gender	Number	Root
1. יִשְׁלָחוּ						
2. עָבַרְנוּ						
3. גָּאֲלָה						
4. אֶקַּח						
5. כָּלִיתִי						
6. תִּמְצָא						
7. נִמְלֹךְ						
8. כָּבֵד						
9. יִפְּלוּ						
10. מָצָאתָ						

Putting It All Together

F. Translate the following.

	1.	לֹא גָדוֹל אֲדוֹן הָעִיר הָרְשָׁעָה
1. The lord of the wicked city is not great.	2.	יָשַׁבְנוּ בָּאֹהֶל תַּחַת הַשָּׁמַיִם
2. We lived in the tent under the sky.	3.	יִבְנוּ הָאִישׁ וְהָאִשָּׁה בַּיִת לַבָּנִים וְלַבָּנוֹת
3. The man and the woman will build a house for the sons and the daughters.	4.	לֹא יִגַּשׁ הַנָּבִיא אֶל־מִזְבַּח־יְהוָה
4. The prophet will not approach the altar of the LORD.	5.	בְּכִיתֶם כָּל־הַיּוֹם וְכָל־הַלָּיְלָה
5. You wept the whole day and the whole night.	6.	תַּעֲשֶׂה לֶחֶם־קֹדֶשׁ לַכֹּהֲנִים הַטְּהוֹרִים
6. She/you (*ms*) will make holy food for the clean priests.	7.	מָצָאתִי אֶת־סֵפֶר־הַבְּרִית בְּבֵית הַמֶּלֶךְ
7. I found the Book of the Covenant in the king's house.	8.	יִסַּע עַם־הָאָרֶץ הֶחָזָק עַל־הַדֶּרֶךְ לַמִּלְחָמָה
8. The strong people of the land will set out on the way for the battle.		

Reading Your Hebrew Bible

G. Translate the following from the Hebrew Bible.

Exodus 20:23	1. אֱלֹהֵי כֶסֶף . . . לֹא תַעֲשׂוּ
Numbers 4:15	2. וְלֹא יִגְּעוּ אֶל־הַקֹּדֶשׁ
Leviticus 10:17	3. לֹא אֲכַלְתֶּם . . . בִּמְקוֹם הַקֹּדֶשׁ
Psalm 78:10	4. לֹא שָׁמְרוּ בְּרִית אֱלֹהִים

16

POSSESSIVE SUFFIXES
ON SINGULAR NOUNS

Possessive Suffixes

16.1 English expresses possession by adding possessive pronouns before nouns, for example, *my* horse, *your* horse, *his* horse.

16.2 Hebrew expresses possession by adding possessive suffixes to the end of nouns. There is a set of suffixes for singular nouns and a related set for plural nouns. In this lesson you are learning the possessive suffixes for singular nouns.

Form of the Suffixes

"his horse"	3ms	סוּסוֹ	=	וֹ	+ סוּס
"her horse"	3fs	סוּסָהּ	=	הָ	+ סוּס
"your horse"	2ms	סוּסְךָ	=	ךָ	+ סוּס
"your horse"	2fs	סוּסֵךְ	=	ךְ	+ סוּס
"my horse"	1cs	סוּסִי	=	י	+ סוּס

"their horse"	3mp	סוּסָם	=	ָם	+ סוּס
"their horse"	3fp	סוּסָן	=	ָן	+ סוּס
"your horse"	2mp	סוּסְכֶם	=	כֶם	+ סוּס
"your horse"	2fp	סוּסְכֶן	=	כֶן	+ סוּס
"our horse"	1cp	סוּסֵנוּ	=	נוּ	+ סוּס

> ➤ *Vocabulary Cards ##954–959*

95

> *The dot in the hey (ה) of the 3fs suffix is called "mappiq" and indicates that the hey is a consonant, not a vowel letter, distinguishing, for example, סוּסָה = "a mare" from סוּסָהּ = "her horse." Mappiq occurs mainly in this suffix.*

Form of Feminine Nouns before the Suffixes

16.3   The same set of possessive suffixes is added to a form of the feminine singular noun, which is related to the construct form = סוּסַת. Because the short *patach* (ַ) of the construct form is in an open pretonic syllable in most suffixed forms, it is lengthened to medium *qamets* (ָ), resulting in סוּסָת, except in the 2*mp* and 2*fp*, where the closed syllable preserves the *patach* (ַ).

"his mare"	3ms	סוּסָתוֹ	=	וֹ	+	סוּסָת
"her mare"	3fs	סוּסָתָהּ	=	הָ	+	סוּסָת
"your mare"	2ms	סוּסָתְךָ	=	ךָ	+	סוּסָת
"your mare"	2fs	סוּסָתֵךְ	=	ךֵ	+	סוּסָת
"my mare"	1cs	סוּסָתִי	=	י	+	סוּסָת

"their mare"	3mp	סוּסָתָם	=	ם	+	סוּסָת
"their mare"	3fp	סוּסָתָן	=	ן	+	סוּסָת
"your mare"	2mp	סוּסַתְכֶם	=	כֶם	+	סוּסַת
"your mare"	2fp	סוּסַתְכֶן	=	כֶן	+	סוּסַת
"our mare"	1cp	סוּסָתֵנוּ	=	נוּ	+	סוּסָת

➤   *Vocabulary Cards ##967–972*

> *Words with a possessive suffix are definite. If such words are (1) modified by an attributive adjective, the adjective has the definite article; (2) the direct object of a verb, the form is preceded by the direct object marker אֶת/אֵת־; or (3) the last word in a construct phrase, the whole phrase is definite.*

Form of Various Nouns before the Suffixes

16.4 Because adding a possessive suffix to a noun results in the accent moving to the suffix, the nature of the preceding syllables will change, and as a result vowels will change in keeping with previously learned rules.

Forms Such as דָּבָר

16.5 Because the addition of the possessive suffix is similar to the addition of the plural suffix, the form of the noun with the possessive suffixes will be similar to the form of the noun in the plural, that is, דְּבָרִים > דָּבָר, so דְּבָרוֹ > דָּבָר = "his word." Other examples are לְבָבוֹ > לֵבָב = "his heart," מְקוֹמוֹ > מָקוֹם = "his place," and נְבִיאוֹ > נָבִיא = "his prophet."

16.6 The main change is that medium vowels in open propretonic syllables reduce to *sheva* (◌ְ).

Forms Such as נֶפֶשׁ, סֵפֶר, and בֹּקֶר

16.7 The vowels in segolate nouns (see Lesson 8) with suffixes *cannot* be explained by the rules of vowel reduction; for example, נַפְשׁוֹ > נֶפֶשׁ. Originally, segolate nouns were one-syllable nouns with either a short "a," "i," or "u" after the first consonant. The original short vowel is preserved in forms with the possessive suffix.

"a" class	"his soul"	נַפְשׁוֹ	נֶפֶשׁ
"i" class	"his book"	סִפְרוֹ	סֵפֶר
"u" class	"his morning"	בָּקְרוֹ	בֹּקֶר

16.8 Nouns with *tsere* (◌ֵ) in the first syllable will always be "i" class segolates. Nouns with *cholem* (◌ֹ) in the first syllable will always be "u" class segolates; the ◌ָ in בָּקְרוֹ is the short "u" class vowel *qamets-chatuf*.

Forms Such as עַם

16.9 Nouns from geminate roots (see Lesson 10) will show gemination when possessive suffixes are added, just as they do when the plural suffix is added, for example, עַמִּים > עַם, so עַמּוֹ > עַם = "his people." Other examples are אִמּוֹ > אֵם = "his mother" and לִבּוֹ > לֵב = "his heart."

Forms Such as בַּיִת

16.10 Because diphthongs contract in unaccented syllables, as in the construct state (see p. 70), the diphthong will contract when a possessive suffix is added, for example, בַּיִת > בֵּיתוֹ = "his house" and עַיִן > עֵינוֹ = "his eye."

Nouns with Odd Forms in the Construct and with Possessive Suffixes

	With Suffix	Construct	
"your father"	אָבִיךָ	אֲבִי	אָב
"your wife"	אִשְׁתְּךָ	אֵשֶׁת	אִשָּׁה
"your daughter"	בִּתְּךָ	בַּת	בַּת

➤ בַּת ("daughter") is actually the noun בֵּן ("son") with the feminine ת added, resulting in בְּנת > בַּת, with the assimilation of the *nun* (נ), indicated by strong *dagesh* when a suffix is added. The original *chireq* (◌ִ) shifted to *patach* (◌ַ), and the original "i" class vowel is preserved in the form with the possessive suffix, בִּתְּךָ. Also note the original *nun* (נ) in the plural בָּנוֹת ("daughters").

Vocabulary

this *m*	זֶה	867	behind, after, west	אַחַר	374
be able	יָכֹל	36	enemy	אֹיֵב	408
go out	יָצָא	9	these	אֵלֶּה (אֵלֶה)	869
go down	יָרַד	39	man	אֱנוֹשׁ	377
go up	עָלָה	16	this *f*	זֹאת	868

Practice

Focusing on New Material

A. Focus on words with possessive suffixes. Match the form with the possessive suffix in the right column with the corresponding absolute singular form in the left column.

אָדוֹן .a	____	קוֹלִי	.1
סוּסָה .b	____	תּוֹרָתְךָ	.2
תּוֹרָה .c	____	אֲדוֹנֵנוּ	.3
סֵפֶר .d	____	כַּסְפְּכֶם	.4
בֹּקֶר .e	____	לִבָּה	.5
קוֹל .f	____	סִפְרוֹ	.6
לֵב .g	____	אִשְׁתִּי	.7
שָׁנָה .h	____	סוּסָתָן	.8
כֶּסֶף .i	____	בְּקָרֶךָ	.9
אִשָּׁה .j	____	שְׁנָתוֹ	.10

B. Focus on words with possessive suffixes. Translate the following words with possessive suffixes.

סוּסָם .4	סוּסֵנוּ .3	סוּסְכֶם .2	סוּסוֹ .1
סוּסָה .8	סוּסְךָ .7	סוּסִי .6	סוּסְךָ .5
דְּבָרוֹ .12	קָדְשָׁם .11	נַפְשְׁךָ .10	מַלְכֵּנוּ .9
עַמִּי .16	בִּגְדֶךָ .15	בֵּיתָה .14	זְהַבְכֶם .13

C. Focus on words with possessive suffixes. Translate the following.

	1.	בָּנִיתִי אֶת־בֵּיתִי
1. I built my house.	2.	נָתַן אָבִינוּ אֶת הַכֶּסֶף
2. Our father gave the money.	3.	דָּרַשׁ לִבְּךָ הַטָּהוֹר לֵאלֹהִים
3. Your pure heart sought for God.	4.	לָקַח אֶת־הַזָּהָב אֶל־אַרְצוֹ

4. He took the gold to his land.	5. הֲלַכְתֶּם לְדַרְכְּכֶם הָרָשָׁע
5. You (*mp*) went on your wicked way. (הָלַךְ + לְ = "go on")	6. יָדַעְנוּ אֶת בַּת אִמָּה
6. We knew the daughter of her mother.	

Reviewing Previous Lessons

D. Focus on the personal pronouns. Translate the personal pronouns, then identify the person, gender, and number.

3fp	they	1.	הֵנָּה
		2.	אַתָּה
		3.	אֲנִי
		4.	הִיא
		5.	אֲנַחְנוּ
		6.	אַתֶּם
		7.	הוּא
		8.	אַתְּ
		9.	הֵם
		10.	אָנֹכִי

E. Parse the following.

Verb	Pattern	Conj.	Person	Gender	Number	Root
1. הֲלַכְתֶּם						
2. אֶגְלֶה						
3. נִמְצָא						
4. עָשִׂיתִי						
5. יַעֲבְדוּ						
6. יִגַּשׁ						
7. חָטָאתָ						

8. גָּאֲלָה						
9. עֲבַרְתֶּן						
10. תִּשָּׂא						

Putting It All Together

F. Translate the following.

	1.	מָצָאתִי אֲנִי אֶת־סִפְרֵךְ הַטּוֹב
1. I myself found your (*fs*) good book.	2.	תִּשָּׂא בַּת־מַלְכֵּנוּ אֶת־בְּנָהּ לַכּוֹהֵן
2. The daughter of our king will carry her son to the priest.	3.	לֹא שְׁמַעְתֶּם אֶת דְּבַר הַנָּבִיא
3. You (*mp*) did not hear the prophet's word.	4.	יִשְׁמְרוּ עַם־הָאָרֶץ אֶת־תּוֹרַת יְהוָה הַקְּדוֹשָׁה
4. The people of the land will keep the holy law of the LORD.	5.	חָזָק הַזָּקֵן מִן־הַנַּעַר
5. The old man (adj. as substantive) is stronger than the boy.	6.	לֹא תִדְרֹשׁ אֵלִים אֲחֵרִים בְּכָל־נַפְשֶׁךָ
6. You (*ms*) will not seek other gods with all your soul.	7.	בָּכוּ הַבָּנִים וְהַבָּנוֹת בְּאָהֳלָם
7. The sons and the daughters wept in their tent.	8.	כָּלְתָה מִלְחֶמֶת הָעַמִּים הַגְּדוֹלָה
8. The great battle of the peoples ended.		

Reading Your Hebrew Bible

G. Translate the following from the Hebrew Bible.

2 Samuel 7:20	וְאַתָּה יָדַעְתָּ אֶת־עַבְדְּךָ	.1
Isaiah 42:24	וְלֹא שָׁמְעוּ בְּתוֹרָתוֹ	.2
Joshua 24:15	וְאָנֹכִי וּבֵיתִי נַעֲבֹד אֶת־יְהוָה	.3

17

DEMONSTRATIVE AND RELATIVE PRONOUNS

Forms of the Demonstrative Pronouns

17.1   Demonstrative pronouns point out the specific person or object referred to, as in English, "*this* boy" and "*these* roads."

17.2   This and These

these *cp*	אֵלֶּה	this *ms*	זֶה
		this *fs*	זֹאת

17.3   That and Those

those *mp*	הֵם	that *ms*	הוּא
those *fp*	הֵנָּה	that *fs*	הִיא

➤   *The Hebrew for "that" and "those" are the same forms as the personal pronouns (see Lesson 5).*

Use of the Demonstrative Pronouns

17.4   The demonstrative pronouns are used like adjectives: attributive and predicate.

➤   An *attributive* demonstrative pronoun must agree in gender, number, and definiteness, and follow the noun it describes. Since a specific/definite person or object is being referred to, the attributive demonstrative usually has the definite article.

"this horse"	הַסּוּס הַזֶּה
"this mare"	הַסּוּסָה הַזֹּאת
"these horses"	הַסּוּסִים הָאֵלֶּה
"these mares"	הַסּוּסוֹת הָאֵלֶּה

"that horse"	הַסּוּס הַהוּא
"that mare"	הַסּוּסָה הַהִיא
"those horses"	הַסּוּסִים הָהֵם
"those mares"	הַסּוּסוֹת הָהֵנָּה

➤ *When a noun is described by an adjective and a demonstrative pronoun, the demonstrative pronoun follows the adjective.*

"this good horse"	הַסּוּס הַטּוֹב הַזֶּה
"this good mare"	הַסּוּסָה הַטּוֹבָה הַזֹּאת
"these good horses"	הַסּוּסִים הַטּוֹבִים הָאֵלֶּה

➤ A *predicate* demonstrative pronoun must agree in gender and number but will not have the definite article and will tend to come before the noun it describes.

"This is the horse."	זֶה הַסּוּס
"This is the mare."	זֹאת הַסּוּסָה
"These are the horses."	אֵלֶּה הַסּוּסִים
"These are the mares."	אֵלֶּה הַסּוּסוֹת
"That is the horse."	הוּא הַסּוּס
"That is the mare."	הִיא הַסּוּסָה
"Those are the horses."	הֵם הַסּוּסִים
"Those are the mares."	הֵנָּה הַסּוּסוֹת

Relative Pronoun (אֲשֶׁר)

17.5 A relative pronoun relates various parts of a sentence to each other, as in English, "the boy *who* sent the gift" or "the gift *that* was sent."

17.6 Hebrew has one primary relative pronoun אֲשֶׁר, translated *who, whom, which, what, where, that,* etc.

17.7 The relative pronoun אֲשֶׁר remains unchanged regardless of the gender or number or definiteness of the word it follows.

הָאִישׁ אֲשֶׁר יָשַׁב בַּבַּיִת

"the man (*ms* and definite) who lived in the house"

הָאִשָּׁה אֲשֶׁר יָשְׁבָה בַּבַּיִת

"the woman (*fs* and definite) who lived in the house"

הָאֲנָשִׁים אֲשֶׁר יָשְׁבוּ בַּבַּיִת

"the men (*mp* and definite) who lived in the house"

אֲנָשִׁים אֲשֶׁר יָשְׁבוּ בַּבַּיִת

"men (*mp* and indefinite) who lived in the house"

17.8　　The relative pronoun אֲשֶׁר follows various parts of a sentence.

נָפַל הָאִישׁ אֲשֶׁר שָׁלַח אֶת־הַנַּעַר

"*The man who* sent the boy fell." (subject)

שָׁלַח אֶת־הַנַּעַר אֲשֶׁר יָשַׁב בַּבַּיִת

"He sent the boy *who lived* in the house." (direct object)

שָׁלַח אֶת־הַנַּעַר לָאִישׁ אֲשֶׁר יָשַׁב בַּבַּיִת

"He sent the boy to the man *who lived* in the house."
(object of preposition)

17.9　　A *pf* in a relative clause may be translated as a past perfect.

נָפַל הָאִישׁ אֲשֶׁר שָׁלַח אֶת־הַנַּעַר

"The man who *had sent* the boy fell."

שָׁלַח אֶת־הַנַּעַר אֲשֶׁר יָשַׁב בַּבַּיִת

"He sent the boy who *had lived* in the house."

Directive Hey (הָ)

17.10　　Directive *hey* (הָ) is an ending added to certain words, expressing "direction toward." Directive *hey* is not accented and is thus distinguished from הָ = the feminine ending.

"to the land"	אַרְצָה (אַרְצָה)	אֶרֶץ
"to the house"	הַבַּיְתָה (הַבַּיְתָה)	הַבַּיִת
"to the city"	הָעִירָה (הָעִירָה)	הָעִיר

Vocabulary

be good	יָטַב	83	animal, cattle	בְּהֵמָה	413
give birth	יָלַד	8	herd	בָּקָר	493
form, create	יָצַר	156	bull	פַּר	542
fear, be afraid	יָרֵא	38	flock	צֹאן	479
inherit	יָרַשׁ	40	be dry, wither	יָבֵשׁ	152

Note:

○ Hebrew בָּקָר is used for large animals such as cows or oxen, and צֹאן is used for small animals such as sheep and goats. If בְּהֵמָה is used in contrast to בָּקָר, then בְּהֵמָה refers to wild animals, in contrast to domesticated animals.

Practice

Focusing on New Material

A. Focus on attributive demonstrative pronouns. Translate the following phrases.

3. הָאֹיְבִים הָאֵלֶּה	2. הַמִּשְׁפָּחָה הַזֹּאת	1. הַפֶּה הַזֶּה
6. הָעֲבָדִים הָהֵם	5. הַבַּת הַהִיא	4. הָרֹאשׁ הַהוּא
9. הַלֶּחֶם הָזֶה	8. הַבֵּן הַהוּא	7. הַתּוֹרָה הַזֹּאת
12. הָרֶגֶל הַטְּמֵאָה הַהִיא	11. הָאֲנָשִׁים הַטּוֹבִים הָהֵם	10. הַמִּלְחָמוֹת הָאֵלֶּה

B. Focus on predicate demonstrative pronouns. Translate the following sentences.

3. אֵלֶּה הַדְּבָרִים	2. זֹאת הָאִשָּׁה	1. זֶה הַבַּיִת
6. הֵם הַסְּפָרִים	5. הִיא הַמַּלְכוּת	4. הוּא הַדֶּרֶךְ
9. זֶה הַמֶּלֶךְ	8. אֵלֶּה הַנָּשִׁים	7. זֹאת הָאָרֶץ

C. Focus on the difference between the attributive and predicate demonstrative pronouns. Read the following lines, then indicate the use (*a* for attributive or *p* for predicate), gender, and number.

Use	Gender	Number		
a	f	s	1.	הָאִשָּׁה הַזֹּאת
			2.	זֶה הָאָדָם
			3.	הַמִּזְבֵּחַ הַזֶּה
			4.	הַבַּת הַהִיא

			5.	אֵלֶּה הָאֵלִים
			6.	הַבְּגָדִים הָהֵם
			7.	הָראשׁ הַזֶּה
			8.	זאת הַמַּלְכוּת
			9.	הָאֹהֶל הַהוּא
			10.	הָאֲרָצוֹת הָאֵלֶּה

D. Focus on the relative pronoun. Translate the following.

1. הַמֶּלֶךְ אֲשֶׁר מָלַךְ   2. הָאִשָּׁה אֲשֶׁר שָׁלְחָה   3. הַנְּבִיאִים אֲשֶׁר אָמְרוּ

4. הַכֶּסֶף אֲשֶׁר בַּבַּיִת   5. מְקוֹמוֹת אֲשֶׁר יָשַׁב   6. הַזָּהָב אֲשֶׁר לָקַח

7. זְבָחִים אֲשֶׁר עַל־מִזְבֵּחַ   8. הַלֶּחֶם אֲשֶׁר אָכַל   9. בָּנִים אֲשֶׁר יָצְאוּ

Reviewing Previous Lessons

E. Parse the following.

Verb	Pattern	Conj.	Person	Gender	Number	Root
1. שְׁמַרְתֶּם						
2. בָּנִיתִי						
3. יִפֹּל						
4. תַּעֲלֶה						
5. יִגְעוּ						
6. כָּלִינוּ						
7. חֲטָאתֶם						
8. אֶגְלֶה						
9. יִשָּׂא						
10. גָּאַלָה						

F. Focus on weak verbs. Translate the following.

1. בָּכוּ הַנְּעָרִים   2. אֶרְאֶה אֶת־הָאֹיֵב   3. קָרָאתָ אֶת־הַתּוֹרָה

4. בְּנִיתֶם בַּיִת   5. יִסַּע הָעָם   6. נִמְצָא אָב

7. יִפֹּל הָאָח   8. יִשְׂאוּ לֶחֶם   9. נִכְלֶה

10. תַּעֲשׂוּ מִזְבֵּחַ   11. יְצָאתֶם   12. חָטָאתִי

Putting It All Together

G. Translate the following.

	1.	בָּנוּ הָאָב וְהַבֵּן אֶת־הַבַּיִת הַזֶּה
1. The father and the son built this house.	2.	לֹא תִגַּע אֶת־זִבְחִי אֲשֶׁר עַל־הַמִּזְבֵּחַ
2. You (ms) will not touch my sacrifice which is on the altar.	3.	מָצָאתִי אֶת־הַכֶּסֶף אֲשֶׁר בַּמָּקוֹם הַהוּא
3. I found the silver which was in that place.	4.	קָרָא נְבִיא יְהוָה בְּקוֹל גָּדוֹל
4. The prophet of the LORD called out with a loud voice.	5.	בָּעֵת הַהִיא תִּדְרֹשׁ אֶת־הָאֱלֹהִים הַחַיִּים בְּכָל־לְבָבְךָ וּבְכָל־נַפְשֶׁךָ
5. At that time, you (ms) will seek the living God with all your heart and with all your soul.	6.	חֲזָקִים עַבְדֵי הַמֶּלֶךְ מֵעַבְדֵי הַכֹּהֵן
6. The king's servants are stronger than the priest's servants.	7.	לֹא עָבַר עַמִּי הַקָּדוֹשׁ אֶת־בְּרִיתִי
7. My holy people did not break my covenant.	8.	זֶה זְהַב אִמֵּנוּ אֲשֶׁר נָתְנָה לַאֲדוֹנָהּ
8. This is our mother's gold, which she gave to her lord.		

Reading Your Hebrew Bible

H. Translate the following from the Hebrew Bible.

1. זֶה הַיּוֹם אֲשֶׁר נָתַן יְהוָה אֶת־סִיסְרָא (Sisera) בְּיָדֶךָ[a]   Judges 4:14

2. בַּיּוֹם הַהוּא כָּרַת יְהוָה אֶת־אַבְרָם[b] (with Abram) בְּרִית   Genesis 15:18

3. זֹאת בְּרִיתִי אֲשֶׁר תִּשְׁמְרוּ   Genesis 17:10

[a] At times, ךָ֫ replaces the expected vocalization of the 2ms suffix (ךָ֖) .

[b] This אֶת־ is not the definite direct object marker but is the preposition "with," which you will learn in Lesson 32.

QAL IMPERFECT:
I YOD AND I ALEF

I Yod Verbs: Imperfect

17.1   I Yod verbs in Biblical Hebrew are placed in two groups: I Yod (Yod) and I Yod (Vav). I Yod (Yod) verbs have always had *yod* as the first root letter. I Yod (Vav) verbs at one time began with a *vav*. (This original *vav* will reappear in forms to be learned later.)

I Yod (Yod)

17.2   These forms follow the standard paradigm, except that (1) the *sheva* (☐) expected under the first root letter is lost and (2) the theme vowel is *patach*.

I Yod (Yod)	Strong	
יִיטַב	יִקְטֹל	*3ms*
תִּיטַב	תִּקְטֹל	*3fs*
תִּיטַב	תִּקְטֹל	*2ms*
תִּיטְבִי	תִּקְטְלִי	*2fs*
אִיטַב	אֶקְטֹל	*1cs*
יִיטְבוּ	יִקְטְלוּ	*3mp*
תִּיטַבְנָה	תִּקְטֹלְנָה	*3fp*
תִּיטְבוּ	תִּקְטְלוּ	*2mp*
תִּיטַבְנָה	תִּקְטֹלְנָה	*2fp*
נִיטַב	נִקְטֹל	*1cp*

I Yod (Vav)

17.3 These forms will vary from the standard paradigm in three ways: (1) the *yod* of the root is lost, (2) the vowel under the prefix is lengthened from short *chireq* (◌) to medium *tsere* (◌) because it is now in an open syllable and unaccented (see "Short vowels," p. 43), and (3) the theme vowel is *tsere* (◌).

I Yod (Vav)	Strong	
יֵשֵׁב	יִקְטֹל	*3ms*
תֵּשֵׁב	תִּקְטֹל	*3fs*
תֵּשֵׁב	תִּקְטֹל	*2ms*
תֵּשְׁבִי	תִּקְטְלִי	*2fs*
אֵשֵׁב	אֶקְטֹל	*1cs*

יֵשְׁבוּ	יִקְטְלוּ	*3mp*
תֵּשַׁבְנָה	תִּקְטֹלְנָה	*3fp*
תֵּשְׁבוּ	תִּקְטְלוּ	*2mp*
תֵּשַׁבְנָה	תִּקְטֹלְנָה	*2fp*
נֵשֵׁב	נִקְטֹל	*1cp*

> The verb הָלַךְ *follows the I Yod (Vav) paradigm in the imperfect >* יֵלֵךְ, *etc. The verb* נָתַן *also has tsere as the theme vowel >* יִתֵּן, *etc. Note also that in the pf of* נָתַן *the final nun* (ן) *assimilates to the tav* (ת) *of the suffix, so* נָתַתָּ > נָתַנְתָּ. *Similarly, in verbs like* כָּרַת *the tav of the root assimilates to the tav of the suffix, so* כָּרַתָּ > כָּרַתְתָּ.

I Alef Verbs: Imperfect

17.4 There are five I Alef verbs that do not follow the I Guttural paradigm but form a paradigm of their own, with three characteristics: (1) the *alef* is silent and therefore has no *sheva* (◌) under it, (2) the vowel of the prefix is *cholem* (◌), and (3) the theme vowel is *patach* (◌).

I Alef	Strong	
יֹאמַר	יִקְטֹל	3ms
תֹּאמַר	תִּקְטֹל	3fs
תֹּאמַר	תִּקְטֹל	2ms
תֹּאמְרִי	תִּקְטְלִי	2fs
אֹמַר	אֶקְטֹל	1cs

יֹאמְרוּ	יִקְטְלוּ	3mp
תֹּאמַרְנָה	תִּקְטֹלְנָה	3fp
תֹּאמְרוּ	תִּקְטְלוּ	2mp
תֹּאמַרְנָה	תִּקְטֹלְנָה	2fp
נֹאמַר	נִקְטֹל	1cp

Notes:

○ In the *1cs* form, the *alef* of the root is lost.

○ The other verbs in this group are אָכַל "eat" (which you have learned), and אָבַד "perish," אָבָה "be willing," and אָפָה "bake" (which you have not learned). ("Once upon a time, an old king *said*, 'I will certainly *perish* if I am not *willing* to *eat* this cake which my wife has *baked* for me.'")

Vocabulary

breath, wind, spirit *f*	רוּחַ	440	nation, Gentile	גּוֹי	416
perish	אָבַד	64	blood	דָּם	417
be willing, want	אָבָה	124	mountain, hill country	הַר	383
be, happen	הָיָה	5	sea	יָם	422
be alive, live	חָיָה	35	army	צָבָא	438

Note:

○ The noun גּוֹי is usually used in reference to non-Israelite nations, while Israel is usually referred to with עַם.

Practice

Focusing on New Material

A. Focus on weak roots. Parse the following.

	Verb	Pattern	Conj.	Person	Gender	Number	Root
1.	יִירַשׁ						
2.	יֵלֵד						
3.	יֹאכַל						
4.	יִיבְשׁוּ						
5.	אֵלֵךְ						
6.	נָתַתִּי						
7.	כְּרַתֶּם						
8.	נֵצֵא						
9.	תִּירָא						
10.	יִתֵּן						

B. Focus on weak roots. Translate the following.

5. יִירָא   4. נָתַתִּי   3. נֵדַע   2. תֵּשֵׁב   1. יֹאמְרוּ

10. אֵלֵד   9. תִּיבְשִׁי   8. תִּירָאוּ   7. יֵצְאוּ   6. אִירַשׁ

15. תֵּלֵךְ   14. אֹמַר   13. נְתַתֶּם   12. תֹּאכַל   11. כָּרַתָּ

Reviewing Previous Lessons

C. Focus on possessive suffixes. Translate the following and indicate the person, gender, and number of the suffix.

Person	Gender	Number		
1	c	s	1.	מַלְכִּי
			2.	מַלְכּוֹ
			3.	מַלְכָּהּ
			4.	מַלְכֵּנוּ

			5.	מַלְכְּכֶם
			6.	מַלְכֵּךְ
			7.	מַלְכְּכֶם
			8.	מַלְכֵּךְ
			9.	מַלְכְּכֶן
			10.	מַלְכָּן

D. Focus on possessive suffixes. Translate the following.

5. סְפְרֵנוּ   4. תּוֹרָתְךָ   3. דְּבָרָהּ   2. אֵלַי   1. מִשְׁפָּטוֹ

10. בֵּיתְכֶם   9. זְהָבֵנוּ   8. עַמּוֹ   7. לִבּוֹ   6. מִשְׁפַּחְתָּם

15. עִירֵנוּ   14. בָּקֶרְךָ   13. עֵינִי   12. עִתָּם   11. נַפְשָׁהּ

Putting It All Together

E. Translate the following.

	1. זֶה הַיּוֹם אֲשֶׁר עָשָׂה יְהוָה
1. This is the day that the LORD has made.	2. נָתַתָּ סְפְרִי לַאֲדוֹן־הַבַּיִת
2. You (ms) gave my book to the master of the house.	3. יִירְאוּ עַבְדֵי מַלְכְּכֶם הַחֲכָמִים אֶת־יְהוָה
3. Your (mp) king's wise servants will fear the LORD.	4. יֵצְאוּ הָאֲנָשִׁים הָאֵלֶּה מֵעִיר־הַמֶּלֶךְ הַגָּדוֹל
4. These men will go out from the great king's city.	5. יְשָׁרִים דִּבְרֵי הַנָּבִיא הַהוּא מִדִּבְרֵי הָאִישׁ הָרָשָׁע
5. The words of that prophet are more correct than the words of the wicked man.	6. אֵשֵׁב בְּבֵית יְהוָה לְעוֹלָם
6. I will live in the house of the LORD forever.	7. נִקַּח אֶת־זְהַב הָעָם הֶחָזָק הַזֶּה אֶל־אָהֳלֵנוּ

7. We will take the gold of this strong people to our tent.	8. תֵּלֵד אִשָּׁה בָּנִים וּבָנוֹת
8. A woman will bear sons and daughters.	9. תֵּלֵךְ בְּדֶרֶךְ־הַבְּרִית אֲשֶׁר כָּרַתִּי לְאָבִיךָ
9. You will walk in the way of the covenant which I made with your father.	

Reading Your Hebrew Bible

F. Translate the following from the Hebrew Bible.

Psalms 26:5	וְעִם רְשָׁעִים לֹא אֵשֵׁב	1.
Deuteronomy 22:16	אֶת־בִּתִּי נָתַתִּי לָאִישׁ הַזֶּה	2.
Psalm 56:5	בֵּאלֹהִים בָּטַחְתִּי לֹא אִירָא	3.
Isaiah 52:6	יֵדַע עַמִּי שְׁמִי[a]	4.

[a] Because שְׁמִי is definite, due to the possessive suffix, you would expect אֶת־ to precede, but the direct object marker is often omitted in poetic texts such as this one.

POSSESSIVE SUFFIXES ON PLURAL NOUNS

Possessive Suffixes on Plural Nouns

19.1   In Lesson 16, you learned that Hebrew expresses "my horse," etc., by adding possessive *suffixes to a singular noun*. In this lesson you learn how Hebrew expresses "my horse*s*," etc., by adding related *suffixes to plural nouns*.

Form of the Suffixes

		Plural	Singular
"his horses"	*3ms*	סוּסָיו	סוּסוֹ
"her horses"	*3fs*	סוּסֶיהָ	סוּסָהּ
"your horses"	*2ms*	סוּסֶיךָ	סוּסְךָ
"your horses"	*2fs*	סוּסַיִךְ	סוּסֵךְ
"my horses"	*1cs*	סוּסַי	סוּסִי
"their horses"	*3mp*	סוּסֵיהֶם	סוּסָם
"their horses"	*3fp*	סוּסֵיהֶן	סוּסָן
"your horses"	*2mp*	סוּסֵיכֶם	סוּסְכֶם
"your horses"	*2fp*	סוּסֵיכֶן	סוּסְכֶן
"our horses"	*1cp*	סוּסֵינוּ	סוּסֵנוּ

➤   *Vocabulary Cards ##960–965*

Notes:

○ The most significant difference between the suffixes on singular nouns and the suffixes on plural nouns is the consistent presence of the *yod* (**'**), which is actually the *yod* of the *mp* construct.

○ The *yod* (**י**) is silent in the 3*ms* suffix, so the suffix is pronounced *av*, as in l<u>a</u>va.

Form of Feminine Plural Nouns before the Suffixes

19.2 The same set of suffixes is added to the *fp* form of the noun.

"his mares"	*3ms*	סוּסוֹתָיו	=	יו ָ	+	סוּסוֹת
"her mares"	*3fs*	סוּסוֹתֶיהָ	=	יהָ ֶ	+	סוּסוֹת
"your mares"	*2ms*	סוּסוֹתֶיךָ	=	יךָ ֶ	+	סוּסוֹת
"your mares"	*2fs*	סוּסוֹתַיִךְ	=	יִךְ ַ	+	סוּסוֹת
"my mares"	*1cs*	סוּסוֹתַי	=	י ַ	+	סוּסוֹת

"their mares"	*3mp*	סוּסוֹתֵיהֶם	=	יהֶם ֵ	+	סוּסוֹת
"their mares"	*3fp*	סוּסוֹתֵיהֶן	=	יהֶן ֵ	+	סוּסוֹת
"your mares"	*2mp*	סוּסוֹתֵיכֶם	=	יכֶם ֵ	+	סוּסוֹת
"your mares"	*2fp*	סוּסוֹתֵיכֶן	=	יכֶן ֵ	+	סוּסוֹת
"our mares"	*1cp*	סוּסוֹתֵינוּ	=	ינוּ ֵ	+	סוּסוֹת

➤ *Vocabulary Cards ##973–978*

The Verb "To Be Able" (יָכֹל)

Imperfect	Perfect	
יוּכַל	יָכֹל	*3ms*
תּוּכַל	יָכְלָה	*3fs*
תּוּכַל	יָכֹלְתָּ	*2ms*
תּוּכְלִי	יָכֹלְתְּ	*2fs*
אוּכַל	יָכֹלְתִּי	*1cs*

Imperfect	Perfect	
יוּכְלוּ	יָכְלוּ	*3c/mp*
תּוּכַלְנָה		*3fp*
תּוּכְלוּ	יְכָלְתֶּם	*2mp*
תּוּכַלְנָה	יְכָלְתֶּן	*2fp*
נוּכַל	יָכֹלְנוּ	*1cp*

Notes:

○ The *pf* varies from the standard paradigm only in that the theme vowel is *cholem* (◌ֹ), which is true of several other stative verbs. The ◌ֳ in the 2*m/fp* is *qamets chatuf*.

○ The *impf* varies from the standard paradigm in that (1) the vowel of the prefix is *shureq* (וּ), (2) the *yod* (י) of the root is lost, and (3) the theme vowel is *patach* (◌ַ), which is characteristic of stative verbs (see Lesson 11).

Vocabulary

because, that	כִּי	911	then	אָז	873
unless, except	כִּי־אִם	912	if	אִם	884
therefore	לָכֵן	919	so that not	בִּלְתִּי	897
in order to	לְמַעַן (לְמַ֫עַן)	921	also, even	גַּם	900
so that not	פֶּן	946	thus	כֹּה	910

Practice

Focusing on New Material

A. Focus on words with possessive suffixes. Match the form with the possessive suffix of the right hand column with the corresponding absolute singular form of the left hand column.

סֵפֶר	.a	____	קוֹלוֹתֵינוּ .1
עִיר	.b	____	תּוֹרוֹתֶיךָ .2
קוֹל	.c	____	אֲדוֹנַי .3
מִשְׁפָּט	.d	____	כַּסְפֵּיכֶם .4
שָׁנָה	.e	____	לְבוֹתֵיהֶם .5
תּוֹרָה	.f	____	סְפָרֶיהָ .6
אָדוֹן	.g	____	דְּבָרָיו .7
לֵב	.h	____	מִשְׁפָּטֶיךָ .8
כֶּסֶף	.i	____	עָרֶיכֶן .9
דָּבָר	.j	____	שְׁנוֹתַיִךְ .10

B. Focus on words with possessive suffixes. Translate the following words with possessive suffixes.

4. סוּסֵיהֶם	3. סוּסֵינוּ	2. סוּסֵיכֶם	1. סוּסָיו
8. סוּסֶיהָ	7. סוּסַיִךְ	6. סוּסַי	5. סוּסֶיךָ
12. דְּבָרָיו	11. זְהָבֵינוּ	10. נַפְשׁוֹתֵיהֶם	9. עֲבָדֵיכֶם
16. יָדָיו	15. מְקוֹמוֹתַי	14. אֲבוֹתַיִךְ	13. מִשְׁפָּטֶיךָ

C. Focus on words with possessive suffixes. Translate the following.

	1.	בָּנִיתִי אֶת־מִזְבְּחוֹתֶיךָ
1. I built your altars.	2.	נָתְנוּ אֲבוֹתֵינוּ אֶת הַכֶּסֶף
2. Our fathers gave the money.	3.	דְּרַשְׁתֶּם לֵאלֹהִים בְּכָל־לְבַבְתֵיכֶם
3. You (*mp*) sought for God with all your hearts.	4.	לָקְחוּ אֶת־הַזָּהָב אֶל־עָרֵיהֶם
4. They took the gold to their cities.	5.	הֲלַכְתֶּן לְדַרְכֵיכֶן הָרְשָׁעִים
5. You (*fp*) went on your wicked ways. (לְ + הָלַךְ = "go on")	6.	רָאִינוּ אֶת סְפָרֶיהָ
6. We saw her books.		

Reviewing Previous Lessons

D. Parse the following.

Verb	Pattern	Conj.	Person	Gender	Number	Root
1. גָּאֲלוּ						
2. תַּעֲמֹד						
3. אֶשָּׂא						
4. בְּכִיתֶם						
5. יוּכַל						
6. נֹאמַר						
7. תַּעֲשׂוּ						
8. כָּבֵד						

9.	יָכֹלְתָּ					
10.	תֵּשְׁבִי					

E. Focus on weak roots. Translate the following.

4. נֵדַע	3. לֹא עֲשִׂיתֶם	2. יִגְעוּ	1. בָּרָאתִי
8. תִּשָּׂא	7. לֹא יַעֲלֶה	6. תֹּאכַל	5. בָּנִינוּ
12. נוּכַל	11. לֹא נְתַתֶּם	10. לֹא אֵלֵד	9. יֹאמְרוּ
15. בָּרָא	14. לֹא נִירָא	13. יִבְכֶּה	

Putting It All Together

F. Translate the following:

1.	יֵצְאוּ צִבְאוֹתֵינוּ לַמִּלְחָמָה הַגְּדוֹלָה
1. Our armies will go out to the great battle.	
2.	נַעֲלֶה בְּהַר־יְהוָה וּבִמְקוֹם קָדְשׁוֹ נֵשֵׁב
2. We will go up into the mountain of the Lord, and we will live in his holy place.	
3.	בְּרֵאשִׁית בָּרָא אֱלֹהִים אֵת הַשָּׁמַיִם וְאֵת הָאָרֶץ וְאֵת הָאָדָם וְאֵת הַבְּהֵמָה
3. In the beginning God created the heavens, the earth, humanity, and the animals.	
4.	לֹא אִירָא אֶת־אֹיְבַי
4. I will not fear my enemies.	
5.	תִּירַשׁ בָּקָר רַב וְצֹאן רַב מֵאָבִיךָ
5. You will inherit many cattle/herds and sheep/flocks from your father.	
6.	אֵלֶּה כֹהֲנֶיךָ הַקְּדוֹשִׁים אֲשֶׁר קָרְאוּ בְּסֵפֶר הַתּוֹרָה
6. These are your holy priests who read in the Book of the Law.	
7.	הָאֲנָשִׁים הָרְשָׁעִים הָהֵם יֵרְדוּ אֶל־הַיָּם
7. Those wicked men will go down to the sea.	
8.	רְאִיתֶם בְּעֵינֵיכֶם וּשְׁמַעְתֶּם בְּאָזְנֵיכֶם
8. You saw with your eyes and heard with your ears.	

Reading Your Hebrew Bible

G. Translate the following from the Hebrew Bible.

1 Kings 8:48   .1   וְהַבַּיִת אֲשֶׁר בָּנִיתִי לִשְׁמֶךָ

Psalm 18:39   .2   יִפְּלוּ תַּחַת רַגְלָי

Genesis 32:31   .3   רָאִיתִי אֱלֹהִים פָּנִים אֶל־פָּנִים

THE VERB: QAL INFINITIVES

Infinitives

20.1 Hebrew has two infinitives: "infinitive construct" and "infinitive absolute." Infinitives are "infinite" conjugations in that they are not marked for person, gender, or number as are, for example, the *pf* and *impf*, which are finite conjugations (see Conjugations, Lesson 6).

20.2 Of the two Hebrew infinitives, the infinitive construct is closer to the English infinitive, as in, "He wanted *to run*."

Infinitive Construct

> *The infinitive construct is abbreviated inf const.*

Form of the Infinitive Construct

20.3 The standard form of the qal *inf const* is קְטֹל. This form is related to the *impf*. Remove the prefix, and the *inf const* is what remains.

Inf const	Impf
קְטֹל	יִקְטֹל

20.4 If the *impf* has a *patach* (◌ַ) as in יִכְבַּד, then the *inf const* has a *patach* as in כְּבַד.

20.5 An *inf const* may have a pronoun suffix added.

➤ The suffixes added are the same as those added to singular nouns.

➤ When a suffix is added, the vowels change, because the accent is on the added syllable > קָטְלוֹ, קָטְלָה, קָטְלְךָ, etc. The ◌ָ is *qamets chatuf*.

20.6   Weak roots have altered forms of the *inf const.*

with suffix	Inf const	Root	Weakness
עָמְדוֹ	עֲמֹד	עמד	I Guttural

➤   *Chatef-patach (◌ֲ) in place of sheva (◌ְ).*

| שָׁמְעוֹ | שְׁמֹעַ | שמע | III Guttural |

➤   *Furtive patach under the final guttural.*

| שִׁבְתּוֹ | שֶׁבֶת | ישב | I Yod (Vav) |

➤   *As in the impf, the yod (י) is lost; a feminine tav (ת) is added to compensate, creating the appearance of three root letters.*

| נָפְלוֹ | נְפֹל | נפל | I Nun |

➤   *Usually the inf const of I Nun verbs is regular.*

| גַּשְׁתּוֹ | גֶּשֶׁת | נגש | I Nun |

➤   *In some I Nun verbs the inf const follows the paradigm of the I Yod (Vav) verbs.*

| גְּלוֹתוֹ | גְּלוֹת | גלה | III Hey |

➤   *The inf const of III Hey verbs is characterized by the וֹת ending.*

The inf const of יָצָא is צֵאת, with a silent alef (א); with the suffix, צֵאתוֹ. Because הָלַךְ follows the I Yod (Vav) paradigm in the impf, the inf const of הָלַךְ is לֶכֶת; with the suffix, לֶכְתּוֹ. The inf const of נָתַן follows the I Yod (Vav) paradigm, but the final nun (ן) of the root is assimilated to the added tav (ת), resulting in תֵּת; with the suffix, תִּתּוֹ. The inf const of לָקַח follows the paradigm of the I Nun verbs that lose the nun (נ), resulting in קַחַת; with the suffix, קַחְתּוֹ.

Use of the Infinitive Construct

20.7   The *inf const* has numerous uses. Several of the the most frequent are introduced in this lesson.

20.8   With the preposition לְ

➤   *In these cases, the suffix is the object of the inf const.*

➤   Verbal complement. The *inf const* is often used to "fill in" the specifics of a verb having a general meaning.

"He is able to judge."	יָכֹל לִשְׁפֹּט
"He wants to judge."	אָבָה לִשְׁפֹּט
"He is afraid to judge you."	יָרֵא לְשָׁפְטְךָ

➤   Purpose. The *inf const* is used to express purpose.

"He sat down to read."	יָשַׁב לִקְרֹא
"He went up to sacrifice."	עָלָה לִזְבֹּחַ
"He went down to find her."	יָרַד לְמָצְאָהּ

➤   The *inf const* is negated by בִּלְתִּי. The לְ is usually placed on the front of בִּלְתִּי.

לְבִלְתִּי מְלֹךְ עַל־הָעִיר

"so as not to reign over the city"

לְבִלְתִּי שְׁמֹעַ אֶת־הַדְּבָרִים

"so as not to hear the words"

לְבִלְתִּי רְאוֹתוֹ

"so as not to see him"

20.9   With the prepositions בְּ and כְּ

➤   *In these cases, the suffix is the subject of the inf const.*

➤   Temporal. The *inf const* is used with the prepositions בְּ and כְּ in temporal clauses. The tense required for translation into English is determined by the context.

"when the king reigned . . . ."	בִּמְלֹךְ הַמֶּלֶךְ
"when the woman wrote . . . ."	כִּכְתֹב הָאִשָּׁה
"when we guarded . . . ."	בְּשָׁמְרֵנוּ

20.10   With time words like יוֹם

➤   Temporal. The *inf const* is used with time words in temporal clauses.

בְּיוֹם מְלֹךְ הַמֶּלֶךְ

"(in the day) when the king reigned . . . ."

בְּיוֹם כְּתֹב הָאִשָּׁה

"(in the day) when the woman wrote . . . ."

בְּיוֹם שָׁמְרֵנוּ

"(in the day) when we guarded . . . ."

Infinitive Absolute

> *The infinitive absolute is abbreviated inf abs.*

Form of the Infinitive Absolute

20.11   The standard form of the qal *inf abs* is קָטוֹל. Note the differences between the *inf abs* and the *inf const*: the *inf abs* has (1) a *qamets* (◌ָ)
under the first root letter, and (2) a *cholem-vav* (וֹ) as the second vowel.

Inf abs	Inf const
קָטוֹל	קְטֹל

> ➤   *In spite of their respective names and vocalizations, the inf const is <u>not</u> the con-*
> *struct form of the inf abs; the two forms are unrelated historically.*

20.12   III Hey verbs (and Hollow verbs; see Lesson 25) vary from the standard
paradigm in the qal *inf abs*.

III Hey	Strong
גָּלֹה / רָאוֹ	קָטוֹל

Use of the Infinitive Absolute

20.13   The *inf abs* has numerous uses. One of the the most frequent is introduced in this lesson.

> ➤   Emphasis. An *inf abs* is placed before another form of the verb from
> the same root to emphasize the kind of action in view.

"You will certainly guard. . . ."	שָׁמוֹר תִּשְׁמֹר
"They will certainly give. . . ."	נָתוֹן יִתְּנוּ
"We will certainly dwell. . . ."	יָשׁוֹב נֵשֵׁב

Vocabulary

until, as far as	עַד	939	ground, land	אֲדָמָה	448	
love	אָהַב	27	light *f*	אוֹר	487	
pour out	יָצַק	155	between	בֵּין	893	
hate, be an enemy	שָׂנֵא	110	loyalty	חֶסֶד (חֶסֶד)	463	
pour out, shed	שָׁפַךְ	122	darkness	חֹשֶׁךְ (חֹשֶׁךְ)	625	

Note:

○ The preposition בֵּין is used before both nouns that it governs, for example, בֵּין אִישׁ וּבֵין אִשָּׁה ("between a man and a woman").

Practice

Focusing on New Material

A. Focus on the forms of the *inf const*. Write the root of each *inf const*.

_____	שְׁמֹעַ	.2	_____	קְטֹל	.1
_____	שֶׁבֶת	.4	_____	עֲמֹד	.3
_____	לֶדֶת	.6	_____	גְּלוֹת	.5
_____	דַּעַת	.8	_____	שְׁלֹחַ	.7
_____	בְּכוֹת	.10	_____	בְּנוֹת	.9
_____	לֶכֶת	.12	_____	רֶדֶת	.11
_____	צֵאת	.14	_____	תֵּת	.13

B. Focus on the use of the *inf const*. Translate the following phrases.

לִמְלֹךְ	.4	לִזְבֹּחַ	.3	לִזְכֹּר	.2	לִכְתֹּב	.1
בְּדַעְתּוֹ	.8	בְּרִדְתּוֹ	.7	לָלֶדֶת	.6	לָשֶׁבֶת	.5
לַעֲשׂוֹתוֹ	.12	לִרְאוֹתוֹ	.11	כִּגְלוֹתוֹ	.10	כִּבְנוֹתוֹ	.9
בְּקַחְתּוֹ	.16	כְּצֵאתוֹ	.15	לָלֶכֶת	.14	לָתֵת	.13

C. Focus on the use of the *inf abs.* Translate the following phrases.

3. זָכוֹר תִּזְכֹּר	2. שָׁלוֹחַ תִּשְׁלַח	1. שָׁמוֹר תִּשְׁמֹר
6. יָדוֹעַ תֵּדַע	5. יָשׁוֹב תֵּשֵׁב	4. הָלוֹךְ תֵּלֵךְ
9. כָּלֹה תִּכְלֶה	8. בָּכֹה תִּבְכֶּה	7. בָּנֹה תִּבְנֶה
12. עָלֹה תַּעֲלֶה	11. יָצוֹא תֵּצֵא	10. נָתוֹן תִּתֵּן

Reviewing Previous Lessons

D. Focus on the use of adjectives. Translate the following phrases and sentences and fill in the blanks for use of adjective (*a* for attributive and *p* for predicative) and for gender and number.

Use	Gender	Number		
a	f	s	1.	הָאִשָּׁה הַטּוֹבָה
			2.	יָשָׁר הָאָדָם
			3.	הַמִּזְבֵּחַ הַטָּהוֹר
			4.	הַבַּת הַטּוֹבָה
			5.	טְמֵאִים הָאֵלִים
			6.	הָאֱלֹהִים הַחַיִּים
			7.	גְּדוֹלִים הַבְּגָדִים
			8.	רְשָׁעָה הַמַּלְכוּת
			9.	לֵב חָכָם
			10.	הָאֲרָצוֹת הָרַבּוֹת

E. Parse the following.

Verb	Pattern	Conj.	Person	Gender	Number	Root
1. קְטֹל						
2. אָבַדְתִּי						
3. אֶכְתֹּב						
4. יֵרֶד						

5.	שֶׁבֶת					
6.	נִרְאֶה					
7.	גְּלוֹת					
8.	אָמוֹר					
9.	לֶכֶת					
10.	תֵּת					

Putting It All Together

F. Translate the following.

	1.	יָכֹלְתִּי לִקְרֹא אֶת־הַסֵּפֶר הַקָּדוֹשׁ
1. I am able to read the holy book. (Stative verbs are present tense.)	2.	יֹאבֶה לָלֶכֶת אֶל־בֵּית־אָבִיךָ
2. He will be willing to go to your father's house.	3.	יִרְאֲנוּ לַעֲבֹר אֶת־תּוֹרַת יְהוָה כִּי יִשְׁפֹּט אֶת־כָּל־עֲבָדָיו
3. We are afraid (stative) to transgress the law of the LORD, because he will judge all his servants.	4.	אָמְרוּ כִּי חֲטָאתֶם כִּי לֹא שְׁמַרְתֶּם אֶת־הַבְּרִית
4. They said that you sinned, because you did not keep the covenant.	5.	נֵצֵא מִן־הָעִיר לִשְׁמֹעַ אֶל־הַנָּבִיא אֲשֶׁר דָּרַשׁ אֶת־יְהוָה
5. We will go out of the city to listen to the prophet who sought the LORD.	6.	זָבוֹחַ תִּזְבַּח זְבָחִים טְהוֹרִים לִפְנֵי יְהוָה כִּי קָדוֹשׁ הוּא
6. You will certainly offer pure sacrifices before the LORD, because he is holy.	7.	בְּשָׁכְבָם בַּלַּיְלָה לֹא יִירָאוּ כִּי אֱלֹהֵיהֶם יִשְׁמֹר אֶת־נַפְשׁוֹתֵיהֶם
7. When they lie down at night, they will not be afraid, because their God will guard their souls.	8.	נַעֲבֹד אֶת־יְהוָה צְבָאוֹת כָּל־יְמֵי־חַיֵּינוּ כִּי טוֹב הוּא
8. We will serve the LORD of Hosts all the days of our life, because he is good.		

Reading Your Hebrew Bible

G. Translate the following from the Hebrew Bible.

1 Samuel 24:21	1. יָדַעְתִּי כִּי מָלוֹךְ תִּמְלוֹךְ [a]
1 Samuel 20:5	2. וְאָנֹכִי יָשׁוֹב אֵשֵׁב עִם הַמֶּלֶךְ לֶאֱכֹל
Deuteronomy 29:3	3. וְלֹא־נָתַן יְהוָה לָכֶם (to you) לֵב לָדַעַת וְעֵינַיִם
	לִרְאוֹת וְאָזְנַיִם לִשְׁמֹעַ

[a]The Hebrew text actually reads מָלֹךְ תִּמְלוֹךְ. The infinitive absolute should be spelled מָלוֹךְ; מָלֹךְ has a "defective" spelling (see p. 129). The imperfect should be spelled תִּמְלֹךְ; the spelling of the imperfect with *cholem vav* for *cholem*, though not rare, is not common.

THE VERB: QAL ACTIVE PARTICIPLE

Participles

21.1   As in English, there are two participles in Hebrew: "active" and "passive." In this lesson you are learning the active participle. English active participles are formed with /ing/, for example, "he is *walking*," "they are *giving*," and so on.

21.2   Hebrew participles are "non-finite" verbs, because they are marked for gender and number but not for person.

> *The active participle is abbreviated ptc.*

Form of the Active Participle

	Plural	Singular
Masculine	קֹטְלִים	קֹטֵל
Feminine	קֹטְלוֹת	קֹטֶלֶת (קֹטֶלֶת) קֹטְלָה

21.3   The *ptc* is declined like the adjective (see p. 56). The *fs* has two forms, but קֹטֶלֶת is the more frequent.

21.4   The first vowel of a *ptc* may be either *cholem* (◌֗) or *cholem-vav* (וֹ). The spelling with *cholem-vav* (וֹ) is "correct"; the spelling with *cholem* (◌֗) is more frequent, but "defective."

> *Defective spelling.   At times, a word should be spelled with a long vowel, a vowel that has a vowel letter, but is spelled without the vowel letter. Such a word is spelled defectively, for example, cholem ($\square$) for cholem-vav (וֹ), chireq ($\square$) for chireq-yod (יִ), or qibbuts ($\square$) for shureq (וּ). The qal ptc is an example of defective spelling: (1) Cholem-vav is a long "a"-class vowel, but cholem is a medium "u"-class vowel. (2) From a comparison with other related languages, we know that the first vowel of the qal ptc is a long "a"-class vowel, and should therefore be spelled with cholem-vav (וֹ). (3) The qal ptc is usually spelled with cholem ($\square$), and is therefore spelled defectively. Other examples of defective spelling are לֹא for לוֹא and נְבִיאִים for נְבִיאִים.*

21.5   The qal *ptc* of weak roots varies from the standard paradigm. The following are the key variations.

	III Hey	III Alef	III Guttural
ms	גֹּלֶה	מֹצֵא	שֹׁמֵעַ
fs	גֹּלָה	מֹצֵאת	שֹׁמַעַת
mp	גֹּלִים	מֹצְאִים	שֹׁמְעִים
fp	גֹּלוֹת	מֹצְאוֹת	שֹׁמְעוֹת

Use of the Active Participle

21.6   Kind of action and time of action.

➤   The *ptc* expresses continuing action.

"writing"	כֹּתֵב
"sitting"	יֹשֵׁב
"walking"	הֹלֵךְ

➤   No tense is indicated by the *ptc*; tense is determined by context.

➤   Action "about to" take place soon (imminent future) can be expressed by the particle הִנֵּה plus the *ptc*.

"I am about to judge"	הִנֵּה אֲנִי שֹׁפֵט
"I am about to walk"	הִנֵּה אֲנִי הֹלֵךְ

21.7   Three uses. The *ptc* has the same three uses as the adjective: "attributive," "predicate," and "substantive" (see Lesson 10).

➤   An attributive *ptc* must agree in gender, number, and definiteness, and follow the noun it describes. Such constructions will usually be definite and are best translated with "who."

"the man *who is writing*"	הָאִישׁ הַכֹּתֵב
"the woman *who is sitting*"	הָאִשָּׁה הַיֹּשֶׁבֶת
"the men *who are walking*"	הָאֲנָשִׁים הַהֹלְכִים

➤   *This use of the ptc with the definite article is equal to the use of a pf or impf with the relative pronoun (*אֲשֶׁר*).*

➤   A predicate *ptc* must agree in gender and number but does not have the definite article and usually <u>follows</u> the noun it describes. [Remember, however, that the predicate adjective tends to come <u>before</u> the noun it describes.]

"The man *is writing* the book."	הָאִישׁ כֹּתֵב אֶת־הַסֵּפֶר
"The woman *is sitting* in the city."	הָאִשָּׁה יֹשֶׁבֶת בָּעִיר
"The men *are walking* to the city."	הָאֲנָשִׁים הֹלְכִים אֶל־הָעִיר

➤   A substantive *ptc* is used as a noun.

"a guard"	שֹׁמֵר
"a judge"	שֹׁפֵט
"the inhabitant"	הַיֹּשֵׁב

➤   *Some participles are used as substantives so frequently that they are listed as nouns in the dictionaries. You have already learned two such nouns,* אֹיֵב *("enemy") and* כֹּהֵן *("priest").*

21.8   Two states. The *ptc* is used in the *cs* as well as the *abs* state.

"the guardian of the covenant"	שֹׁמֵר־הַבְּרִית
"the judge of the wicked"	שֹׁפֵט־הָרְשָׁעִים
"the inhabitants of the city"	יֹשְׁבֵי הָעִיר

21.9   With suffixes. The *ptc* can take pronoun suffixes.

➤   The suffix is usually the object of the verb.

"all who find me"	כָּל־מֹצְאַי
"those who know him"	יֹדְעָיו

Vocabulary

there	שָׁם	950	mighty man	גִּבּוֹר	494
imprison	אָסַר	126	generation	דּוֹר	495
camp	חָנָה	79	wall	חוֹמָה	498
be hot, angry	חָרָה	147	heat, anger	חֵמָה	502
capture	לָכַד	90	now	עַתָּה	944

Note:

○ An idiom for anger in Hebrew is חָרָה אַף. The literal translation of חָרָה אַפּוֹ is "his nose was hot," which is idiomatically translated "he was angry." A related idiom is אֶרֶךְ אַפַּיִם "length of nose" > "it takes a long time for one's nose to get hot" > "patient."

Practice

Focusing on New Material

A. Focus on the form of the active participle. Parse the following.

	Verb	Pattern	Conj.	Person	Gender	Number	Root
1.	כֹּרֵת						
2.	הֹלֶכֶת						
3.	עֹבְרִים						
4.	שֹׁלְחוֹת						
5.	שׁוֹלֵחַ						
6.	נֹשֵׂאת						
7.	בּוֹנִים						
8.	בֹּכָה						
9.	גּוֹלוֹת						
10.	רֹאֶה						

B. Focus on the use of the active participle. Translate the following (present progressive is fine, since there is no context) and indicate the use (*a* for attributive, *p* for predicate, or *s* for substantive).

Use		
a	1.	הַמֶּלֶךְ הַיּשֵׁב
	2.	הַמֶּלֶךְ יֹשֵׁב
	3.	יוֹשְׁבֵי הָעִיר
	4.	אֲנַחְנוּ אֹכְלִים
	5.	הִנֵּה אֲנַחְנוּ אֹכְלִים
	6.	הָעֲבָדִים בֹּנִים
	7.	הָעֲבָדִים הַבֹּנִים
	8.	הָאִם בֹּכָה
	9.	הָאִם יוֹצֵאת
	10.	שֹׁפֵט־הָרְשָׁעִים

Reviewing Previous Lessons

C. Focus on possessive suffixes. Translate the following nouns, paying attention to the number of the noun and the person, gender, and number of the suffix.

4. קוֹלָהּ   3. זְרוֹעֹתֶיךָ   2. אֵלֶךְ   1. אוֹרִי

8. דְּבָרִי   7. מִשְׁפְּחוֹתֵיהֶם   6. מִשְׁפַּחְתָּם   5. קוֹלֶיהָ

12. סְפָרָיו   11. סִפְרוֹ   10. זִבְחֵיכֶם   9. דְּבָרַי

16. עֵינַיִךְ   15. עֵינֶךָ   14. מַלְכֵּנוּ   13. מְלָכֵינוּ

D. Parse the following.

Verb	Pattern	Conj.	Person	Gender	Number	Root
1. עֲבַדְתֶּם						
2. אֶמְצָא						
3. יִתֵּן						

4. גָּלִינוּ						
5. שָׁפַט						
6. שֹׁמְרִים						
7. בְּנוֹת						
8. בָּנוֹת						
9. יֵרְדוּ						
10. שָׁבַת						

Putting It All Together

E. Translate the following.

	1.	יָדַעְתִּי אֶת־הָאֲנָשִׁים הַשֹּׁמְעִים בִּדְבַר־יְהוָה
1. I knew the men who were obeying the word of the LORD. (Remember: שָׁמַע בְּ means "obey.")	2.	יָדַעְתִּי אֶת־הָאֲנָשִׁים אֲשֶׁר שָׁמְעוּ בִּדְבַר־יְהוָה
2. I knew the men who obeyed the word of the LORD.	3.	הִנֵּה הוּא עֹלֶה אֶל־הַר־הָאֱלֹהִים לִזְבֹּחַ שָׁם
3. He is about to go up to the mountain of God to sacrifice there.	4.	לֹא תֵשֵׁב מִשְׁפַּחַת הַמֶּלֶךְ הַגְּדוֹלָה בִּמְקוֹם הַמִּלְחָמָה
4. The great (*fs*) family (*fs*) of the king (*ms*) will not dwell near the place of the battle.	5.	אֲבִיתֶם לִשְׁפֹּךְ דָּם כִּי לֹא יְרֵאתֶם אֶת־הָאֱלֹהִים הַחַיִּים
5. You were willing to shed blood, because you did not fear the living God.	6.	הַנָּבִיא הַקָּדוֹשׁ כֹּתֵב אֶת סִפְרוֹ לַמֶּלֶךְ הָרָשָׁע הַהוּא
6. The holy prophet is writing his book to that wicked king.	7.	נִזְכֹּר אֶת־תּוֹרַת אֱלֹהֵינוּ וּמִשְׁפָּטָיו לְעוֹלָם כִּי טוֹבִים הֵם
7. We will remember forever the law of our God and his judgments, for they are good.	8.	יֵרֵד הָאֹיֵב לָקַחַת אֶת־בָּנֶיךָ וּבְנוֹתֶיךָ לְעִירָם
8. The enemy will go down to take your sons and your daughters to their city.		

Reading Your Hebrew Bible

F. Translate the following from the Hebrew Bible.

1. וְהִנֵּה אָנֹכִי הוֹלֵךְ הַיּוֹם בְּדֶרֶךְ כָּל־הָאָרֶץ   Joshua 23:14

2. אַתָּה נֹתֵן אֶת־עַבְדְּךָ בְּיַד אַחְאָב (Ahab)   1 Kings 18:9

3. שׁוֹמֵר יְהוָה אֶת־כָּל־אֹהֲבָיו   Psalm 145:20

PRONOUN SUFFIXES
ON PREPOSITIONS

Form of Pronoun Suffixes on Prepositions

22.1   The pronoun suffixes added to prepositions are the same as those added to nouns. Prepositions are neither singular nor plural, but some
prepositions take the suffixes added to singular nouns and others take
the suffixes added to plural nouns.

Prepositions Taking the Suffixes Added to Singular Nouns

		Preposition	Noun
"to him"	*3ms*	לוֹ	סוּסוֹ
"to her"	*3fs*	לָהּ	סוּסָהּ
"to you"	*2ms*	לְךָ	סוּסְךָ
"to you"	*2fs*	לָךְ	סוּסֵךְ
"to me"	*1cs*	לִי	סוּסִי

		Preposition	Noun
"to them"	*3mp*	לָהֶם	סוּסָם
"to them"	*3fp*	לָהֶן	סוּסָן
"to you"	*2mp*	לָכֶם	סוּסְכֶם
"to you"	*2fp*	לָכֶן	סוּסְכֶן
"to us"	*1cp*	לָנוּ	סוּסֵנוּ

135

➤ Other prepositions following this paradigm are:

"in him"	בּוֹ	בְּ
"within him"	בְּתוֹכוֹ	בְּתוֹךְ
"with him"	עִמּוֹ	עִם

Prepositions Taking the Suffixes Added to Plural Nouns

			Preposition	Noun
"to him"	3ms		אֵלָיו	סוּסָיו
"to her"	3fs		אֵלֶיהָ	סוּסֶיהָ
"to you"	2ms		אֵלֶיךָ	סוּסֶיךָ
"to you"	2fs		אֵלַיִךְ	סוּסַיִךְ
"to me"	1cs		אֵלַי	סוּסַי

			Preposition	Noun
"to them"	3mp		אֲלֵיהֶם	סוּסֵיהֶם
"to them"	3fp		אֲלֵיהֶן	סוּסֵיהֶן
"to you"	2mp		אֲלֵיכֶם	סוּסֵיכֶם
"to you"	2fp		אֲלֵיכֶן	סוּסֵיכֶן
"to us"	1cp		אֵלֵינוּ	סוּסֵינוּ

➤ Other prepositions following this paradigm are:

"before him"	לְפָנָיו	לִפְנֵי
"on him"	עָלָיו	עַל
"under him"	תַּחְתָּיו	תַּחַת

The Preposition מִן with Suffixes

22.2   In some forms the preposition מִן is written twice, resulting in מִן + מִן = מִמֶּנ as the base form.

"from him"	3ms	מִמֶּנּוּ
"from her"	3fs	מִמֶּנָּה
"from you"	2ms	מִמְּךָ
"from you"	2fs	מִמֵּךְ
"from me"	1cs	מִמֶּנִּי

"from them"	3mp	מֵהֶם
"from them"	3fp	מֵהֶן
"from you"	2mp	מִכֶּם
"from you"	2fp	מִכֶּן
"from us"	1cp	מִמֶּנּוּ

The Preposition כְּ with Suffixes

22.3   In addition to the regular form כְּ there is an expanded form כְּמוֹ. This expanded form is the base form for most forms with a suffix.

"like him"	3ms	כָּמוֹהוּ
"like her"	3fs	כָּמוֹהָ
"like you"	2ms	כָּמוֹךָ
"like you"	2fs	
"like me"	1cs	כָּמוֹנִי

"like them"	3mp	כָּהֶם
"like them"	3fp	כָּהֶן
"like you"	2mp	כָּכֶם
"like you"	2fp	
"like us"	1cp	כָּמוֹנוּ

The Direct Object Marker (אֶת־ / אֵת) with Suffixes

22.4   When a pronoun is the direct object of a verb, the suffixes can be added to the direct object marker (אֶת־ / אֵת). Except in the 2*mp*, the first vowel is *cholem-vav* (וֹ).

"him"	3ms	אֹתוֹ
"her"	3fs	אֹתָהּ
"you"	2ms	אֹתְךָ
"you"	2fs	אֹתָךְ
"me"	1cs	אֹתִי

"them"	3mp	אֹתָם	
"them"	3fp	אֹתָן	(1×)
"you"	2mp	אֶתְכֶם	
"you"	2fp		
"us"	1cp	אֹתָנוּ	

"The king sent the prophet."	שָׁלַח הַמֶּלֶךְ אֶת־הַנָּבִיא
"The king sent him."	שָׁלַח הַמֶּלֶךְ אֹתוֹ
"The king sent the prophets."	שָׁלַח הַמֶּלֶךְ אֶת־הַנְּבִיאִים
"The king sent them."	שָׁלַח הַמֶּלֶךְ אֹתָם

Resumptive Pronouns on Prepositions

22.5   In English, a preposition is placed at the beginning of a relative clause; for example, "the place *in which he dwelled*." In Hebrew, the preposition is placed at the end of the relative clause and a pronoun (that agrees with the noun being modified) is placed on the preposition. This pronoun is called "resumptive" because it resumes or picks up again the noun being modified.

"the place in which he dwelled"	הַמָּקוֹם אֲשֶׁר יָשַׁב בּוֹ
"the city to which he walked"	הָעִיר אֲשֶׁר הָלַךְ אֵלֶיהָ
"the king before whom we stood"	הַמֶּלֶךְ אֲשֶׁר עָמַדְנוּ לְפָנָיו

Vocabulary

peace	שָׁלוֹם	484	there is/are not	אֵין	879
be full, fill	מָלֵא	46	there is/are	יֵשׁ	511
abandon	עָזַב	98	glory, honor	כָּבוֹד	464
approach	קָרַב	105	very	מְאֹד	467
drink	שָׁתָה	63	messenger, angel	מַלְאָךְ	471

Practice

Focusing on New Material

A. Focus on prepositions with pronoun suffixes. Translate the following prepositional phrases.

5. לְךָ	4. בְּתוֹכִי	3. עִמָּהּ	2. בְּךָ	1. לוֹ
10. אֵלָיו	9. לָכֶן	8. בָּכֶם	7. בְּתוֹכֵנוּ	6. עִמָּהֶם
15. לִפְנֵיהֶם	14. אֵלֵינוּ	13. תַּחְתֶּיהָ	12. לְפָנַי	11. עָלֶיךָ
20. אֲלֵיכֶן	19. לִפְנֵיהֶן	18. אֵלַיִךְ	17. עֲלֵיכֶם	16. תַּחְתֵּינוּ
25. בָּנוּ	24. אֵלַי	23. לִי	22. לְפָנֵינוּ	21. עִמָּנוּ

B. Translate the following.

	1.	נָתַן אֶת־הַזֶּבַח לָהֶם
1. He gave the sacrifice to them (*mp*).	2.	הָלְכוּ עִמָּנוּ
2. They walked with us.	3.	לָקַחְתָּ אֶת־הַכֶּסֶף מִמֶּנִּי
3. You took the silver from me.	4.	תַּחְתֶּיךָ זְרוֹעַ־יְהוָה
4. The arm of the LORD is under you (*ms*).	5.	גָּדוֹל הָאִישׁ אֲשֶׁר עָמַדְנוּ לְפָנָיו
5. The man before whom we stood is great.	6.	בָּטַחְנוּ בּוֹ
6. We trust in him. (Stative = present)	7.	יָצַק אֶת־הַמַּיִם עֲלֵיכֶם

7. He poured out the water on you (*mp*).	8. לָכְדוּ אֶת־הָעִיר מֵהֶם
8. They captured the city from them (*mp*).	

Reviewing Previous Lessons

C. Focus on the construct state. Translate the following phrases.

1. דְּבַר הַנָּבִיא   2. דִּבְרֵי הַנָּבִיא   3. צְבָא הַשָּׁמַיִם

4. תּוֹרַת הָאָרֶץ   5. מִשְׁפַּחַת הַמֶּלֶךְ   6. זִבְחֵי הָאֱלֹהִים

7. נַפְשׁוֹת הָעַמִּים   8. יוֹם יְהוָה   9. יְמֵי הַשָּׁנָה

10. אֲדוֹן־כָּל־הָאָרֶץ   11. רֵאשִׁית דַּרְכּוֹ   12. בְּרִית אֱלֹהֵינוּ

D. Focus on adjectives and the construct state. Translate the following phrases, paying attention to which noun is modified by the adjective.

1. יוֹם יְהוָה הַגָּדוֹל   2. צְבָא הַשָּׁמַיִם הָרַב

3. רֵאשִׁית דַּרְכּוֹ הַטּוֹבָה   4. זִבְחֵי הַכֹּהֵן הַטָּמֵא

5. דְּבַר הַנְּבִיאִים הָרְשָׁעִים   6. יְמֵי הַשָּׁנָה הַטּוֹבִים

7. תּוֹרַת יְהוָה הַטְּהוֹרָה   8. בְּרִית אֱלֹהֵינוּ הַטּוֹבָה

9. נַפְשׁוֹת הָעַמִּים הַטְּהוֹרוֹת   10. דִּבְרֵי הַנָּבִיא הַגָּדוֹל

11. אֲדוֹן־כָּל־הָאָרֶץ הַגָּדוֹל   12. מִשְׁפַּחַת הַמֶּלֶךְ הַגָּדוֹל

E. Parse the following.

Verb	Pattern	Conj.	Person	Gender	Number	Root
1. כְּתַבְתֶּם						
2. נֵרֵד						
3. עֲשׂוֹת						
4. בֹּנִים						
5. מָצָאנוּ						
6. אַתֶּן						

7.	שָׁבַת					
8.	כָּתֹב					
9.	לְכֹוד					
10.	יַעֲלוּ					

Putting It All Together

F. Translate the following.

1. The men of the city will walk to the house of the priest with us.	1. יֵלְכוּ אַנְשֵׁי הָעִיר עִמָּנוּ אֶל־בֵּית־הַכֹּהֵן
2. The LORD is giving the land to us forever.	2. יְהוָה נֹתֵן אֶת־הָאָרֶץ לָנוּ לְעוֹלָם
3. The prophet of the LORD will come down from the mountain to read the book of the law of the covenant to you (*mp*).	3. נְבִיא יְהוָה יֵרֵד מִן־הָהָר לִקְרֹא אֶת־סֵפֶר תּוֹרַת הַבְּרִית אֲלֵיכֶם
4. The boy who found the gold sent it to me.	4. הַנַּעַר אֲשֶׁר מָצָא אֶת הַזָּהָב שָׁלַח אֹתוֹ לִי
5. The man who has a pure heart within is good.	5. טוֹב הָאִישׁ אֲשֶׁר לֵב טָהוֹר בְּתוֹכוֹ
6. I am going up to the mountains to live there.	6. אֲנִי עֹלֶה אֶל־הֶהָרִים לָשֶׁבֶת שָׁם
7. That brother is not able to stand before you because you are holy, but he is not holy.	7. לֹא יָכֹל הָאָח הַהוּא לַעֲמֹד לְפָנֶיךָ כִּי קָדוֹשׁ אַתָּה וְלֹא קָדוֹשׁ הוּא
8. The Lord of the whole earth is willing to care for you.	8. אָבָה אֲדוֹן כָּל־הָאָרֶץ לִפְקָדֶךָ

Reading Your Hebrew Bible

G. Translate the following from the Hebrew Bible.

Deuteronomy 1:30	1. יְהוָה אֱלֹהֵיכֶם הַהֹלֵךְ לִפְנֵיכֶם
Joshua 22:31	2. הַיּוֹם יָדַעְנוּ כִּי־בְתוֹכֵנוּ יְהוָה
Genesis 41:38	3. אִישׁ אֲשֶׁר רוּחַ אֱלֹהִים בּוֹ

THERE IS (NOT)
AND HAVE (NOT)

There Is (Not) in Hebrew

23.1 There Is (Present Time)

➤ To express "there is" in present time the particle יֵשׁ is used.

"There is a boy in the house."	יֵשׁ נַעַר בַּבַּיִת
"There are boys in the house."	יֵשׁ נְעָרִים בַּבַּיִת

➤ *יֵשׁ is not marked for person, gender, or number.*

➤ To express "there is not" in present time, the particle אֵין is used.

"There is not a boy in the house."	אֵין נַעַר בַּבַּיִת
"There are not boys in the house."	אֵין נְעָרִים בַּבַּיִת

➤ *אֵין is not marked for person, gender, or number.*

23.2 There Was (Past Time)

➤ To express "there was" in past time, the 3*ms* and 3*cp* forms of the verb הָיָה are used.

"There was a boy in the house."	הָיָה נַעַר בַּבַּיִת
"There were boys in the house."	הָיוּ נְעָרִים בַּבַּיִת

➤ To express "there was not" in past time, לֹא is added.

"There was not a boy in the house."	לֹא הָיָה נַעַר בַּבַּיִת
"There were not boys in the house."	לֹא הָיוּ נְעָרִים בַּבַּיִת

Have (Not) in Hebrew

23.3 Have (Present Time)

➤ To express "have" in present time the particle יֵשׁ is used with the preposition לְ.

"The father has a son."　　　　　　　יֵשׁ לָאָב בֵּן

"I have a son."　　　　　　　　　　יֵשׁ לִי בֵּן

➤ To express "not have" in present time, the particle אֵין is used with the preposition לְ.

"The father does not have a son."　　אֵין לָאָב בֵּן

"I do not have a son."　　　　　　אֵין לִי בֵּן

23.4　Have (Past Time)

➤ To express "have" in past time the *pf* of הָיָה is used with the preposition לְ.

"The father had a son."　　　　　הָיָה לָאָב בֵּן

"I had a son."　　　　　　　　　הָיָה לִי בֵּן

"The father had sons."　　　　　הָיוּ לָאָב בָּנִים

"I had sons."　　　　　　　　　הָיוּ לִי בָּנִים

➤ *The form of* הָיָה *must agree with whatever is possessed.*

➤ To express "not have" in past time לֹא is added.

"The father did not have a son."　　לֹא הָיָה לָאָב בֵּן

"I did not have a son."　　　　　לֹא הָיָה לִי בֵּן

23.5　Have (Future Time)

➤ To express "have" in future time the *impf* of הָיָה is used with the preposition לְ.

"The father will have a son."　　　יִהְיֶה לָאָב בֵּן

"I will have sons."　　　　　　　יִהְיוּ לִי בָּנִים

➤ *The form of* הָיָה *must agree with whatever is possessed.*

➤ To express "not have" in future time לֹא is added.

"The father will not have a son."　　לֹא יִהְיֶה לָאָב בֵּן

"I will not have sons."　　　　　לֹא יִהְיוּ לִי בָּנִים

Another Use of הָיָה לְ

23.6　הָיָה לְ is used in the sense of "become."

"The man became a father."　　　הָיָה הָאִישׁ לְאָב

"The woman will become a mother."　תִּהְיֶה הָאִשָּׁה לְאֵם

Another Use of אֵין

➤ אֵין is used to negate sentences with predicate participles.

"You (ms) are not walking."	אֵין אַתָּה הֹלֵךְ
"You (fs) are not walking."	אֵין אַתְּ הֹלֶכֶת

➤ In such constructions, אֵין is usually used with pronoun suffixes, rather than independent personal pronouns.

"You (ms) are not walking."	אֵינְךָ הֹלֵךְ
"You (fs) are not walking."	אֵינֵךְ הֹלֶכֶת

➤ Here are the forms of אֵין with the pronoun suffixes.

3mp	אֵינָם		3ms	אֵינֶנּוּ
3fp			3fs	אֵינֶנָּה
2mp	אֵינְכֶם		2ms	אֵינְךָ
2fp			2fs	אֵינֵךְ
1cp	אֵינֶנּוּ		1cs	אֵינֶנִּי

Vocabulary

sin, guilt	עָוֹן	478	sin	חַטָּאת	461
choose	בָּחַר	128	decree, law	חֹק	506
flee	בָּרַח	133	commandment	מִצְוָה	525
cling to	דָּבַק	134	in front of	נֶגֶד (נֶגֶד)	936
want, desire	חָפֵץ	146	around	סָבִיב	938

Notes:

○ The word עָוֹן is spelled defectively for עָווֹן.

○ The verb בָּחַר often takes its object through the preposition בְּ, for example, בָּחַר בַּנַּעַר, "He chose the boy."

○ The plural of מִצְוָה is usually spelled defectively, מִצְוֹת for מִצְווֹת.

○ The plural of חֹק is spelled חֻקִּים.

Practice

Focusing on New Material

A. Focus on "there is/was (not)." Translate the following, paying attention to the difference between past/present and positive/negative.

3. אֵין נָבִיא בָּאָרֶץ	2. לֹא הָיָה נָבִיא בָּאָרֶץ	1. הָיָה נָבִיא בָּאָרֶץ
6. אֵין גִּבּוֹר שָׁם	5. יֵשׁ שָׁלוֹם בַּמַּלְכוּת	4. יֵשׁ נָבִיא בָּאָרֶץ
9. יֵשׁ גִּבּוֹר עַל־הַדֶּרֶךְ	8. אֵין זֶבַח עַל־הַמִּזְבֵּחַ	7. לֹא הָיָה גִּבּוֹר שָׁם

B. Focus on "have/had (not)." Translate the following, paying attention to the difference between past/present and positive/negative.

3. אֵין לָאִישׁ בְּהֵמוֹת	2. לֹא הָיוּ לָאִישׁ בְּהֵמוֹת	1. הָיוּ לָאִישׁ בְּהֵמוֹת
6. אֵין לָנוּ שָׁלוֹם	5. יֵשׁ לְךָ עֲבָדִים	4. יֵשׁ לָאִישׁ בְּהֵמוֹת
9. יֵשׁ לָעִיר חוֹמָה	8. אֵין לַבַּת אָח	7. לֹא הָיָה לָכֶם כָּבוֹד

C. Focus on אֵין negating predicate participles. Translate the following.

3. אֵין אַתָּה שֹׁמֵעַ	2. אֵינֶנִּי כֹתֵב	1. אֵין אֲנִי כֹתֵב
6. אֵינְכֶם בֹּטְחִים	5. אֵין אַתֶּם בֹּטְחִים	4. אֵינְךָ שֹׁמֵעַ
9. אֵינֶנּוּ כֹּרְתִים בְּרִית	8. אֵינֶנּוּ מֶלֶךְ	7. אֵין הוּא מֶלֶךְ

Reviewing Previous Lessons

D. Focus on infinitives. Translate the following, paying attention to the use of the *inf const* and *inf abs*.

	1.	לֹא אָבִיתָ לִשְׁכַּב עַל־הָאֲדָמָה
1. You are not willing (stative = present) to lie down on the ground.	2.	יָכֹלְנוּ לַחֲנוֹת תַּחַת הַשָּׁמַיִם
2. We are able (stative = present) to camp under the sky.	3.	יֵלֵךְ לִרְאוֹת אֶת־הַמִּלְחָמָה

3. He will go to see the battle.	4. . . . כְּלֶכְתּוֹ לִרְאוֹת אֶת־הַמִּלְחָמָה
4. When he goes to see the battle . . .	5. . . . בְּכָתְבִי אֶת־הַסֵּפֶר
5. When I write/wrote the book . . .	6. בְּיוֹם אֲכָלְךָ מִמֶּנּוּ אָבוֹד תֹּאבֵד
6. In the day when you eat (*inf const*) from it you will surely (*inf abs*) perish.	7. נֵצֵא מִן־הַבַּיִת לָרֶדֶת מִן־הָהָר
7. We will go out of/from the house to go down from the mountain.	8. שָׁלַח אֶת־הָאֲנָשִׁים לִבְנוֹת חוֹמָה
8. He sent the men to build a wall.	

E. Parse the following.

	Verb	Pattern	Conj.	Person	Gender	Number	Root
1.	כְּתַבְתֶּם						
2.	נִבְטַח						
3.	עֲשׂוֹת						
4.	גְלוֹת						
5.	דַּעַת						
6.	אֶתֵּן						
7.	בְּרָאתָ						
8.	תֵּצֵא						
9.	תֹּאכְלוּ						
10.	אָבוֹד						

Putting It All Together

F. Translate the following.

	1. לֹא יֶחֱרֶה אַף יְהֹוָה בְּעַמּוֹ לְעוֹלָם
1. The anger of the LORD will not burn against his people forever.	2. וּבַיּוֹם הַהוּא יִהְיֶה שָׁלוֹם בְּכָל־הָאָרֶץ
2. And in that day there will be peace in the whole earth.	3. יֵשׁ כָּבוֹד לָאִישׁ אֲשֶׁר יָרֵא אֶת־יְהֹוָה בְּכָל־נַפְשׁוֹ

3. There is honor for the man who fears (stative = present) the LORD with all his soul.	4.	בָּכֹה בָּכִינוּ כִּי לֹא הָיָה לָנוּ כֹּהֵן לִזְבֹּחַ זִבְחֵי קֹדֶשׁ לָנוּ
4. We really wept, because we had no priest to offer holy sacrifices for us.	5.	הִנֵּה יָצָא הַצָּבָא הָרַב הַזֶּה לַמִּלְחָמָה אֲשֶׁר בֵּין הֶהָרִים וּבֵין הַיָּם
5. This large army is about to go out to the battle which is between the mountains and the sea.	6.	הָעֲבָדִים הַבֹּנִים אֶת־הַחוֹמָה יוֹשְׁבִים עַל־הָאֲדָמָה לֶאֱכֹל וְלִשְׁתּוֹת
6. The servants who are building the wall are sitting on the ground to eat and to drink.	7.	גָּאוֹל תִּגְאַל זְרוֹעַ יְהוָה הַחֲזָקָה אוֹתָנוּ כִּי עַמּוֹ אֲנַחְנוּ
7. The strong arm (ƒs) of the LORD will surely redeem us, because we are his people.	8.	טוֹבִים דִּבְרֵי הָאִשָּׁה הַיֹּדַעַת אֶת־דֶּרֶךְ הַשָּׁלוֹם
8. The words of the woman who knows the way of peace are good.		

Reading Your Hebrew Bible

G. Translate the following from the Hebrew Bible.

Isaiah 57:21	אֵין שָׁלוֹם אָמַר אֱלֹהַי לָרְשָׁעִים .1
1 Samuel 17:46	(Israel) וְיֵדְעוּ כָּל־הָאָרֶץ כִּי יֵשׁ אֱלֹהִים לְיִשְׂרָאֵל .2
2 Kings 17:26	אֵינָם יֹדְעִים אֶת־מִשְׁפַּט אֱלֹהֵי הָאָרֶץ .3

24

THE VERB:
QAL VOLITIVES

Volitives

24.1 Volitives (from Latin *volo* "to will" and related to English "volition" = "will") are verb forms that are used to express the *will* of the speaker. Hebrew has three volitives:

➤ Cohortative: volitive of the first person, for example, "Let me listen!"

➤ Imperative: volitive of the second person, for example, "Listen!"

➤ Jussive: volitive of the third person, for example, "Let him listen!"

24.2 Volitives have special *forms* as well as the special *use* of expressing the will of the speaker.

> *There is a "jussive of the second person" that has a __form__ similar to a jussive but the __use__ of expressing the will of the second person. This "jussive of the second person" is used primarily in one context; see below on Negating Volitives.*

Cohortative

> *Cohortative is abbreviated coh.*

24.3 Qal Strong Verb

➤ The cohortative is the first person *impf*, to which הָ is added. This הָ is not to be confused with הָ = the *fs* marker.

	Cohortative	Imperfect
"Let me write."	אֶכְתְּבָה	אֶכְתֹּב
"Let us write."	נִכְתְּבָה	נִכְתֹּב

148

➤ *Since the medium cholem ($\square$) ends up in an open pretonic syllable, cholem reduces to sheva, as in* יְקַטְלוּ < יִקְטֹל.

24.4 Qal Weak Verbs

	Cohortative	Imperfect	
"Let me fall."	אֶפְּלָה	אֶפֹּל	I Nun
"Let me dwell."	אֵשְׁבָה	אֵשֵׁב	I Yod (Vav)
"Let me stand."	אֶעֶמְדָה	אֶעֱמֹד	I Guttural

➤ *Two vocal shevas in a row are not permitted in Hebrew, so the expected chatef-segol ($\square$) under the ayin (ע) is changed to the corresponding short vowel, segol ($\square$).*

	Cohortative	Imperfect	
"Let me go away."	אֶגְלֶה	אֶגְלֶה	III Hey

➤ *Because the first-person form already ends in a vowel, the expected* הַ $\square$ *cannot be added. Context will determine whether an impf or a coh translation is appropriate.*

Imperative

> *Imperative is abbreviated impv.*

24.5 Qal Strong Verbs

➤ The imperative, like the *inf const*, is related to the imperfect. Basically, the *impv* is the second person *impf* without the prefix.

Imperative	Imperfect	
קְטֹל	תִּקְטֹל	*2ms*
קִטְלִי	תִּקְטְלִי	*2fs*

Imperative	Imperfect	
קִטְלוּ	תִּקְטְלוּ	*2mp*
קְטֹלְנָה	תִּקְטֹלְנָה	*2fp*

➤ *With the prefix gone, the first sheva becomes vocal, resulting in two vocal shevas in a row in the fs and mp forms, so the first sheva becomes chireq in these forms.*

➤ If the *impf* has a *patach* as the theme vowel, so does the *impv*.

Imperative	Imperfect	
בְּטַח	תִּבְטַח	*2ms*

24.6   Qal Weak Verbs

	Imperative	Imperfect		
"Stand!"	עֲמֹד	תַּעֲמֹד	*2ms*	I Guttural
"Stand!"	עִמְדִי	תַּעַמְדִי	*2fs*	
"Stand!"	עִמְדוּ	תַּעַמְדוּ	*2mp*	
"Stand!"	עֲמֹדְנָה	תַּעֲמֹדְנָה	*2fp*	
"Fall!"	נְפֹל	תִּפֹּל	*2ms*	I Nun
"Fall!"	נִפְלִי	תִּפְּלִי	*2fs*	
"Fall!"	נִפְלוּ	תִּפְּלוּ	*2mp*	
"Fall!"	נְפֹלְנָה	תִּפֹּלְנָה	*2fp*	
"Dwell!"	שֵׁב	תֵּשֵׁב	*2ms*	I Yod (Vav)
"Dwell!"	שְׁבִי	תֵּשְׁבִי	*2fs*	
"Dwell!"	שְׁבוּ	תֵּשְׁבוּ	*2mp*	
"Dwell!"	שֵׁבְנָה	תֵּשַׁבְנָה	*2fp*	

Since הלך and נתן follow the paradigm of ישב in the impf, they do so in the impv, resulting in לֵךְ and תֵּן.

	Imperative	Imperfect		
"Go away!"	גְּלֵה	תִּגְלֶה	2ms	III Hey
"Go away!"	גְּלִי	תִּגְלִי	2fs	
"Go away!"	גְּלוּ	תִּגְלוּ	2mp	
"Go away!"	גְּלֶינָה	תִּגְלֶינָה	2fp	

Jussive

> *Jussive is abbreviated jus.*

24.7   Qal Strong Verb

➤ In the strong verb, the *jus* and the *impf* are identical in form. Context determines whether a *jus* or an *impf* translation is required.

24.8   Qal Weak Verbs

➤ In most weak verbs, the *jus* and the *impf* are identical in form. One exception is III Hey verbs. In III Hey verbs, the *jus* is a shortened form of the *impf*.

	Jussive fs	Jussive ms	Imperfect
"Let him/her go away!"	תִּגֶל	יִגֶל	יִגְלֶה
"Let him/her cry!"	תֵּבְךְּ	יֵבְךְּ	יִבְכֶּה
"Let him/her go up!"	תַּעַל	יַעַל	יַעֲלֶה

Negating Volitives

➤ The *coh* and *jus* are negated with אַל, "not."

"Let us not send him!"   אַל נִשְׁלָחָה אוֹתוֹ

"Let him not build it!"   אַל יִבֶן אוֹתוֹ

➤ The *impv* is never negated. To express a negative command in the second person, a "jussive of the second person" is used. The form is that of a jussive, being short, but used in the second person.

"Do not build it!"   אַל תִּבֶן אֹתוֹ

"Do not cry!"   אַל תֵּבְךְּ

➤ אַל־תֵּבְךְּ *could also mean "Don't let her cry."*

Indirect Volitives

➤ In addition to their use for expressing the "direct" will of the speaker, the volitives are also used to express the "indirect" will of the speaker. An indirect volitive will most often be translated as a purpose clause in English, "so that. . . ."

➤ Whenever there is a sequence of volitive + וְ + volitive, the second volitive is usually "indirect," unless the volitives are the same person.

שְׁלַח אוֹתָנוּ וְנִזְבְּחָה זְבָחִים

"Send us, so that we may offer sacrifices." (*impv* + וְ + *coh*)

שְׁלַח אֹתוֹ וְיִבֶן מִזְבֵּחַ

"Send him, so that he may build an altar." (*impv* + וְ + *jus*)

נִשְׁלְחָה אוֹתוֹ וְיִבֶן מִזְבֵּחַ

"Let us send him, so that he may build an altar." (*coh* + וְ + *jus*)

יִבֶן מִזְבֵּחַ וְנִזְבְּחָה זְבָחִים

"Let him build an altar, so that we may offer sacrifices."
(*jus* + וְ + *coh*)

Vocabulary

arise, stand	קוּם	20	go in , enter	בּוֹא	3
be high, exalted	רוּם	59	be ashamed	בּוֹשׁ	66
run	רוּץ	107	understand	בִּין	68
put, place	שִׂים	23	die	מוּת	12
turn, return, repent	שׁוּב	24	turn aside	סוּר	54

Note:

○ These forms are qal *inf const* of a weak verb, which is the subject of the next chapter.

Practice

Focusing on New Material

A. Focus on the form of the volitives. Parse the following.

Verb	Pattern	Conj.	Person	Gender	Number	Root
1. אֶשְׁפְּטָה						
2. זִבְחוּ						
3. יִבֶן						
4. שֵׁב						
5. לֵךְ						
6. נִתְּנָה						
7. בְּכֵה						
8. אֵדְעָה						
9. קְחוּ						
10. כִּתְבִי						

B. Focus on the use of the volitives. Translate the following.

4. אַל יַעַל　　　3. יִבֶן　　　2. נִכְרְתָה　　　1. פְּקֹד

8. בְּנוּ　　　7. אַל אֵרְדָה　　　6. דְּבְקִי　　　5. שִׁלְחוּ

12. אַל תֵּבְךְ　　　11. תַּעַשׂ　　　10. לְכוּ　　　9. צְאוּ

C. Focus on the use of the indirect volitives. Translate the following.

	1. כְּתֹב סֵפֶר וְאֶקְרְאָה אוֹתוֹ
1. Write a book, so that I may read it.	2. בְּנוּ בַיִת וְנֵשְׁבָה בּוֹ
2. Build a house so that we may live in it.	3. נִזְכְּרָה אֶת־יְהוָה וְנַעַבְדָה אוֹתוֹ
3. Let us remember the LORD, and let us serve him.	4. יַעַל אֶת־הָהָר וְיִבֶן מִזְבֵּחַ
4. Let him go up the mountain, and let him build an altar.	5. תֶּן מַיִם לָהּ וְתֵשְׁתְּ
5. Give water to her, so that she may drink.	

Reviewing Previous Lessons

D. Parse the following.

Verb	Pattern	Conj.	Person	Gender	Number	Root
1. מָלַכְתָּ						
2. יִבְטְחוּ						
3. שְׁלָחִי						
4. זֹבְחִים						
5. אָבוֹד						
6. לְקַחְתֶּם						
7. תִּשְׁמְעוּ						
8. שָׁמֶרֶת						
9. נָפַלְתִּי						
10. תִּפְקֹד						

Putting It All Together

E. Translate the following.

	1.	שְׁמַע אֶת־דִּבְרֵי הַנָּבִיא הַיְשָׁרִים
1. Listen to the upright words of the prophet.	2.	אַל נִירָאָה לָלֶכֶת אֶל־בֵּית יְהוָה הַיּוֹם כִּי מֶלֶךְ־כָּל־הָאָרֶץ הוּא
2. Let us not be afraid to go to the house of the LORD today, for he is the king of all the earth.	3.	הַנָּשִׁים דְּבֵקוֹת לַבְּרִית אֲשֶׁר כָּרְתוּ אִמּוֹתֵיהֶן עִמָּן
3. The women are clinging to the covenant which their mothers made with them.	4.	יִבְרַח הַנַּעַר הַמֹּצֵא אֶת־הַסֵּפֶר מֵאֹיְבָיו הַחֲזָקִים
4. The boy who finds the book will flee from his strong enemies.	5.	דְּעוּ כִּי לֹא תֵשְׁבוּ עַל־הָאֲדָמָה לְעוֹלָם כִּי עֲבַרְתֶּם אֶת־מִצְוֹת־יְהוָה וְחֻקָּיו
5. Know that you (*mp*) will not live on the land forever, because you transgressed the commandments of the LORD and his statutes.	6.	יָכֹלְנוּ לִלְכֹּד אֶת־הַגִּבּוֹרִים הַגְּדוֹלִים אֲשֶׁר שָׁפְכוּ אֶת־דַּם־בָּנֵינוּ
6. We are (stative) able to capture the great warriors who shed the blood of our sons.	7.	אֵין הַצָּבָא אֹבֶה לַעֲזֹב אֶת מִלְחֶמֶת הַקֹּדֶשׁ
7. The army is not willing to leave the holy battle.	8.	נִשְׁלְחָה אֶת־עַבְדֵי הַמֶּלֶךְ אֶל־הָעִיר וְיִבְנוּ בַיִת לוֹ שָׁם
8. Let us send the king's servants to the city, so that they may build a house for him there.		

Reading Your Hebrew Bible

F. Translate the following from the Hebrew Bible.

Psalm 62:9	בִּטְחוּ בוֹ בְכָל־עֵת . . . שִׁפְכוּ־לְפָנָיו לְבַבְכֶם	.1
Deuteronomy 4:1	וְעַתָּה יִשְׂרָאֵל שְׁמַע אֶל־הַחֻקִּים וְאֶל־הַמִּשְׁפָּטִים לְמַעַן תִּחְיוּ	.2
Isaiah 2:5	לְכוּ וְנֵלְכָה בְּאוֹר יְהוָה	.3

QAL: HOLLOW VERBS

Hollow Verbs

➤ A hollow verb is weak, because the root is not made up of three consonants but only of two consonants, with a long vowel in between, for example, קוּם, שִׂים, and בּוֹא.

25.1 Infinitive Construct

➤ The characteristic long vowel is present in the *inf const*, which is the dictionary form of hollow verbs, for example, קוּם, שִׂים, and בּוֹא.

25.2 Imperfect

➤ The characteristic long vowel is also present in the *impf.*

	בּוֹא	שִׂים	קוּם
3ms	יָבוֹא	יָשִׂים	יָקוּם
3fs	תָּבוֹא	תָּשִׂים	תָּקוּם
2ms	תָּבוֹא	תָּשִׂים	תָּקוּם
2fs	תָּבוֹאִי	תָּשִׂימִי	תָּקוּמִי
1cs	אָבוֹא	אָשִׂים	אָקוּם

	בּוֹא	שִׂים	קוּם
3mp	יָבוֹאוּ	יָשִׂימוּ	יָקוּמוּ
3fp	תְּבוֹאֶינָה	תְּשִׂימֶינָה	תְּקוּמֶינָה
2mp	תָּבוֹאוּ	תָּשִׂימוּ	תָּקוּמוּ
2fp		תְּשִׂימֶינָה	תְּקוּמֶינָה
1cp	נָבוֹא	נָשִׂים	נָקוּם

25.3   Imperative

➤ The characteristic long vowel is also present in the *impv*, because the *impv* is related in form to the *inf const* and the *impf*.

				Imperfect
2ms	בּוֹא	שִׂים	קוּם	תָּקוּם
2fs	בּוֹאִי	שִׂימִי	קוּמִי	תָּקוּמִי
2mp	בּוֹאוּ	שִׂימוּ	קוּמוּ	תָּקוּמוּ
2fp			קֹמְנָה	תְּקוּמֶינָה

25.4   Cohortative

➤ The *coh* is simply the *impf* with the הָ added on, for example, אָקוּמָה.

25.5   Jussive

➤ As in III Hey verbs, the *jus* is a shortened form of the *impf*, for example, יָקֹם (*impf* יָקוּם) and יָשֵׂם (*impf* יָשִׂים).

25.6   Perfect

➤ The characteristic long vowel is not found in the *pf*. Most hollow verbs are action verbs, and the vowel of the *pf* is an "a"-class vowel. Several hollow verbs are stative verbs, and in these cases the vowel of the *pf* is an "i"- or "u"-class vowel.

	מוּת	בּוֹשׁ	בּוֹא	שִׂים	קוּם
3ms	מֵת	בּוֹשׁ	בָּא	שָׂם	קָם
3fs	מֵתָה	בּוֹשָׁה	בָּאָה	שָׂמָה	קָמָה
2ms	מַתָּה		בָּאתָ	שַׂמְתָּ	קַמְתָּ
2fs		בֹּשְׁתְּ	בָּאת	שַׂמְתְּ	קַמְתְּ
1cs	מַתִּי	בֹּשְׁתִּי	בָּאתִי	שַׂמְתִּי	קַמְתִּי

	מוּת	בּוֹשׁ	בּוֹא	שִׂים	קוּם
3cp	מֵתוּ	בּוֹשׁוּ	בָּאוּ	שָׂמוּ	קָמוּ
2mp			בָּאתֶם	שַׂמְתֶּם	קַמְתֶּם
2fp				שַׂמְתֶּן	קַמְתֶּן
1cp	מַתְנוּ	בּוֹשְׁנוּ	בָּאנוּ	שַׂמְנוּ	קַמְנוּ

25.7 Participle

➤ The qal *ptc* has the same form as the 3*ms* of the *pf*, onto which the *ptc* endings are added.

	מוּת	בּוֹשׁ	בּוֹא	שִׂים	קוּם
ms	מֵת	בּוֹשׁ	בָּא	שָׂם	קָם
fs	מֵתָה		בָּאָה	שָׂמָה	קָמָה
mp	מֵתִים	בּוֹשִׁים	בָּאִים	שָׂמִים	קָמִים
fp			בָּאוֹת	שָׂמוֹת	קָמוֹת

25.8 Infinitive Absolute

➤ The *inf abs* has the *cholem-vav* (וֹ) characteristic of every qal *inf abs*.

מוֹת   בּוֹשׁ   בּוֹא   שׂוֹם   קוֹם

Vocabulary

field	שָׂדֶה	441	stone *f*	אֶבֶן (אָבֶן)	447
gather	אָסַף	28	border, boundary	גְּבוּל	459
think	חָשַׁב	80	seed, offspring	זֶרַע (זֶרַע)	460
add, do again	יָסַף	37	therefore	עַל־כֵּן	942
answer, be humble	עָנָה	56	tree, wood	עֵץ	433

Practice

Focusing on New Material

A. Focus on the forms of qal Hollow verbs. Memorize the forms of the qal Hollow verbs before parsing the following.

	Verb	Pattern	Conj.	Person	Gender	Number	Root
1.	קָם						
2.	שַׂמְנוּ						
3.	בָּאתָ						

4.	שְׁבוּ					
5.	תָּרוּץ					
6.	אָבִין					
7.	תָּבוֹאוּ					
8.	רָמִים					
9.	שִׂימוּ					
10.	בָּאוֹת					
11.	מוֹת					
12.	יֵבוֹשׁוּ					
13.	נָסוּרָה					
14.	יָשֵׂם					
15.	יָקֹם					
16.	רָצִים					
17.	מֵתוּ					
18.	בּוֹשִׁי					
19.	מַתָּה					
20.	תָּרוּמוּ					

Reviewing Previous Lessons

B. Focus on the use of the *pf* and *impf*. Translate the following verb forms.

.1 שָׁמַע   .2 כָּבֵד   .3 יִבְטַח   .4 אֶשְׁפֹּט   .5 עָמְדוּ

.6 רְאִיתֶם   .7 נַעֲשָׂה   .8 בָּנִינוּ   .9 תִּקְחִי   .10 יַעֲלוּ

C. Focus on the forms of the *pf* and *impf*. Parse the following.

	Verb	Pattern	Conj.	Person	Gender	Number	Root
1.	יֹאבֶה						
2.	אֹמַר						
3.	יֵרְדוּ						

4. מָצָאתִי						
5. עֲלִיתֶם						
6. אֵשֵׁב						
7. נָתַתָּ						
8. נִקַּח						
9. תֵּלְכוּ						
10. תִּשָּׂאִי						

Putting It All Together

D. Translate the following.

	1. רָצוּ אֹיְבֵי אֱלֹהֵינוּ אֶל־עִיר־קָדְשׁוֹ כִּי רָם הוּא
1. The enemies of our God ran to his holy city (*fs*) because he (*ms*) is exalted.	2. לֹא טָהוֹר הַמָּקוֹם אֲשֶׁר זָבְחוּ הַכֹּהֲנִים הָרְשָׁעִים בּוֹ
2. The place in which the wicked priests sacrificed is not clean.	3. לֹא יֵבוֹשׁוּ אֲנָשִׁים יְשָׁרִים כָּל־יְמֵי־חַיֵּיהֶם
3. Upright men will not be ashamed all the days of their lives.	4. הַבֹּטְחִים בַּיהוָה יָקוּמוּ לְעוֹלָם כִּי הוּא יִשְׁמֹר נַפְשׁוֹתֵיהֶם
4. Those who trust in the LORD will stand/endure forever, for he himself will guard their souls.	5. אֶשָּׂא אֶת־חַטָּאתְךָ וַעֲוֹנְךָ כִּי אָהַבְתִּי אוֹתְךָ מֵעוֹלָם
5. I will forgive your sin (*ms*) and your (*ms*) iniquity/guilt, for I have loved you (*ms*) from eternity.	6. יָסוּר בֵּן חָכָם מִכָּל־דֶּרֶךְ רָשָׁע
6. A wise son will turn aside from every wicked path.	7. נָסַע הָעָם בַּבֹּקֶר וְלֹא חָנָה עַד־הָעֶרֶב כִּרְאוֹתָם אֶת־הֶהָרִים
7. The people started out in the morning and did not set up camp until evening, when they saw the mountains.	8. קְחוּ אֶת־הַכֶּסֶף וְאֶת־הַזָּהָב לַשֹּׁמֵר אֲשֶׁר יָשִׂים אוֹתָם בַּבַּיִת
8. Take (*mp*) the silver and the gold to the guard who will place them in the house.	

Reading Your Hebrew Bible

E. Translate the following from the Hebrew Bible.

1. וְקָרָא זֶה אֶל־זֶה וְאָמַר קָדוֹשׁ קָדוֹשׁ קָדוֹשׁ יְהוָה צְבָאוֹת   Isaiah 6:3

      מְלֹא[a] כָל־הָאָרֶץ כְּבוֹדוֹ

2. אֵלֶּה הַחֻקִּים וְהַמִּשְׁפָּטִים אֲשֶׁר תִּשְׁמְרוּן[b] לַעֲשׂוֹת   Deuteronomy 12:1

      בָּאָרֶץ אֲשֶׁר נָתַן יְהוָה אֱלֹהֵי אֲבֹתֶיךָ לְךָ לְרִשְׁתָּהּ[c] כָּל־הַיָּמִים

      אֲשֶׁר־אַתֶּם חַיִּים עַל־הָאֲדָמָה

[a] This form is a noun in the construct state and means "fulness of."

[b] Some times a 2*mp impf* has an extra *nun* (נ) on the end; there is no effect on the meaning. The sense of שָׁמַר here is "guard" > "be careful."

[c] This form is the preposition לְ + the *inf const* of יָרַשׁ + the 3*fs* object suffix, which agrees with הָאָרֶץ (*fs*).

THE VERB: VAV-RELATIVE

Vav-Relative

➤ The *vav*-relative is a special use of the conjunction *vav* (וֹ) when attached to a *pf* or *impf* verb. This *vav* "relates" the verb to which it is attached to a previous verb.

Form of Vav-Relative

26.1 Form of Vav-Relative Imperfect

➤ Vav-relative *impf* is made up of *vav* + *patach* + strong *dagesh* (⊡ וַ), prefixed to the *impf/jus*.

וַיִּקְטֹל

וַתִּקְטֹל

וָאֶקְטֹל

➤ *Note the compensatory lengthening on the 1cs form.*

➤ The verb form used is actually the *jus* not the *impf*, as is clear from the vav-relative *impf* of some forms of III Hey and Hollow verbs.

Vav-Relative	Jussive	Imperfect
וַיִּבֶן	יִבֶן	יִבְנֶה
וַיֵּבְךְּ	יֵבְךְּ	יִבְכֶּה
וַיָּקָם	יָקֹם	יָקוּם
וַיָּשֶׂם	יָשֵׂם	יָשִׂים

➤ *To identify the root as III Hey or Hollow, look at the vowel of the verb prefix. If the vowel is a ◌ָ, then the root is Hollow.*

➤ Often, but not always, the accent moves to the right, thus explaining the difference between the *jus* יָקֹם and the vav-relative *impf* וַיָּקָם (the second *qamets* = *qamets-chatuf*) and the *jus* יָשֵׂם and the vav-relative *impf* וַיָּשֶׂם.

> The classical name of vav is "waw." Vav-relative goes by a variety of names, waw-consecutive being quite common. Because of the frequent use of the term *waw-consecutive* imperfect, vav-relative imperfect is abbreviated *wci* in this grammar.

26.2   Form of Vav-Relative Perfect

➤ Vav-relative perfect is made up of the simple *vav* (וְ) prefixed to the *pf*.

$$וְקָטַל$$

$$וּקְטַלְתֶּם$$

➤ Often, but not always, the accent will move to the final syllable.

וְקָטַלְתָּ	קָטַלְתָּ
וְקָטַלְתִּי	קָטַלְתִּי

> Vav-relative perfect is abbreviated *wcp*.

Use of Vav-Relative

➤ Vav-relative is used in a variety of ways, but the most frequent use is to express <u>temporal succession</u>: "The next thing that happened (or will happen)."

26.3   Use of Vav-Relative Imperfect

➤ In an earlier phase of Hebrew, there were two imperfects: a "long imperfect" and a "short imperfect."

○ The long imperfect was used as a present and a future. This long imperfect is found in Biblical Hebrew as the imperfect = present/future (יָקוּם).

○ The short imperfect was used as a <u>jussive</u> and for <u>past time</u>. This short imperfect is found in Biblical Hebrew as a <u>jussive</u> (יָקֹם) and in the vav-relative impf (וַיָּקָם), which expresses <u>temporal succession in past time</u>.

➤ *One traditional name for the vav-relative is waw-conversive, which presumes that an imperfect = present/future is converted to a past tense by the addition of* וַ *as a prefix. However, this is not the case. The vav-relative imperfect = past time is simply the preservation of an old use of the short imperfect.*

"He sat then wrote in the book."   יָשַׁב וַיִּכְתֹּב בַּסֵּפֶר

"They sat then made a covenant."   יָשְׁבוּ וַיִּכְרְתוּ בְּרִית

"He sat then said to me. . ."   יָשַׁב וַיֹּאמֶר אֵלַי

שָׁלַחְתִּי אֶת־הַנַּעַר וַיִּמְצָא אֶת־הַכֶּסֶף

"I sent the boy, then he found the money."

26.4   Use of Vav-Relative Perfect

➤ The original use of the vav-relative *pf* was probably to mark the "then" clause in an "if . . . then" statement.

"If you go with me, then I will go."   אִם תֵּלֵךְ עִמִּי וְהָלַכְתִּי

"If you listen, then you will know."   אִם תִּשְׁמַע וְיָדַעְתָּ

➤ Because the "then" clause is by definition a future situation, the vav-relative *pf* is used to express <u>temporal succession in future time</u> when following an *impf* verb.

"We will go, then we will sacrifice."   נֵלֵךְ וְזָבַחְנוּ

"You will sit down, then you will eat."   תֵּשֵׁב וְאָכַלְתָּ

אֶזְבַּח וְיָשַׁבְתָּ וְאָכַלְתָּ

"I will sacrifice, then you will sit down and eat."

Vocabulary

burnt offering	עוֹלָה	431	after, behind	אַחֲרֵי	875
be great, wealthy	גָּדַל	71	just as, when	כַּאֲשֶׁר	909
clothe, dress, wear	לָבַשׁ	88	what?	מָה	927
reach out, extend	נָטָה	50	who?	מִי	930
be much, many	רָבָה	58	gift, grain offering	מִנְחָה	472

Practice

Focusing on New Material

A. Focus on the form of the vav-relative imperfect (*wci*). Parse the following.

Verb	Pattern	Conj.	Person	Gender	Number	Root
1. וַיִּבְטַח						
2. וָאֶבְטַח						
3. וַנָּקָם						
4. וַתִּבֶן						
5. וַתַּעַל						
6. וַיִּתֵּן						
7. וַתָּשֶׂם						
8. וַיֵּבְךְּ						
9. וַיַּעַשׂ						
10. וַתִּפֹּל						

B. Focus on the use of the vav-relative perfect and the vav-relative imperfect. Translate the following forms.

.1 וַיִּזְבְּחוּ   .2 וְזָבְחוּ   .3 וְעָלָה   .4 וַיַּעַל   .5 וַתָּקָם

.6 וְקַמְתָּ   .7 וַיֹּאמֶר   .8 וַנֵּבְךְּ   .9 וַיָּרוּצוּ   .10 וָאֶעֱמֹד

.11 וּנְתַתֶּם   .12 וַיַּעֲלוּ   .13 וִידַעְנוּ   .14 וַיִּשָּׂא   .15 וַיִּפֹּל

C. Focus on the use of the vav-relative perfect and the vav-relative imperfect. Translate the following sentences.

	1.	אִם תֶּחֱטָא וָמַתָּה
1. If you (*ms*) sin, you (*ms*) will die.	2.	חָטְאוּ וַיָּמוּתוּ
2. They sinned, then they died.	3.	בָּאוּ בְּבֵית־יְהוָה וַיִּזְבְּחוּ אֶת־זִבְחֵיהֶם

3. They entered the house of the LORD, then they offered their sacrifices.	4. רָאִיתָ אֶת־הַבֶּגֶד וַתִּקַּח אוֹתוֹ אֶל־בֵּיתֶךָ
4. You (ms) saw the garment, then you (ms) took it to your house.	5. וַיָּקָם וַיֵּלֶךְ עַל־הַדֶּרֶךְ וַיָּשָׁב אֶל־מִשְׁפַּחְתּוֹ וַיִּשְׂאוּ אֶת־עֲוֺנוֹ
5. He arose, went along the road, and returned to his family. Then they forgave his sin.	6. יָקוּם וְהָלַךְ עַל־הַדֶּרֶךְ וְשָׁב אֶל־מִשְׁפַּחְתּוֹ וְנָשְׂאוּ אֶת־עֲוֺנוֹ
6. He will arise, go along the road, and return to his family. Then they will forgive his sin.	

Reviewing Previous Lessons

D. Focus on the form of the infinitive construct. Parse the following.

Verb	Pattern	Conj.	Person	Gender	Number	Root
1. כְּתֹב						
2. בִּין						
3. תֵּת						
4. בְּכוֹת						
5. רֶדֶת						
6. קַחַת						
7. לֶכֶת						
8. עֲשׂוֹת						
9. שׁוּב						
10. בּוֹא						

E. Focus on the use of the infinitive construct in temporal clauses. Translate the following.

1. כְּשֹׁלֹחַ הָאִישׁ אֶת־הַנַּעַר   2. כְּשָׁלְחוֹ אֶת־הַנַּעַר   3. כְּשָׁלְחוֹ אוֹתוֹ

4. בְּקוּם אֹיְבֵינוּ עָלֵינוּ   5. בְּשָׁכְבְּךָ וּבְקוּמֶךָ   6. כַּעֲלוֹת הַכֹּהֲנִים

7. בְּצֵאתוֹ וּבְבוֹאוֹ   8. בְּלֶדֶת הָאִשָּׁה אֶת־בְּנָהּ   9. בִּבְנוֹתְכֶם מִזְבֵּחַ

Putting It All Together

F. Translate the following.

	1. אִם שָׁמוֹר תִּשְׁמְרוּ אֶת מִשְׁפְּטֵי יְהוָה אֱלֹהֵיכֶם וְחֻקָּיו וַחְיִיתֶם וּבָאתֶם בָּאָרֶץ אֲשֶׁר יְהוָה נֹתֵן לָכֶם לְרִשְׁתָּהּ
1. If you (*mp*) carefully (*inf abs*) keep the judgments of the LORD your (*mp*) God and his statutes, then you will live and enter the land which the LORD is giving you to possess [it].	2. וַיֹּאמֶר הַנָּבִיא אֶל הַכֹּהֲנִים הָרְשָׁעִים הָהֵם כִּי עֲזַבְתֶּם אֶת־יְהוָה וְעָזַב אֶתְכֶם וַאֲבַדְתֶּם
2. The prophet said to those wicked priests, "Because you abandoned the LORD, he will abandon you and you will perish."	3. זֶה הַבֹּקֶר אֲשֶׁר נִסַּע בּוֹ וְהָלַכְנוּ אֶל־הֶהָרִים וּמָצָאנוּ עֵצִים לִבְנוֹת בָּתִּים לָנוּ וּלְבָנֵינוּ
3. This is the morning on which we will set out and go to the mountains and find wood to build houses for ourselves and for our sons.	4. וַיַּעֲלוּ גִבּוֹרֵי הַגּוֹיִם מִן־הַיָּם וַיִּלְכְּדוּ אֶת־עָרֵיכֶם וַיִּקְחוּ אֶת־נְשֵׁיכֶם וְאֶת־בְּנוֹתֵיכֶם וַיִּבְרְחוּ וְלֹא יְכָלְתֶּם לַעֲמֹד עֲלֵיהֶם
4. The mighty men of the nations came up from the sea, captured your (*mp*) cities, and took your (*mp*) wives and your (*mp*) daughters. And they fled, and you (*mp*) were not able to stand against them.	

Reading Your Hebrew Bible

G. Translate the following from the Hebrew Bible.

1.   וַיֹּאמֶר יְהוֹשֻׁעַ[a] אֶל־הָעָם לֹא תוּכְלוּ לַעֲבֹד אֶת־יְהוָה
כִּי־אֱלֹהִים קְדֹשִׁים הוּא

Joshua 24:19

2.   וַיֹּאמְרוּ הָעָם[b] אֶל־יְהוֹשֻׁעַ אֶת־יְהוָה אֱלֹהֵינוּ נַעֲבֹד
וּבְקוֹלוֹ נִשְׁמָע:[c] וַיִּכְרֹת יְהוֹשֻׁעַ בְּרִית לָעָם בַּיּוֹם הַהוּא
וַיָּשֶׂם לוֹ[d] חֹק וּמִשְׁפָּט בִּשְׁכֶם[e]

Joshua 24:24-25

^a "Joshua"

^bA collective noun—that is, a singular noun referring to a group or collection of items—often takes a plural verb in Hebrew.

^cThe symbol ׃ is called *sof passuq* ("end of verse") and marks the end of a verse.

^dThe *ms* suffix refers back to the collective עַם and so is translated with a plural, "to them."

^e "In Shechem"

27

CLAUSES:
TEMPORAL AND INTERROGATIVE

Temporal Clauses

➤ Hebrew has various ways of expressing temporal clauses, clauses introduced with before, when, after, etc. Three common ways are introduced in this lesson.

27.1 Preposition + Infinitive Construct

➤ The *inf const* preceded by בְּ or כְּ and used as a temporal clause was introduced in Lesson 20. Other prepositions are also used to form temporal clauses.

"when he sent the prophet"	בְּשָׁלְחוֹ אֶת־הַנָּבִיא
"when he sent the prophet"	כְּשָׁלְחוֹ אֶת־הַנָּבִיא
"after he sent the prophet"	אַחֲרֵי שָׁלְחוֹ אֶת־הַנָּבִיא
"until he sent the prophet"	עַד שָׁלְחוֹ אֶת־הַנָּבִיא

➤ The time of such clauses is indicated by context. Two frequent indicators at the beginning of clauses are: (1) וַיְהִי (*wci* of הָיָה) for past time and (2) וְהָיָה (*wcp* of הָיָה) for future time.

"when he sent the prophet"	וַיְהִי כְּשָׁלְחוֹ אֶת־הַנָּבִיא
"after he sent the prophet"	וַיְהִי אַחֲרֵי שָׁלְחוֹ אֶת־הַנָּבִיא
"when he sends the prophet"	וְהָיָה כְּשָׁלְחוֹ אֶת־הַנָּבִיא

➤ וַיְהִי *and* וְהָיָה *need not be translated, because they simply function to indicate the time.*

➤ The main clause is usually introduced by a *wci* for past time or a *wcp* for future time.

וַיְהִי כְּשָׁלְחוֹ אֶת־הַנָּבִיא וַיֵּלֶךְ הַנָּבִיא אֶל־הָעִיר

"When he sent the prophet, the prophet went to the city."

וַיְהִי אַחֲרֵי שָׁלְחוֹ אֶת־הַנָּבִיא וַיִּשְׁלַח אֶת־הַכֹּהֵן

"After he sent the prophet, he sent the priest."

וְהָיָה כְּשָׁלְחוֹ אֶת־הַנָּבִיא וְהָלַךְ הַנָּבִיא אֶל־הָעִיר

"When he sends the prophet, the prophet will go to the city."

27.2   Preposition or Particle + Perfect or Imperfect

וַיְהִי כִּי שָׁלַח אֶת־הַנָּבִיא וַיֵּלֶךְ הַנָּבִיא אֶל־הָעִיר

"When he sent the prophet, the prophet went to the city."

וַיְהִי אַחֲרֵי שָׁלַח אֶת־הַנָּבִיא וַיִּשְׁלַח אֶת־הַכֹּהֵן

"After he sent the prophet, he sent the priest."

וְהָיָה כִּי יִשְׁלַח אֶת־הַנָּבִיא וְהָלַךְ הַנָּבִיא אֶל־הָעִיר

"When he sends the prophet, the prophet will go to the city."

27.3   Time Words

וַיְהִי בַּיּוֹם הַהוּא וַיִּשְׁלַח אֶת־הַנָּבִיא

"In that day, he sent the prophet."

וְהָיָה בַּיּוֹם הַהוּא וְשָׁלַח אֶת־הַנָּבִיא

"In that day, he will send the prophet."

וַיְהִי בַּבֹּקֶר וַיֵּלֶךְ אֶל־הָעִיר

"In the morning, he went to the city."

וְהָיָה בַּבֹּקֶר וְהָלַךְ אֶל־הָעִיר

"In the morning, he will go to the city."

Interrogative Clauses

➤   Hebrew has two ways of asking questions.

27.4   Interrogative Pronouns

➤   Questions are often introduced with an interrogative pronoun.

"Who went to the city?"	מִי הָלַךְ אֶל־הָעִיר
"Who will go to the city?"	מִי יֵלֶךְ אֶל־הָעִיר
"What did he say to you?"	מָה אָמַר אֵלֶיךָ
"What will he say to you?"	מָה יֹאמַר אֵלֶיךָ

27.5   Interrogative Particle הַ

➤ The interrogative particle הַ is not an independent word but is prefixed to another word.

➤ The interrogative particle הַ is distinguished from the definite article in that the definite article never has *chatef-patach* (◌) as the vowel and the interrogative particle does not have strong *dagesh* as an element.

"He went to the city."	הָלַךְ אֶל־הָעִיר
"Did he go to the city?"	הֲהָלַךְ אֶל־הָעִיר
"He will go to the city."	יֵלֵךְ אֶל־הָעִיר
"Will he go to the city?"	הֲיֵלֵךְ אֶל־הָעִיר

Vocabulary

Qal: speak	דָּבַר	4	ark	אָרוֹן	454
Piel: speak	דִּבֶּר		righteous	צַדִּיק	336
	הָלַל	75	righteousness	צֶדֶק / צְדָקָה	545/6
Piel: praise	הִלֵּל			בָּקַשׁ	30
	כָּפַר	87	Piel: seek	בִּקֵּשׁ	
Piel: atone	כִּפֶּר		Qal: be blessed	בָּרַךְ	31
	צָוָה	19	Piel: bless	בֵּרֵךְ	
Piel: command	צִוָּה				
Qal: be holy	קָדַשׁ	103			
Piel: sanctify	קִדֵּשׁ				

Note:

○ The piel verb pattern is introduced in the next lesson. When a verb occurs in the qal and the piel, both spellings are given in the vocabulary list, for example, קָדַשׁ and קִדֵּשׁ. If a verb occurs in the piel only, both spellings are given, but a meaning is given for the piel only, for example, כִּפֶּר and כָּפַר.

Practice

Focusing on New Material

A. Focus on temporal clauses. Translate the following clauses.

2. וְהָיָה בִּכְתֹב הָאִישׁ סֵפֶר		1. וַיְהִי בִּכְתֹב הָאִישׁ סֵפֶר	
4. וַיְהִי כִּי כָתַב סֵפֶר		3. וַיְהִי אַחֲרֵי כָתְבוֹ סֵפֶר	
6. וַיְהִי לִפְנֵי כָתַב סֵפֶר		5. וַיְהִי כְּכָתְבוֹ סֵפֶר	
8. וַיְהִי בַּשָּׁנָה הַהִיא		7. וְהָיָה בַּיּוֹם הַהוּא	
10. וַיְהִי כִּשְׁפֹט יְהוָה אֶת־עַמּוֹ		9. וְהָיָה כִּשְׁפֹט יְהוָה אֶת־הַגּוֹיִם	

B. Focus on temporal clauses within sentences. Translate the following.

	1. וַיְהִי אַחֲרֵי כְּתֹב הָאִישׁ אֶת־הַסֵּפֶר וָאֶקְרָא אוֹתוֹ
1. After the man wrote the book, I read it.	2. וְהָיָה בַּיּוֹם הַהוּא וּבָא יְהוָה לִשְׁפֹּט אֶת־הַגּוֹיִם
2. On that day, the Lord will come to judge the nations.	3. וַיְהִי כִּרְאוֹתִי אֶת־הָאִשָּׁה וָאָשֵׁב לְבֵיתִי
3. When I saw the woman, I returned to my house.	4. וְהָיָה בִּזְבֹּחַ הַכֹּהֵן אֶת־הַזֶּבַח וְאָכַלְנוּ לִפְנֵי הָאֱלֹהִים
4. When the priest offers the sacrifice, we will eat in the presence of God.	5. וַיְהִי לִפְנֵי זָבְחוּ אֶת־הַזֶּבַח וַנֵּשֶׁב עַל־הָאֲדָמָה
5. Before he offered the sacrifice, we sat down on the ground.	

C. Focus on interrogative clauses. Translate the following clauses.

2. הֲשָׁמַע אֶת־הַדְּבָרִים		1. מִי שָׁמַע אֶת־הַדְּבָרִים	
4. הֲתִשְׁמַע אֵלַי		3. מָה שָׁמַע	
6. מִי מֶלֶךְ הָעִיר		5. הַאַתָּה מֶלֶךְ הָעִיר	
8. הֲיִזְבַּח זְבָחִים		7. מָה אָמַר אֵלֶיךָ	
10. מִי הָלַךְ עִמָּנוּ		9. מָה אַתָּה עֹשֶׂה	

Reviewing Previous Lessons

D. Parse the following.

Verb	Pattern	Conj.	Person	Gender	Number	Root
1. שָׁכַבְתִּי						
2. אֶפְקֹד						
3. מָלַכְתָּ						
4. זְכַרְתֶּם						
5. נִכְתֹּב						
6. יִדְרְשׁוּ						
7. תִּדְבְּקוּ						
8. אָכְלוּ						
9. אָסַפְנוּ						
10. תִּמְצָאִי						

E. Focus on nouns with pronoun suffixes. Translate the following words.

1. שְׁלוֹמְךָ   2. שְׁלוֹמְכֶם   3. שְׁלוֹמוֹ   4. שְׁלוֹמִי   5. שְׁלוֹמֵנוּ

6. דְּבָרָם   7. דִּבְרֵיהֶם   8. דְּבָרֶיךָ   9. דְּבָרַי   10. דְּבָרֶיהָ

11. זְבָחוֹ   12. זְבָחָיו   13. זִבְחֵיהֶם   14. זְבָחֵינוּ   15. זִבְחֵיכֶן

Putting It All Together

F. Translate the following.

	1. וַיְהִי בְּלֶכֶת מַלְכֵּנוּ אֶל־הָעִיר וַיַּרְא אֶת־הַכֹּהֵן הַיֹּשֵׁב שָׁם וַיֹּאמֶר לוֹ מַה שְׁמֶךָ
1. When our king came to the city, he saw the priest who was living there. Then he said to him, "What is your name?"	2. וְהָיָה לִפְנֵי צֵאתִי לַמִּלְחָמָה וְדָרַשְׁתִּי אֶת־יְהוָה וְשַׁבְתִּי מֵחַטָּאתִי לְמַעַן יֵצֵא עַמִּי

2. Before I go out to the battle, I will seek the LORD and turn from my sin, so that he will go out with me.	3. וַיְהִי בְּלָכֹד אֹיְבֵינוּ אֶת־מִשְׁפְּחוֹתֵינוּ וַיִּקְחוּ אוֹתָם אֶל־אַרְצָם וַיַּאַסְרוּ אוֹתָם וַנֹּאמַר נֵלְכָה אַחֲרֵיהֶם פֶּן יֹאבֵדוּ
3. When our enemies captured our families, they took them to their country and imprisoned them. Then we said, "Let's go after them, lest they perish."	4. וַיְהִי בְּרִדְתִּי מִן־הָהָר וָאֶמְצָא אֶת הָעָם חֹטְאִים לֵאלֹהַי וָאֵשֵׁב עַל־הָאֲדָמָה וָאֶבְכֶּה מְאֹד
4. When I came down from the mountain, I found the people sinning against my God. Then I sat down on the ground and really wept.	

Reading Your Hebrew Bible

G. Translate the following from Josh 1:1–2.

(1) וַיְהִי אַחֲרֵי מוֹת[a] מֹשֶׁה[b] עֶבֶד יְהוָה וַיֹּאמֶר יְהוָה אֶל־יְהוֹשֻׁעַ[c] בִּן־נוּן[d] מְשָׁרֵת[e] מֹשֶׁה לֵאמֹר[f]:

(2) מֹשֶׁה עַבְדִּי מֵת וְעַתָּה קוּם עֲבֹר אֶת־הַיַּרְדֵּן[g] הַזֶּה אַתָּה וְכָל־הָעָם הַזֶּה אֶל־הָאָרֶץ אֲשֶׁר אָנֹכִי נֹתֵן לָהֶם לִבְנֵי יִשְׂרָאֵל[h]:

[a] "the death of"

[b] "Moses"

[c] "Joshua"

[d] "son of Nun"

[e] "servant of"

[f] The *inf const* of אָמַר is used to introduce a quotation and is often left untranslated.

[g] "Jordan"

[h] "Israel"

THE PIEL:
STRONG ROOTS

Meaning of the Piel

➤ The piel is the second of the seven major verb patterns you will learn. The qal makes up 69% of all verbs in the Hebrew Bible; the piel, 9%.[1]

➤ Like the qal, the piel has a *pf, impf, jus, coh, impv, ptc, inf const,* and *inf abs.*

➤ To change verb pattern is to **change the meaning** of the verb.

Piel	Qal	Root
"destroy"	"perish"	אבד
"finish"	"be finished"	כלה
"fill"	"be full"	מלא
"set free"	"send"	שׁלח

➤ Some verbs occur only (or mainly) in the piel without a corresponding qal.

"seek"		בקשׁ
"speak"		דבר
"command"		צוה

Form of the Piel

➤ The primary characteristic of the piel is the strong *dagesh* in the middle root consonant.

---

1. B. Waltke and M. O'Connor, *Syntax,* §21.2.3e.

28.1   Perfect

Piel	Qal	
קִטֵּל	קָטַל	3ms
קִטְּלָה	קָטְלָה	3fs
קִטַּלְתָּ	קָטַלְתָּ	2ms
קִטַּלְתְּ	קָטַלְתְּ	2fs
קִטַּלְתִּי	קָטַלְתִּי	1cs

קִטְּלוּ	קָטְלוּ	3cp
קִטַּלְתֶּם	קְטַלְתֶּם	2mp
קִטַּלְתֶּן	קְטַלְתֶּן	2fp
קִטַּלְנוּ	קָטַלְנוּ	1cp

28.2   Imperfect

Piel	Qal	
יְקַטֵּל	יִקְטֹל	3ms
תְּקַטֵּל	תִּקְטֹל	3fs
תְּקַטֵּל	תִּקְטֹל	2ms
תְּקַטְּלִי	תִּקְטְלִי	2fs
אֲקַטֵּל	אֶקְטֹל	1cs

יְקַטְּלוּ	יִקְטְלוּ	3mp
תְּקַטֵּלְנָה	תִּקְטֹלְנָה	3fp
תְּקַטְּלוּ	תִּקְטְלוּ	2mp
תְּקַטֵּלְנָה	תִּקְטֹלְנָה	2fp
נְקַטֵּל	נִקְטֹל	1cp

28.3   Imperative

Imperative	Imperfect	
קַטֵּל	תְּקַטֵּל	*2ms*
קַטְּלִי	תְּקַטְּלִי	*2fs*
קַטְּלוּ	תְּקַטְּלוּ	*2mp*
קַטֵּלְנָה	תְּקַטֵּלְנָה	*2fp*

28.4   Infinitives

Infinitive Construct	Imperative
קַטֵּל	קַטֵּל

Infinitive Absolute
קַטֵּל / קַטֹּל

28.5   Participle

Piel	Qal	
מְקַטֵּל	קֹטֵל	*ms*
מְקַטֶּלֶת	קֹטֶלֶת	*fs*
מְקַטְּלִים	קֹטְלִים	*mp*
מְקַטְּלוֹת	קֹטְלוֹת	*fp*

28.6   Cohortative

Piel	Qal	
אֲקַטְּלָה	אֶקְטְלָה	*1cs*
נְקַטְּלָה	נִקְטְלָה	*1cp*

28.7   Jussive

Piel	Qal	
יְקַטֵּל	יִקְטֹל	*3ms*

Vocabulary

Piel: pollute, begin	חִלֵּל		sword *f*	חֶרֶב (חֶרֶב)	421
	כָּסָה	86	utensil	כְּלִי	423
Piel: conceal, cover	כִּסָּה	86	meeting	מוֹעֵד	468
Qal: count	סָפַר	97	congregation	עֵדָה	536
Piel: report, tell	סִפֵּר		yet, still	עוֹד	940
Qal: be glad	שָׂמַח	109	only	רַק	948
Piel: make glad	שִׂמֵּחַ			חָלָל	78

Practice

Focusing On New Material

A. Focus on the form of the piel. Parse the following.

Verb	Pattern	Conj.	Person	Gender	Number	Root
1. דִּבַּרְתִּי						
2. יְכַפֵּר						
3. מְקַדֵּשׁ						
4. הַלְלוּ						
5. תְּבַקְשִׁי						
6. דִּבַּרְתֶּם						
7. הִלְלוּ						
8. נְקַדֵּשׁ						
9. בַּקֵּשׁ						
10. מְדַבְּרִים						
11. אֲהַלְלָה						
12. כַּפֵּר						
13. תְּבַקֵּשׁ						
14. קִדַּשְׁתָּ						
15. תְּדַבְּרוּ						

Reviewing Previous Lessons

B. Focus on strong verbs in the qal and piel. Parse the following.

	Verb	Pattern	Conj.	Person	Gender	Number	Root
1.	יִמְלֹךְ						
2.	יְדַבֵּר						
3.	הֲלַכְתָּ						
4.	הֲלַכְתְּ						
5.	שָׁפְטוּ						
6.	דִּבְּרוּ						
7.	מְקַדֵּשׁ						
8.	שִׁמֵּר						
9.	תְּכַפְּרוּ						
10.	בִּקַּשְׁתֶּם						

C. Focus on III Hey verbs in the qal. Parse the following.

	Verb	Pattern	Conj.	Person	Gender	Number	Root
1.	בָּכִינוּ						
2.	יִבְנֶה						
3.	עֹלִים						
4.	רְאוֹת						
5.	יִגְלוּ						
6.	עָשׂוּ						
7.	בְּנֵה						
8.	בְּכוּ						
9.	כְּלוֹת						
10.	נְטִיתֶם						

Putting It All Together

D. Translate the following.

	1.	וַיְהִי כְּבוֹא הַנָּבִיא וַיְדַבֵּר אֶל־כָּל־הָעָם לֵאמֹר הַלְלוּ אֶת־יְהוָה כִּי לְעוֹלָם חַסְדּוֹ
1. When the prophet came, he spoke to all the people saying, "Praise the LORD, because his faithfulness is/lasts forever."	2.	לֹא חָרָה עָלֵינוּ אַף־יְהוָה כִּי בִקַּשְׁנוּ אֶת־פָּנָיו וַנְּקַדֵּשׁ אֶת־שְׁמוֹ הַגָּדוֹל
2. The anger of the LORD did not burn against us, because we sought his face and sanctified his great name.	3.	תְּכַפֵּר אֶת־הַמִּזְבֵּחַ וְקִדַּשְׁתָּ אוֹתוֹ וְכָל־הַנֹּגֵעַ בּוֹ יִקְדָּשׁ
3. You will atone for the altar and sanctify it. Then all who touch it will be holy. (נגע usually takes its object through the preposition בְּ).	4.	וָאֶשְׁמַע קוֹל מְדַבֵּר וָאֹמַר מִי אַתָּה וַיֹּאמֶר אֵלַי אֲנִי יְהוָה אֱלֹהֶיךָ הַמְכַפֵּר לְכָל־אֲשֶׁר עָשִׂיתָ
4. I heard a voice speaking and I said, "Who are you?" Then he said to me, "I am the LORD your God, who atones for every-thing/all which you have done."		

Reading Your Hebrew Bible

E. Translate the following from 1 Samuel 11.

(4) וַיָּבֹאוּ הַמַּלְאָכִים גִּבְעַת[a] שָׁאוּל[b] וַיְדַבְּרוּ אֶת־הַדְּבָרִים בְּאָזְנֵי הָעָם וַיִּשְׂאוּ[c] כָל־הָעָם אֶת־קוֹלָם וַיִּבְכּוּ: (5) וְהִנֵּה[d] שָׁאוּל בָּא אַחֲרֵי הַבָּקָר מִן־הַשָּׂדֶה וַיֹּאמֶר שָׁאוּל מַה־לָּעָם[e] כִּי יִבְכּוּ וַיְסַפְּרוּ[f]־לוֹ אֶת־דִּבְרֵי אַנְשֵׁי יָבֵישׁ[h]: (6) וַתִּצְלַח[i] רוּחַ־אֱלֹהִים עַל־שָׁאוּל בְּשָׁמְעוֹ אֶת־הַדְּבָרִים הָאֵלֶּה וַיִּחַר אַפּוֹ מְאֹד:

[a] "To Gibeah of"

[b] "Saul"

^cThe form should be וַיִּשְׂאוּ with strong *dagesh* in the שׂ, since the נ of the root has
    assimilated. Frequently, however, a consonant with strong *dagesh* and vocal
    sheva will lose the strong *dagesh*.

^d"Just then"

^eLiterally, "What to the people" = "What is wrong with the people?"

^f*Impf* for present time.

^g"They reported"

^h"Jabesh"

ⁱ"Rushed"

THE PIEL: WEAK ROOTS

Weak Roots in the Piel

➤ Weak roots cause piel verbs to vary from the standard paradigm, as is the case in the qal. The variations are similar to those learned in the qal. II Guttural and III Hey roots show variations.

29.1 II Guttural

➤ Because the middle consonant is a guttural, which cannot take the strong *dagesh* that is characteristic of the piel, II Guttural verbs vary from the standard paradigm (1) by not having *dagesh* in the middle consonant and (2) by having compensatory lengthening of the preceding vowel. (א, ה, ח, and ע may have virtual doubling.)

II Guttural Imperfect	Standard Imperfect	II Guttural Perfect	Standard Perfect	
יְבָרֵךְ	יְקַטֵּל	בֵּרֵךְ	קִטֵּל	*3ms*
תְּבָרֵךְ	תְּקַטֵּל	בֵּרְכָה	קִטְלָה	*3fs*
תְּבָרֵךְ	תְּקַטֵּל	בֵּרַכְתָּ	קִטַּלְתָּ	*2ms*
תְּבָרְכִי	תְּקַטְּלִי	בֵּרַכְתְּ	קִטַּלְתְּ	*2fs*
אֲבָרֵךְ	אֲקַטֵּל	בֵּרַכְתִּי	קִטַּלְתִּי	*1cs*

II Guttural Imperfect	Standard Imperfect	II Guttural Perfect	Standard Perfect	
יְבָרְכוּ	יְקַטְּלוּ	בֵּרְכוּ	קִטְּלוּ	*3c/mp*
תְּבָרֵכְנָה	תְּקַטֵּלְנָה			*3fp*
תְּבָרְכוּ	תְּקַטְּלוּ	בֵּרַכְתֶּם	קִטַּלְתֶּם	*2mp*
תְּבָרֵכְנָה	תְּקַטֵּלְנָה	בֵּרַכְתֶּן	קִטַּלְתֶּן	*2fp*
נְבָרֵךְ	נְקַטֵּל	בֵּרַכְנוּ	קִטַּלְנוּ	*1cp*

II Guttural Participle	Standard Participle	II Guttural Imperative	Standard Imperative	
מְבָרֵךְ	מְקַטֵּל	בָּרֵךְ	קַטֵּל	*2ms*
מְבָרֶכֶת	מְקַטֶּלֶת	בָּרְכִי	קַטְּלִי	*2fs*
מְבָרְכִים	מְקַטְּלִים	בָּרֲכוּ	קַטְּלוּ	*2mp*
מְבָרְכוֹת	מְקַטְּלוֹת	בָּרֵכְנָה	קַטֵּלְנָה	*2fp*

II Guttural Inf abs	Standard Inf abs	II Guttural Inf const	Standard Inf const
בָּרֵךְ / בָּרוֹךְ	קַטֵּל	בָּרֵךְ	קַטֵּל

29.2   III Hey

III Hey Piel Imperfect	III Hey Qal Imperfect	III Hey Piel Perfect	III Hey Qal Perfect	
יְגַלֶּה	יִגְלֶה	גִּלָּה	גָּלָה	*3ms*
תְּגַלֶּה	תִּגְלֶה	גִּלְּתָה	גָּלְתָה	*3fs*
תְּגַלֶּה	תִּגְלֶה	גִּלִּיתָ	גָּלִיתָ	*2ms*
תְּגַלִּי	תִּגְלִי	גִּלִּית	גָּלִית	*2fs*
אֲגַלֶּה	אֶגְלֶה	גִּלִּיתִי	גָּלִיתִי	*1cs*

יְגַלּוּ	יִגְלוּ	גִּלּוּ	גָּלוּ	*3c/mp*
תְּגַלֶּינָה	תִּגְלֶינָה			3fp
תְּגַלּוּ	תִּגְלוּ	גִּלִּיתֶם	גְּלִיתֶם	*2mp*
תְּגַלֶּינָה	תִּגְלֶינָה	גִּלִּיתֶן	גְּלִיתֶן	*2fp*
נְגַלֶּה	נִגְלֶה	גִּלִּינוּ	גָּלִינוּ	*1cp*

III Hey Piel Participle	III Hey Qal Participle	III Hey Piel Imperative	III Hey Qal Imperative	
מְגַלֶּה	גֹּלֶה	גַּלֵּה	גְּלֵה	2ms
מְגַלָּה	גֹּלָה	גַּלִּי	גְּלִי	2fs
מְגַלִּים	גֹּלִים	גַּלּוּ	גְּלוּ	2mp
מְגַלּוֹת	גֹּלוֹת		גְּלֶינָה	2fp

III Hey Piel Inf abs	III Hey Qal Inf abs	III Hey Piel Inf const	III Hey Qal Inf const
גַּלֹּה	גָּלֹה	גַּלּוֹת	גְּלוֹת

III Hey Piel Wci	III Hey Qal Wci	III Hey Piel Jussive	III Hey Qal Jussive	
וַיְגַל	וַיִּגֶל	יְגַל	יִגֶל	3ms

The Root צוה

> The root צוה is not Hollow; the *vav* (ו) is a consonant. This root is used as a verb mainly in the piel ("to command"). (It is also used in the noun מִצְוָה, "commandment.") In verb forms from this root, ו is not *shureq*, but *vav* with strong *dagesh*; for example, יְצַוֶּה, צָוָה, צִוִּיתִי, and מְצַוֶּה. The *inf const* is usually spelled defectively, צַוֹּת for צַוּוֹת.

Vocabulary

seven	שִׁבְעָה	403	one	אֶחָד	373
eight	שְׁמֹנָה	561	two	שְׁנַיִם (שְׁנֵים)	406
nine	תִּשְׁעָה	723	three	שְׁלֹשָׁה	443
ten	עֲשָׂרָה	434	four	אַרְבָּעָה	410
one hundred	מֵאָה	391	five	חֲמִשָּׁה	420
one thousand	אֶלֶף (אָלֶף)	409	six	שִׁשָּׁה	485

Practice

Focusing on New Material

A. Focus on the form of the piel from weak roots. Parse the following.

	Verb	Pattern	Conj.	Person	Gender	Number	Root
1.	כִּסָּה						
2.	בֵּרֵךְ						
3.	יְגַלֶּה						
4.	אֲבָרֵךְ						
5.	מְכַסִּים						
6.	מְבָרְכוֹת						
7.	גִּלִּינוּ						
8.	בֵּרַכְנוּ						
9.	בָּרֵךְ						
10.	כַּסּוֹת						

B. Focus on the piel from strong and weak roots. Parse the following.

	Verb	Pattern	Conj.	Person	Gender	Number	Root
1.	שִׂמַּחְתֶּם						
2.	יְהַלְלוּ						
3.	יְכַסּוּ						
4.	צִוִּיתָ						
5.	מְבַקֶּשֶׁת						
6.	מְגַלָּה						
7.	קִדְּשׁוּ						
8.	בָּרְכוּ						
9.	צַוֹּת						
10.	תְּבָרֵךְ						

C. Focus on the difference in meaning when a verb occurs in both the qal and the piel. Translate the following verb forms. If you encounter a root you have not yet learned in the qal or piel, consult the vocabulary at the back of the grammar for the meaning.

1. שָׂמְחוּ   2. שִׂמְחוּ   3. סָפַרְתִּי   4. סִפַּרְתִּי   5. קָדַשׁ

6. קִדֵּשׁ   7. גָּדַלְנוּ   8. גִּדַּלְנוּ   9. כְּלִיתֶם   10. כִּלִּיתֶם

Reviewing Previous Lessons

D. Focus on the construct state. Translate the following.

1. תּוֹרַת יְהוָה   2. עֲדַת הַקֹּדֶשׁ   3. שְׁלוֹם הָאָרֶץ   4. מִשְׁפַּט הַמֶּלֶךְ

5. עַבְדֵי הָאִישׁ   6. חוֹמַת הָעִיר   7. כְּבוֹד הַגִּבּוֹר   8. מִלְחֶמֶת הַשָּׁנָה

9. אַדְמַת קֹדֶשׁ   10. אֱלֹהֵי הַשָּׁמַיִם   11. צִדְקַת הָעָם   12. דְּבַר הַנָּבִיא

E. Focus on verbs in the qal and the piel. Parse the following.

Verb	Pattern	Conj.	Person	Gender	Number	Root
1. מִלֵּא						
2. זָקֵן						
3. הַלְלוּ						
4. יְשַׂמַּח						
5. תְּסַפְּרוּ						
6. כַּסּוֹת						
7. בֹּנוֹת						
8. מְצֻוִּים						
9. דִּבַּרְתֶּם						
10. גִּלִּיתִי						

Putting It All Together

F. Translate the following.

	1. וַיְדַבְּרוּ כֹהֲנֵי הַבַּיִת לָעָם וַיֹּאמְרוּ לָהֶם בָּרְכוּ וְגַדְּלוּ אֶת־שֵׁם־יְהוָה הַגָּדוֹל
1. The temple priests spoke to the people and said to them, "Bless and magnify the great name of the LORD."	2. וַיְהִי כְּכַלּוֹת הַנָּבִיא לְדַבֵּר וַיִּפְּלוּ הָאֲנָשִׁים עַל־פְּנֵיהֶם וַיִּבְכּוּ וַיָּקוּמוּ וַיֹּאמְרוּ חָטָאנוּ מְאֹד
2. When the prophet finished speaking, the men fell on their faces and wept. Then they got up and said, "We have sinned greatly."	3. וְהָיָה בַּיּוֹם הַהוּא וְכָרַת יְהוָה בְּרִית לְכָל־הַגּוֹיִם וְשָׂמְחוּ בוֹ וְהִלְלוּ אוֹתוֹ לְעוֹלָם
3. In that day the LORD will make a covenant for all nations. And they will rejoice in him and praise him forever.	4. אָבִיתִי לְסַפֵּר לְךָ אֶת־כָּל־אֲשֶׁר עָשָׂה לִי יְהוָה אַחֲרֵי בִקַּשְׁתִּי אוֹתוֹ בְּכָל־נַפְשִׁי
4. I want to tell you everything which the LORD did for me after I sought him with all my soul.	

Reading Your Hebrew Bible

G. Translate the following from Joshua 22:2–3

(2) וַיֹּאמֶר אֲלֵיהֶם אַתֶּם שְׁמַרְתֶּם אֵת כָּל־אֲשֶׁר צִוָּה אֶתְכֶם מֹשֶׁה[a] עֶבֶד יְהוָה וַתִּשְׁמְעוּ בְקוֹלִי לְכֹל אֲשֶׁר צִוִּיתִי אֶתְכֶם: (3) לֹא עֲזַבְתֶּם אֶת־אֲחֵיכֶם

[a]"Moses"

30

NUMBERS
AND "SURPRISE"

Numbers

30.1 Cardinals and Ordinals from One to Ten

	Cardinals			Ordinals	
	Feminine	*Masculine*		*Feminine*	*Masculine*
1	אַחַת	אֶחָד	1st	רִאשׁוֹנָה	רִאשׁוֹן
2	שְׁתַּיִם	שְׁנַיִם	2nd	שֵׁנִית	שֵׁנִי
3	שָׁלֹשׁ	שְׁלֹשָׁה	3rd	שְׁלִישִׁית	שְׁלִישִׁי
4	אַרְבַּע	אַרְבָּעָה	4th	רְבִיעִית	רְבִיעִי
5	חָמֵשׁ	חֲמִשָּׁה	5th	חֲמִישִׁית	חֲמִישִׁי
6	שֵׁשׁ	שִׁשָּׁה	6th	שִׁשִּׁית	שִׁשִּׁי
7	שֶׁבַע	שִׁבְעָה	7th	שְׁבִיעִית	שְׁבִיעִי
8	שְׁמֹנֶה	שְׁמֹנָה	8th	שְׁמִינִית	שְׁמִינִי
9	תֵּשַׁע	תִּשְׁעָה	9th	תְּשִׁיעִית	תְּשִׁיעִי
10	עֶשֶׂר	עֲשָׂרָה	10th	עֲשִׂירִית	עֲשִׂירִי

➤ The cardinal number *one* agrees in gender and follows the noun it modifies, for example, אִישׁ אֶחָד, "one man," and אִשָּׁה אַחַת, "one woman."

➤ The cardinal number *two* agrees in gender but may come before or after the noun it modifies, for example, שְׁנַיִם אֲנָשִׁים, "two men," and נָשִׁים שְׁתַּיִם, "two women."

➤ The cardinal numbers *three* through *ten* may come before or after the noun they modify, but the form that looks feminine is used with a masculine noun and the form that looks masculine is used with a feminine noun, for example, שְׁלֹשָׁה אֲנָשִׁים, "three men," and נָשִׁים שָׁלֹשׁ, "three women."

➤ The cardinal numbers *two* through *ten* may also be used in the construct state and are then placed before the noun that they modify, for example, שְׁלֹשֶׁת אֲנָשִׁים, "three men," and שְׁלֹשׁ נָשִׁים, "three women."

➤ The ordinal numbers are used just like adjectives, for example, הַיּוֹם הַשְּׁבִיעִי, "the seventh day."

30.2   "Teens"

➤ The numbers *eleven* through *nineteen* are made up of a combination of the "ones" plus a form of "ten." The form of "ten" with masculine nouns is עָשָׂר, resulting in, for example, שְׁלֹשָׁה עָשָׂר, "thirteen." The form of "ten" with feminine nouns is עֶשְׂרֵה, resulting in, for example, שְׁלֹשׁ עֶשְׂרֵה, "thirteen."

30.3   "Tens"

➤ The "tens" (i.e., 20, 30, 40, etc.) are formed with masculine plurals. "Twenty" is formed with the plural of ten, עֶשְׂרִים. "Thirty" through "ninety" are the plurals of the corresponding "ones," for example, שְׁלֹשִׁים, "thirty," and אַרְבָּעִים, "forty."

30.4   "Hundreds"

➤ The "hundreds" are formed by placing a construct form of the "ones" in front of the plural of "hundred," for example, חֲמֵשֶׁת מֵאוֹת, "five hundred," and שֵׁשֶׁת מֵאוֹת, "six hundred."

30.5   "Thousands"

➤ The "thousands" are formed by placing a construct form of the "ones" in front of the plural of "thousand," for example, שִׁבְעַת אֲלָפִים, "seven thousand," and שְׁמֹנַת אֲלָפִים, "eight thousand."

"Surprise"

30.6   The particle הִנֵּה, traditionally translated "behold," often introduces something "unexpected" or a "surprise."

➤ In reports of dreams, הִנֵּה often occurs.

וְהִנֵּה מַלְאֲכֵי אֱלֹהִים

"There were angels of God!" (Genesis 28:12)

➤ Sometimes an author draws attention to the marvelous with הִנֵּה.

וַיַּרְא אֱלֹהִים אֶת־כָּל־אֲשֶׁר עָשָׂה וְהִנֵּה־טוֹב מְאֹד

"And God saw everything that he had made, and it was very good!" (Genesis 1:31)

➤ An event about to take place in the immediate future is often expressed by הִנֵּה followed by a participle.

הִנֵּה אָנֹכִי עֹשֶׂה דָבָר

"I am about to do something. . . !" (1 Samuel 3:11)

➤ הִנֵּה is used to show existence.

הִנֵּה אִשְׁתְּךָ קַח וָלֵךְ

"Here is your wife! Take her and go!" (Genesis 12:19)

➤ הִנֵּה may have pronoun suffixes added to it.

הִנְּךָ שֹׁכֵב עִם אֲבֹתֶיךָ

"You are about to lie down with your fathers." (Deut 31:16)

Vocabulary

Qal: be provoked	כָּעַס	159	strength, virtue	חַיִל (חֵיל)	462
Hiph: provoke	הִכְעִיס		staff, tribe	מַטֶּה	470
Qal: remain	שָׁאַר	113	inheritance	נַחֲלָה	476
Hiph: leave	הִשְׁאִיר		leader	שַׂר	442
	שָׁבַע	114	sabbath	שַׁבָּת	557
Hiph: make swear	הִשְׁבִּיעַ		gate	שַׁעַר (שָׁעַר)	445
	שָׁלַךְ	120			
Hiph: throw; reject	הִשְׁלִיךְ				

Practice

Focusing on New Material

A. Focus on cardinal numbers one through ten. Translate the following.

3. שְׁנַיִם מְלָכִים   2. אֵם אַחַת   1. מֶלֶךְ אֶחָד

6. שָׁלֹשׁ אַמּוֹת   5. שְׁלֹשָׁה מְלָכִים   4. שְׁתַּיִם אַמּוֹת

9. חֲמִשָּׁה מְלָכִים   8. שִׁבְעָה מְלָכִים   7. תֵּשַׁע אַמּוֹת

12. אַרְבַּע אַמּוֹת   11. שֵׁשׁ אַמּוֹת   10. עֲשָׂרָה מְלָכִים

B. Focus on ordinal numbers one through ten. Translate the following.

3. הַמֶּלֶךְ הַשְּׁלִישִׁי   2. הָאֵם הָרִאשׁוֹנָה   1. הַמֶּלֶךְ הָרִאשׁוֹן

6. הַמֶּלֶךְ הַשְּׁמִינִי   5. הָאֵם הָרְבִיעִית   4. הָאֵם הַשְּׁלִישִׁית

9. הַמֶּלֶךְ הַשִּׁשִּׁי   8. הָאֵם הַתְּשִׁיעִית   7. הַמֶּלֶךְ הַשְּׁבִיעִי

C. Focus on higher cardinal numbers. Decipher the following.

2. שְׁלֹשִׁים וּשְׁלֹשָׁה   1. שְׁלֹשִׁים

4. תִּשְׁעִים וְשֵׁשׁ   3. אַרְבָּעָה וַחֲמִשִּׁים

6. שְׁלֹשׁ מֵאוֹת וּשְׁלֹשָׁה   5. שְׁלֹשׁ מֵאוֹת

8. שְׁלֹשׁ מֵאוֹת וּשְׁלֹשִׁים וְשָׁלֹשׁ   7. שְׁלֹשׁ מֵאוֹת וּשְׁלֹשִׁים

10. שְׁלֹשֶׁת אֲלָפִים וּשְׁלֹשׁ מֵאוֹת   9. שְׁלֹשֶׁת אֲלָפִים
     וּשְׁלֹשִׁים וְשָׁלֹשׁ

Reviewing Previous Lessons

D. Focus on the qal and piel of strong roots. Parse the following.

Verb	Pattern	Conj.	Person	Gender	Number	Root
1. שָׁלַחְתָּ						
2. דִּבַּרְתָּ						
3. נִכְתֹּב						
4. נְסַפֵּר						

5.	מָלְכוּ						
6.	אֲהַלֵּל						
7.	קַדְּשׁוּ						
8.	קַדְּשׁוּ						
9.	מְשַׂמְּחִים						
10.	בְּקַשְׁתֶּם						

E. Focus on negatives. Translate the following, paying attention to the different negative particles used.

		1.	לֹא נִשְׁלַח אֶת־הַנַּעַר
1. We will not send the boy.		2.	אַל נִשְׁלְחָה אֶת־הַנַּעַר
2. Let's not send the boy.		3.	לֹא תִבְנֶה אֶת־הַבַּיִת
3. You (*ms*)/she will not build the house.		4.	אַל תִּבֶן אֶת־הַבַּיִת
4. Don't build/let her build the house.		5.	יָשַׁב לְבִלְתִּי עָמְדוֹ כָּל־הַיּוֹם
5. He sat down, so as not to stand the whole day.		6.	אָסְרוּ אוֹתוֹ לְבִלְתִּי מָלְכוֹ עַל־הָעִיר
6. They imprisoned him, so that he would not reign over the city.			

Putting It All Together

F. Translate the following.

		1.	רָאִינוּ אֶת־שְׁלֹשֶׁת הַנְּבִיאִים הַמְדַבְּרִים לְזִקְנֵי הָעִיר
1. We saw the three prophets who were speaking to the elders of the city.		2.	יָצְאוּ אַרְבָּעִים גִּבּוֹרִים לַמִּלְחָמָה הַגְּדוֹלָה וַיָּמוּתוּ שָׁם וְלֹא שָׁבוּ לְמִשְׁפְּחוֹתֵיהֶם

2. Forty warriors went out to the great battle and died there. They did not return to their families.	3. וַיֵּלְכוּ חֲמֵשׁ מֵאוֹת וַחֲמִשִּׁים עַבְדֵי הַמֶּלֶךְ לִמְצֹא אֶת־בְּנוֹ וַיְהִי בְמָצְאָם אוֹתוֹ וַיָּשׁוּבוּ לְבֵית הַמֶּלֶךְ וַיֹּאמֶר לוֹ הַמֶּלֶךְ אַל תֵּלֵךְ אֶל־הַשָּׂדֶה כִּי־אִם שְׁנַיִם עֲבָדִים עִמְּךָ
3. Five hundred and fifty of the king's servants went to find his son. And when they found him, they returned to the king's palace. Then the king said to him, "Don't go into the field unless two servants are with you."	4. וְהִנֵּה בַּיּוֹם הַהוּא יָבוֹא יְהוָה לִשְׁפֹּט אֶת־כָּל־הָאָרֶץ וְכָל־בְּנֵי־הָאָדָם יִרְאוּ אֶת־כְּבוֹדוֹ וְעָבְדוּ אוֹתוֹ עַמּוֹ לְעוֹלָם
4. And in that day the LORD will come to judge the whole earth. All mankind will see his glory. And his people will serve him forever!	

Reading Your Hebrew Bible

G. Translate the following from 2 Samuel 5:4–5.

(4) בֶּן־שְׁלֹשִׁים[a] שָׁנָה דָּוִד בְּמָלְכוֹ אַרְבָּעִים שָׁנָה מָלָךְ:

(5) בְּחֶבְרוֹן[b] מָלַךְ עַל־יְהוּדָה[c] שֶׁבַע שָׁנִים וְשִׁשָּׁה חֳדָשִׁים וּבִירוּשָׁלִַם[d] מָלַךְ שְׁלֹשִׁים וְשָׁלֹשׁ שָׁנָה עַל כָּל־יִשְׂרָאֵל[e] וִיהוּדָה[c]

[a] Lit. "son of thirty years" = "thirty years old"; a common noun like שָׁנָה is often in the singular when used with teens or tens.

[b] "In Hebron"

[c] "Judah"

[d] "Jerusalem"; spelled defectively for יְרוּשָׁלַיִם

[e] "Israel"

THE HIPHIL: STRONG ROOTS

The Meaning of the Hiphil

➤ The hiphil is the third of the seven major verb patterns you will learn. The hiphil makes up 13% of all verbs in the Hebrew Bible.[1] The qal, piel, and hiphil make up 91% of all verbs.

➤ Like the qal and the piel, the hiphil has a *pf, impf, jus, coh, impv, ptc, inf const*, and *inf abs*.

➤ To change verb pattern is to **change the meaning** of the verb.

Hiphil	Qal	Root
"boast"	"be great"	גדל
"make king"	"be king"	מלך
"appoint"	"visit"	פקד
"treat as holy"	"be holy"	קדשׁ

➤ Some verbs occur only (or mainly) in the hiphil, without a corresponding qal.

"tell"		נגד
"deliver"		נצל
"throw"		שׁלך

The hiphil is abbreviated hiph.

---

1. B. Waltke and M. O'Connor, *Syntax*, §21.2.3e.

Form of the Hiphil

➤ The primary characteristics of the hiphil are: (1) a prefixed ה and
(2) ִי◌ as the theme vowel.

31.1 Perfect

Hiphil	Qal	
הִקְטִיל	קָטַל	*3ms*
הִקְטִילָה	קָטְלָה	*3fs*
הִקְטַלְתָּ	קָטַלְתָּ	*2ms*
הִקְטַלְתְּ	קָטַלְתְּ	*2fs*
הִקְטַלְתִּי	קָטַלְתִּי	*1cs*

הִקְטִילוּ	קָטְלוּ	*3cp*
הִקְטַלְתֶּם	קְטַלְתֶּם	*2mp*
הִקְטַלְתֶּן	קְטַלְתֶּן	*2fp*
הִקְטַלְנוּ	קָטַלְנוּ	*1cp*

31.2 Imperfect

➤ The characteristic ה is dropped in the *impf,* as is the ה of the definite
article with an inseparable preposition, for example, לַבַּיִת for לְהַבַּיִת.

Hiphil	Qal	
יַקְטִיל	יִקְטֹל	*3ms*
תַּקְטִיל	תִּקְטֹל	*3fs*
תַּקְטִיל	תִּקְטֹל	*2ms*
תַּקְטִילִי	תִּקְטְלִי	*2fs*
אַקְטִיל	אֶקְטֹל	*1cs*

יַקְטִילוּ	יִקְטְלוּ	*3mp*
תַּקְטֵלְנָה	תִּקְטֹלְנָה	*3fp*
תַּקְטִילוּ	תִּקְטְלוּ	*2mp*

Hiphil	Qal	
תַּקְטֵלְנָה	תִּקְטֹלְנָה	*2fp*
נַקְטִיל	נִקְטֹל	*1cp*

31.3 Imperative

Imperative	Imperfect	
הַקְטֵל	תַּקְטִיל	*2ms*
הַקְטִילִי	תַּקְטִילִי	*2fs*
הַקְטִילוּ	תַּקְטִילוּ	*2mp*
הַקְטֵלְנָה	תַּקְטֵלְנָה	*2fp*

31.4 Infinitives

Inf. Const.	Imperative
הַקְטִיל	הַקְטֵל
Inf. Abs.	
הַקְטֵל	

31.5 Participle

➤ The characteristic ה is dropped in the *ptc.*

Hiphil	Qal	
מַקְטִיל	קֹטֵל	*ms*
מַקְטֶלֶת	קֹטֶלֶת	*fs*
מַקְטִילִים	קֹטְלִים	*mp*
מַקְטִילוֹת	קֹטְלוֹת	*fp*

31.6 Cohortative

➤ The characteristic ה is dropped in the *coh.*

Hiphil	Qal	
אַקְטִילָה	אֶקְטְלָה	*1cs*
נַקְטִילָה	נִקְטְלָה	*1cp*

31.7   Jussive

➤   The *jus* is a short form; see §24.8 and §25.5.

Jussive	Imperfect	
יַקְטֵל	יַקְטִיל	3ms

31.8   Vav-relative

Vav-relative	Jussive	
וַיַּקְטֵל	יַקְטֵל	3ms

Vocabulary

Qal: be silent	חָרַשׁ	149	faithfulness, truth	אֱמֶת	65
Hiph: be silent, silence	הֶחֱרִישׁ			
	נָבַט	170	camp	מַחֲנֶה	469
Hiph: look	הִבִּיט			
	נָגַד	49	work, product	מַעֲשֶׂה	473
Hiph: tell	הִגִּיד			
	נָדַח	171	middle	קֶרֶב (קֶרֶב)	480
Hiph: scatter	הִדִּיחַ			
	נָצַל	53		אָמֵן	65
Hiph: deliver	הִצִּיל		Hiph: believe, trust	הֶאֱמִין	

Practice

Focusing on New Material

A. Focus on the form of the hiphil. Parse the following.

	Verb	Pattern	Conj.	Person	Gender	Number	Root
1.	הִכְעִיסוּ						
2.	הַשְׁלִיכוּ						

3.	הִשְׁאִיר					
4.	אַשְׂבִּיעַ					
5.	מַכְעִיסִים					
6.	הִשְׁלַכְתֶּם					
7.	תַּשְׂבִּיעוּ					
8.	וַתַּכְעֵס					
9.	מַשְׁאֶרֶת					
10.	הִשְׁלַכְתִּי					

B. Focus on the difference in meaning when a verb occurs in both the qal and the hiphil. Translate the following verb forms. If you encounter a root that you have not yet learned in the qal or hiphil, consult the vocabulary at the back of the grammar for the meaning.

5. קָדַשְׁתָּ   4. הִשְׁאַרְתִּי   3. שָׁאַרְתִּי   2. הִכְעִיס   1. כָּעַס

10. הִגְדַּלְתֶּם   9. גְּדַלְתֶּם   8. הִזְכַּרְנוּ   7. זָכַרְנוּ   6. הִקְדַּשְׁתָּ

Reviewing Previous Lessons

C. Focus on the form of verbs in the qal from I Guttural roots. Parse the following.

	Verb	Pattern	Conj.	Person	Gender	Number	Root
1.	חֲזַקְתֶּם						
2.	עֲזַבְתֶּם						
3.	יֶחֱזַק						
4.	אֶעֱמֹד						
5.	עֲמֹד						
6.	חֲשַׁבְתֶּם						

D. Focus on qal verbs from I Nun roots. Parse the following.

	Verb	Pattern	Conj.	Person	Gender	Number	Root
1.	יִתֵּן						
2.	אֶפֹּל						
3.	אֶפְּלָה						
4.	נִסַּע						
5.	תִּגַּשׁ						
6.	יִשָּׂא						
7.	יִטֶּה						
8.	נְתַתֶּם						

Putting It All Together

E. Translate the following.

	1.	חָטָא אִישׁ אֶחָד וַיַּכְעֵס אֶת־יְהוָה וַיִּחַר אַפּוֹ עָלָיו עַד שָׁב מֵחַטָּאתוֹ
1. One man sinned and provoked the LORD, so his anger burned against him, until he turned from his sin.	2.	לֹא אָבִינוּ לְהַשְׁאִיר אֶת־הַצֹּאן בֶּהָרִים וַנִּקַּח אוֹתוֹ לַשָּׂדֶה
2. We were not willing to leave the flock in the mountains, so we took it to the field.	3.	הִשְׁבִּיעַ הַמֶּלֶךְ אֶת־שְׁנַיִם הַמַּלְאָכִים כִּי לֹא יְדַבְּרוּ לְזִקְנֵי הָעִיר וַיִּשְׁלַח אוֹתָם מִבֵּיתוֹ בַּלַּיְלָה
3. The king made the two messengers swear that they would not speak to the elders of the city, then he sent them from his palace at night.	4.	בִּשְׂאֵת הַשַּׂר אֶת־מַטּוֹ עַל־רֹאשׁוֹ וַיָּקוּמוּ כָּל־הָאֲנָשִׁים וַיַּעַמְדוּ לְפָנָיו וַיֹּאמֶר אֲלֵיהֶם צְאוּ לַמִּלְחָמָה וְאַל־תִּירָאוּ כִּי יְהוָה עִמָּכֶם
4. When the leader raised his staff above his head, all the men arose and stood before him. Then he said to them, "Go out to the battle, and do not be afraid, for the LORD is with you."		

Reading Your Hebrew Bible

F. Translate the following from the Hebrew Bible.

1. וַיְהִי כִּשְׁמֹעַ כָּל־יִשְׂרָאֵל כִּי־שָׁב יָרָבְעָםᵃ וַיִּשְׁלְחוּ וַיִּקְרְאוּ
   אֹתוֹ אֶל־הָעֵדָה וַיַּמְלִיכוּ אֹתוֹ עַל־כָּל־יִשְׂרָאֵל
   1 Kings 12:20

2. וַיֹּאמֶר יְהוֹשֻׁעַᵇ אֶל־הַכֹּהֲנִים לֵאמֹר שְׂאוּᶜ אֶת־אֲרוֹן הַבְּרִית
   וְעִבְרוּ לִפְנֵי הָעָם וַיִּשְׂאוּᵈ אֶת־אֲרוֹן הַבְּרִית וַיֵּלְכוּ
   לִפְנֵי הָעָם
   Joshua 3:6

ᵃ "Jeroboam"

ᵇ "Joshua"

ᶜ From the root נשׂא.

ᵈ The form should be וַיִּשְּׂאוּ, with strong *dagesh* in the שׂ, but strong *dagesh* is often lost when the consonant is followed by vocal *sheva*.

32

THE HIPHIL:
I GUTTURAL AND I NUN

I Guttural

➤ Because the first consonant is a guttural, which usually does not take simple *sheva*, I Guttural verbs vary from the standard paradigm by having *chatef-segol* (◌ֱ) under the first root letter in the *pf* and *chatef-patach* (◌ֲ) under the first root letter in the other forms.

I Guttural Imperfect	Standard Imperfect	I Guttural Perfect	Standard Perfect	
יַעֲמִיד	יַקְטִיל	הֶעֱמִיד	הִקְטִיל	*3ms*
תַּעֲמִיד	תַּקְטִיל	הֶעֱמִידָה	הִקְטִילָה	*3fs*
תַּעֲמִיד	תַּקְטִיל	הֶעֱמַדְתָּ	הִקְטַלְתָּ	*2ms*
תַּעֲמִידִי	תַּקְטִילִי	הֶעֱמַדְתְּ	הִקְטַלְתְּ	*2fs*
אַעֲמִיד	אַקְטִיל	הֶעֱמַדְתִּי	הִקְטַלְתִּי	*1cs*

יַעֲמִידוּ	יַקְטִילוּ	הֶעֱמִידוּ	הִקְטִילוּ	*3m/cp*
תַּעֲמֵדְנָה	תַּקְטֵלְנָה			*3fp*
תַּעֲמִידוּ	תַּקְטִילוּ	הֶעֱמַדְתֶּם	הִקְטַלְתֶּם	*2mp*
תַּעֲמֵדְנָה	תַּקְטֵלְנָה	הֶעֱמַדְתֶּן	הִקְטַלְתֶּן	*2fp*
נַעֲמִיד	נַקְטִיל	הֶעֱמַדְנוּ	הִקְטַלְנוּ	*1cp*

I Guttural Participle	Standard Participle	I Guttural Imperative	Standard Imperative	
מַעֲמִיד	מַקְטִיל	הַעֲמֵד	הַקְטֵל	*2ms*
מַעֲמֶדֶת	מַקְטֶלֶת	הַעֲמִידִי	הַקְטִילִי	*2fs*

201

I Guttural Participle	Standard Participle	I Guttural Imperative	Standard Imperative	
מַעֲמִידִים	מַקְטִילִים	הַעֲמִידוּ	הַקְטִילוּ	2mp
מַעֲמִידוֹת	מַקְטֵילוֹת	הַעֲמֵדְנָה	הַקְטֵלְנָה	2fp

I Guttural Inf abs	Standard Inf abs	I Guttural Inf const	Standard Inf const
הַעֲמֵד	הַקְטֵל	הַעֲמִיד	הַקְטִיל

I Guttural Vav-rel.	Standard Vav-rel.	I Guttural Jussive	Standard Jussive	
וַיַּעֲמֵד	וַיַּקְטֵל	יַעֲמֵד	יַקְטֵל	3ms

I Nun

➤ The *nun* of the root will always assimilate to the second root consonant in these forms.

Participle	Imperative	Imperfect	Perfect	
מַצִּיל		יַצִּיל	הִצִּיל	3ms
מַצֶּלֶת		תַּצִּיל	הִצִּילָה	3fs
	הַצֵּל	תַּצִּיל	הִצַּלְתָּ	2ms
	הַצִּילִי	תַּצִּילִי	הִצַּלְתְּ	2fs
		אַצִּיל	הִצַּלְתִּי	1cs

Participle	Imperative	Imperfect	Perfect	
מַצִּילִים		יַצִּילוּ	הִצִּילוּ	3c/mp
מַצִּילוֹת		תַּצֵּלְנָה		3fp
	הַצִּילוּ	תַּצִּילוּ	הִצַּלְתֶּם	2mp
	הַצֵּלְנָה	תַּצֵּלְנָה	הִצַּלְתֶּן	2fp
		נַצִּיל	הִצַּלְנוּ	1cp

Vav-rel.	Jussive	Inf abs	Inf const
וַיַּצֵּל	יַצֵּל	הַצֵּל	הַצִּיל

Vocabulary

friend	רֵעַ	482	fire	אֵשׁ	411
	יָכַח	153	fire offering	אִשֶּׁה	587
Hiph: rebuke	הוֹכִיחַ				
	יָשַׁע	41	with	אֵת	889
Hiph: save	הוֹשִׁיעַ				
	יָתַר	84	flesh, meat	בָּשָׂר	458
Hiph: leave behind	הוֹתִיר				
Qal: learn	לָמַד	162	declaration	נְאֻם	475
Piel: teach	לִמֵּד				

Note:

○ The preposition אֵת must not be confused with the direct object marker אֵת/אֶת־. With the pronoun suffix, the preposition אֵת has the form אִתּוֹ, in contrast to the direct object marker, which has the form אוֹתוֹ.

Practice

Focusing on New Material

A. Focus on the the form of the hiphil from I Guttural and I Nun roots. Parse the following.

Verb	Pattern	Conj.	Person	Gender	Number	Root
1. הֶאֱמִינוּ						
2. אַבִּיט						
3. תַּגִּידוּ						

4. הַגִּידוּ					
5. הִגִּידוּ					
6. נַחֲרִישׁ					
7. הַאֲמִין					
8. הֶאֱמִין					
9. הֶחֱרֵשׁ					
10. יַצֵּל					
11. וַיַּצֵּל					
12. הִבַּטְתֶּם					
13. מַאֲמִין					
14. יַחֲרֵשׁ					
15. מַבִּיטִים					

Reviewing Previous Lessons

B. Focus on the form of all verbs learned to this point. Parse the following.

Verb	Pattern	Conj.	Person	Gender	Number	Root
1. מָצָאתָ						
2. גַּלּוֹת						
3. יַאֲמִינוּ						
4. מְבָרֵךְ						
5. יִתֵּן						
6. בֹּנֶה						
7. דִּבֶּר						
8. יֵרֶד						
9. קַמְתֶּם						
10. גְּלוֹת						

C. Focus on qal verbs from I Yod roots. Parse the following.

	Verb	Pattern	Conj.	Person	Gender	Number	Root
1.	יֵשֵׁב						
2.	יִיבַשׁ						
3.	יֵלְדוּ						
4.	נִירָא						
5.	יֵיטַב						
6.	אֵדַע						
7.	תֵּצְאִי						
8.	תִּירְשִׁי						

Putting It All Together

D. Translate the following.

1.	לֹא הֶאֱמִינוּ בַּיהוָה אֱלֹהֵיהֶם וְלֹא אָבָה לְאַבֵּד אוֹתָם כִּי עַמּוֹ הֵם אֲשֶׁר אָהַב אוֹתָם

1.	They did not believe in the LORD their God, but he was not willing to destroy them, because they were his people, whom he loved.	2.	נַאֲמִינָה בֵּאלֹהֵינוּ וְיַצֵּל אוֹתָנוּ מִכָּל־אֹיְבֵינוּ וְעָבַדְנוּ אוֹתוֹ לְעוֹלָם
2.	Let us trust in our God, so that he will save us from all our enemies. Then we will serve him forever.	3.	כְּמָצְאָם אֶת־הָאִישׁ הָרָשָׁע בְּקֶרֶב הַמַּחֲנֶה וַיִּקְחוּ אוֹתוֹ אֶל־הַזְּקֵנִים אֲשֶׁר שָׁפְטוּ אוֹתוֹ וַיָּשָׁב מֵחַטָּאתוֹ
3.	When they found the wicked man within the camp, they took him to the elders, who judged him. Then he repented from his sin.	4.	אַגִּיד אֶת־שִׁמְךָ לְכָל־הַגּוֹיִם וְיָדְעוּ כִּי אַתָּה הָאֱלֹהִים הַחַיִּים וְכִי תַּעֲמֹד אֲמִתְּךָ לְדוֹר וָדוֹר
4.	I will declare your name to all the nations. Then they will know that you are the living God, and that your truth endures for all generations (lit. "to generation and generation").		

Reading Your Hebrew Bible

E. Translate the following from 2 Chronicles 9:5–6. The first verb is *3fs* and refers to the Queen of Sheba.

(5) וַתֹּאמֶר אֶל־הַמֶּלֶךְ אֱמֶת הַדָּבָר אֲשֶׁר שָׁמַעְתִּי בְּאַרְצִי
עַל־דְּבָרֶיךָ וְעַל־חָכְמָתֶךָ[a]: (6) וְלֹא־הֶאֱמַנְתִּי לְדִבְרֵיהֶם
עַד[b] אֲשֶׁר־בָּאתִי וַתִּרְאֶינָה עֵינַי

[a]The noun חָכְמָה (*qamets-chatuf*) means wisdom.

[b]עַד and עַד אֲשֶׁר mean the same thing.

THE HIPHIL: I YOD

I Yod (Yod)

➤ I Yod (Yod) verb forms originally were הַיְטִיב, יַיְטִיב, etc., before the initial *patach* changed to a *chireq*. But because the unaccented diphthong יְ◌ contracts to י◌ (see "diphthong," p. 70), the forms are הֵיטִיב, יֵיטִיב, etc.

I Yod (Yod) Imperfect	Standard Imperfect	I Yod (Yod) Perfect	Standard Perfect	
יֵיטִיב	יַקְטִיל	הֵיטִיב	הִקְטִיל	*3ms*
תֵּיטִיב	תַּקְטִיל	הֵיטִיבָה	הִקְטִילָה	*3fs*
תֵּיטִיב	תַּקְטִיל	הֵיטַבְתָּ	הִקְטַלְתָּ	*2ms*
תֵּיטִיבִי	תַּקְטִילִי	הֵיטַבְתְּ	הִקְטַלְתְּ	*2fs*
אֵיטִיב	אַקְטִיל	הֵיטַבְתִּי	הִקְטַלְתִּי	*1cs*

יֵיטִיבוּ	יַקְטִילוּ	הֵיטִיבוּ	הִקְטִילוּ	*3m/cp*
תֵּיטֵבְנָה	תַּקְטֵלְנָה			*3fp*
תֵּיטִיבוּ	תַּקְטִילוּ	הֵיטַבְתֶּם	הִקְטַלְתֶּם	*2mp*
תֵּיטֵבְנָה	תַּקְטֵלְנָה	הֵיטַבְתֶּן	הִקְטַלְתֶּן	*2fp*
נֵיטִיב	נַקְטִיל	הֵיטַבְנוּ	הִקְטַלְנוּ	*1cp*

I Yod (Yod) Participle	Standard Participle	I Yod (Yod) Imperative	Standard Imperative	
מֵיטִיב	מַקְטִיל	הֵיטֵב	הַקְטֵל	*2ms*
מֵיטֶבֶת	מַקְטֶלֶת	הֵיטִיבִי	הַקְטִילִי	*2fs*

I Yod (Yod) Participle	Standard Participle	I Yod (Yod) Imperative	Standard Imperative	
מֵיטִיבִים	מַקְטִילִים	הֵיטִיבוּ	הַקְטִילוּ	2mp
מֵיטִיבוֹת	מַקְטִילוֹת	הֵיטֵבְנָה	הַקְטֵלְנָה	2fp

I Yod (Yod) Inf abs	Standard Inf abs	I Yod (Yod) Inf const	Standard Inf const
הֵיטֵב	הַקְטֵל	הֵיטִיב	הַקְטִיל

I Yod (Yod) Wci	Standard Wci	I Yod (Yod) Jussive	Standard Jussive	
וַיֵּיטֶב	וַיַּקְטֵל	יֵיטֵב	יַקְטֵל	3ms

I Yod (Vav)

➤ I Yod (Vav) verb forms should be יַוְשִׁיב, הַוְשִׁיב, etc. But because the unaccented diphthong וְ‎ contracts to וֹ, the forms are יוֹשִׁיב, הוֹשִׁיב, etc.

I Yod (Vav) Imperfect	Standard Imperfect	I Yod (Vav) Perfect	Standard Perfect	
יוֹשִׁיב	יַקְטִיל	הוֹשִׁיב	הִקְטִיל	3ms
תּוֹשִׁיב	תַּקְטִיל	הוֹשִׁיבָה	הִקְטִילָה	3fs
תּוֹשִׁיב	תַּקְטִיל	הוֹשַׁבְתָּ	הִקְטַלְתָּ	2ms
תּוֹשִׁיבִי	תַּקְטִילִי	הוֹשַׁבְתְּ	הִקְטַלְתְּ	2fs
אוֹשִׁיב	אַקְטִיל	הוֹשַׁבְתִּי	הִקְטַלְתִּי	1cs
יוֹשִׁיבוּ	יַקְטִילוּ	הוֹשִׁיבוּ	הִקְטִילוּ	3m/cp
תּוֹשֵׁבְנָה	תַּקְטֵלְנָה			3fp
תּוֹשִׁיבוּ	תַּקְטִילוּ	הוֹשַׁבְתֶּם	הִקְטַלְתֶּם	2mp
תּוֹשֵׁבְנָה	תַּקְטֵלְנָה	הוֹשַׁבְתֶּן	הִקְטַלְתֶּן	2fp
נוֹשִׁיב	נַקְטִיל	הוֹשַׁבְנוּ	הִקְטַלְנוּ	1cp

I Yod (Vav) Participle	Standard Participle	I Yod (Vav) Imperative	Standard Imperative	
מוֹשִׁיב	מַקְטִיל	הוֹשֵׁב	הַקְטֵל	2ms
מוֹשֶׁבֶת	מַקְטֶלֶת	הוֹשִׁיבִי	הַקְטִילִי	2fs
מוֹשִׁיבִים	מַקְטִילִים	הוֹשִׁיבוּ	הַקְטִילוּ	2mp
מוֹשִׁיבוֹת	מַקְטִילוֹת	הוֹשֵׁבְנָה	הַקְטֵלְנָה	2fp

I Yod (Vav) Inf abs	Standard Inf abs	I Yod (Vav) Inf const	Standard Inf const
הוֹשֵׁב	הַקְטֵל	הוֹשִׁיב	הַקְטִיל

I Yod (Vav) Wci	Standard Wci	I Yod (Vav) Jussive	Standard Jussive	
וַיּוֹשֶׁב	וַיַּקְטֵל	יוֹשֵׁב	יַקְטֵל	3ms

Known I Yod (Vav) Verbs in the Hiphil

	Hiphil		Qal
"dry up"	הוֹבִישׁ	"be dry"	יָבֵשׁ
"inform"	הוֹדִיעַ	"know"	יָדַע
"father"	הוֹלִיד	"give birth"	יָלַד
"bring out"	הוֹצִיא	"go out"	יָצָא
"bring down"	הוֹרִיד	"go down"	יָרַד
"dispossess"	הוֹרִישׁ	"inherit"	יָרַשׁ
"settle"	הוֹשִׁיב	"dwell"	יָשַׁב

Vocabulary

Qal: shoot, throw	יָדָה	82	belly, womb *f*	בֶּטֶן (בֶּטֶן)	589
Hiph: praise, confess	הוֹדָה				

Qal: shoot, throw	יָרָה	157	palm, sole *f*	כַּף	465
Hiph: teach	הוֹרָה				
	כּוּן	42	tongue	לָשׁוֹן	519
Hiph: make firm	הֵכִין				
Qal: rest	נוּחַ	172	bone *f*	עֶצֶם (עָצֶם)	539
Hiph: give rest, settle	הֵנִיחַ				
	נָכָה	51	lip	שָׂפָה	555
Hiph: strike	הִכָּה				

Practice

Focusing on New Material

A. Focus on the form of the hiphil from I Yod roots. Parse the following.

Verb	Pattern	Conj.	Person	Gender	Number	Root
1. הֵיטִיב						
2. הוֹשִׁיב						
3. יוֹשִׁיב						
4. יֵיטִיב						
5. מוֹלִידִים						
6. הוֹרַדְתֶּם						
7. תֵּיטִיבוּ						
8. וַנּוֹשֶׁב						
9. הוֹשַׁע						
10. הוֹשִׁיבִי						

○ The Qal and the Hiphil of יָרָה and הוֹרָה appear to be from the same root. This is not the case. These were two different roots historically that have merged into one. Hebrew dictionaries will distinguish such cases by the use of roman numerals, e.g., I ידה and II ידה. The same is the case with יָרָה and הוֹרָה.

B. **Focus on the difference in meaning when a verb occurs in both the qal and the hiphil.** Translate the following verb forms. If you encounter a root that you have not yet learned in the qal or hiphil, consult the vocabulary at the back of the grammar for the meaning.

5. יָרַד	4. הוֹבִישׁ	3. יָבֵשׁ	2. הוֹצִיא	1. יָצָא
10. הוֹדִיעַ	9. יָדַע	8. הוֹרִישׁ	7. יָרַשׁ	6. הוֹרִיד
15. הוֹדַעְתֶּם	14. הוֹרַדְתֶּם	13. הוֹצֵאתֶם	12. הוֹלִיד	11. יָלְדָה

Reviewing Previous Lessons

C. **Focus on the form of qal and piel verbs from III Hey roots.** Parse the following.

	Verb	Pattern	Conj.	Person	Gender	Number	Root
1.	גָּלָה						
2.	גִּלָּה						
3.	יְכַסֶּה						
4.	יְכַסֶּה						
5.	גָּלוֹת						
6.	גְּלוֹת						
7.	כִּסִּיתָ						
8.	כָּסִיתָ						
9.	יִגְלוּ						
10.	יְגַלּוּ						

D. **Focus on the form of qal verbs from Hollow roots.** Parse the following.

	Verb	Pattern	Conj.	Person	Gender	Number	Root
1.	קָם						
2.	יָקוּם						
3.	קוּם						

4.	קַמְתֶּם					
5.	תָּקֹם					
6.	וַתָּקָם					
7.	קַמְתְּ					
8.	תָּקוּמוּ					
9.	קוּמוּ					
10.	אָקוּמָה					

Putting It All Together

E. Translate the following.

1.	יָרַד הַנָּבִיא מִן־הָהָר וַיּוֹרֶד אֶת־הָעָם עִמּוֹ וַיֵּלְכוּ אֶל־הָעִיר לָשֶׁבֶת שָׁם

1. The prophet came down from the mountain and brought the people down with him. Then they went to the city to live there.	2. כְּבוֹא הַכֹּהֵן לָאֲנָשִׁים וַיֹּאמֶר אֲלֵיהֶם הוֹצִיאוּ אֶת־הָאִישׁ הָרָשָׁע לְמַעַן אֶשְׁפֹּט אוֹתוֹ כִּי חָטָא לַיהוָה

2. When the priest came to the men he said to them, "Bring out the wicked man, that I may judge him, for he has sinned against the Lᴏʀᴅ."	3. יָכֹל יְהוָה לְהוֹבִישׁ אֶת־הַיָּם הַגָּדוֹל כִּי מֶלֶךְ הוּא עַל־כָּל־הָאָרֶץ וְעָבַדְנוּ אוֹתוֹ כָּל־יְמֵי־חַיֵּינוּ

3. The Lᴏʀᴅ is able to dry up the great sea, because he is king over all the earth. And we will serve him all the days of our life (The adj חַי is used in the plural for "life.")	4. יוֹשִׁיב יְהוָה אוֹתְךָ בְּאֶרֶץ טוֹבָה וְיָשַׁבְתָּ שָׁם שָׁנוֹת רַבּוֹת וְהוּא יִהְיֶה אֱלֹהֶיךָ וְאַתָּה תִּהְיֶה עַמּוֹ

4. The Lᴏʀᴅ will settle you in a good land and you will live there many years. He will be your God, and you will be his people.

Reading Your Hebrew Bible

F. Translate the following from Judges 7:4, 5, 7.

(4) וַיֹּאמֶר יְהֹוָה אֶל־גִּדְעוֹן ^a עוֹד הָעָם רַב

הוֹרֵד אוֹתָם אֶל־הַמָּיִם. . . . (5) וַיּוֹרֶד אֶת־הָעָם אֶל־הַמָּיִם:

(7) וַיֹּאמֶר יְהֹוָה אֶל־גִּדְעוֹן בִּשְׁלֹשׁ מֵאוֹת הָאִישׁ ^b . . . אוֹשִׁיעַ אֶתְכֶם. . . .

^a "Gideon."

^b הָאִישׁ is here a collective singular for a plural = "men."

THE HIPHIL:
III HEY AND HOLLOW

III Hey

➤ The hiphil of verbs from III Hey roots varies from the standard paradigm with the same endings as in the qal and the piel.

III Hey Hiphil Imperfect	III Hey Qal Imperfect	III Hey Hiphil Perfect	III Hey Qal Perfect	
יַגְלֶה	יִגְלֶה	הִגְלָה	גָּלָה	3ms
תַּגְלֶה	תִּגְלֶה	הִגְלְתָה	גָּלְתָה	3fs
תַּגְלֶה	תִּגְלֶה	הִגְלִיתָ	גָּלִיתָ	2ms
תַּגְלִי	תִּגְלִי	הִגְלִית	גָּלִית	2fs
אַגְלֶה	אֶגְלֶה	הִגְלִיתִי	גָּלִיתִי	1cs

III Hey Hiphil Imperfect	III Hey Qal Imperfect	III Hey Hiphil Perfect	III Hey Qal Perfect	
יַגְלוּ	יִגְלוּ	הִגְלוּ	גָּלוּ	3c/mp
תַּגְלֶינָה	תִּגְלֶינָה			3fp
תַּגְלוּ	תִּגְלוּ	הִגְלִיתֶם	גְּלִיתֶם	2mp
תַּגְלֶינָה	תִּגְלֶינָה	הִגְלִיתֶן	גְּלִיתֶן	2fp
נַגְלֶה	נִגְלֶה	הִגְלִינוּ	גָּלִינוּ	1cp

III Hey Hiphil Participle	III Hey Qal Participle	III Hey Hiphil Imperative	III Hey Qal Imperative	
מַגְלֶה	גֹּלֶה	הַגְלֵה	גְּלֵה	2ms
מַגְלָה	גֹּלָה	הַגְלִי	גְּלִי	2fs
מַגְלִים	גֹּלִים	הַגְלוּ	גְּלוּ	2mp
מַגְלוֹת	גֹּלוֹת		גְּלֶינָה	2fp

214

III Hey Hiphil Inf abs	III Hey Qal Inf abs	III Hey Hiphil Inf const	III Hey Qal Inf const
הַגְלֵה	גָּלֹה	הַגְלוֹת	גְּלוֹת

III Hey Hiphil Wci	III Hey Qal Wci	III Hey Hiphil Jussive	III Hey Qal Jussive
וַיֶּגֶל	וַיִּגֶל	יֶגֶל	יִגֶל

The Hiphil of נכה

➤ The hiphil of נכה is fairly frequent, occurring more than 500 times, and is doubly weak, being I Nun and III Hey.

Participle	Imperative	Imperfect	Perfect	
מַכֶּה	הַכֵּה	יַכֶּה	הִכָּה	*3ms*

Wci	Jussive	Inf abs	Inf const	
וַיַּךְ	יַךְ	הַכֵּה	הַכּוֹת	*3ms*

Hollow

➤ The hiphil of verbs from Hollow roots will in most forms have ◌ִי as the theme vowel.

Hollow Hiphil Imperfect	Hollow Qal Imperfect	Hollow Hiphil Perfect	Hollow Qal Perfect	
יָקִים	יָקוּם	הֵקִים	קָם	*3ms*
תָּקִים	תָּקוּם	הֵקִימָה	קָמָה	*3fs*
תָּקִים	תָּקוּם	הֲקִימוֹתָ	קַמְתָּ	*2ms*
תָּקִימִי	תָּקוּמִי	הֲקִימוֹת	קַמְתְּ	*2fs*
אָקִים	אָקוּם	הֲקִימוֹתִי	קַמְתִּי	*1cs*

Hollow Hiphil Imperfect	Hollow Qal Imperfect	Hollow Hiphil Perfect	Hollow Qal Perfect	
יָקִימוּ	יָקוּמוּ	הֵקִימוּ	קָמוּ	3c/mp
תְּקִימֶינָה	תְּקוּמֶינָה			
תָּקִימוּ	תָּקוּמוּ	הֲקִימוֹתֶם	קַמְתֶּם	2mp
תְּקִימֶינָה	תְּקוּמֶינָה	הֲקִימוֹתֶן	קַמְתֶּן	2fp
נָקִים	נָקוּם	הֲקִימוֹנוּ	קַמְנוּ	1cp

Hollow Hiphil Participle	Hollow Qal Participle	Hollow Hiphil Imperative	Hollow Qal Imperative	
מֵקִים	קָם	הָקֵם	קוּם	2ms
מְקִימָה	קָמָה	הָקִימִי	קוּמִי	2fs
מְקִימִים	קָמִים	הָקִימוּ	קוּמוּ	2mp
מְקִימוֹת	קָמוֹת	הָקֵמְנָה	קֹמְנָה	2fp

Hollow Hiphil Inf abs	Hollow Qal Inf abs	Hollow Hiphil Inf const	Hollow Qal Inf const
הָקֵם	קוֹם	הָקִים	קוּם

Hollow Hiphil Wci	Hollow Qal Wci	Hollow Hiphil Jussive	Hollow Qal Jussive
וַיָּקֵם	וַיָּקָם	יָקֵם	יָקֹם

Known Hollow Verbs in the Hiphil

	Hiphil		Qal
"bring"	הָבִיא	"come"	בּוֹא
"kill"	הֵמִית	"die"	מוּת
"remove"	הֵסִיר	"turn aside"	סוּר
"raise"	הָקִים	"rise"	קוּם
"return" (transitive)	הֵשִׁיב	"return" (intransitive)	שׁוּב

Vocabulary

width	רֹחַב (רֹחַב)	552	end	אַחֲרִית	574	
Qal: sojourn	גּוּר	72	length	אֹרֶךְ (אֹרֶךְ)	586	
Qal: kill	הָרַג	76	right, south *f*	יָמִין	510	
Qal: flee	נוּס	94	north *f*	צָפוֹן	547	
Qal: turn	פָּנָה	99	first, former	רִאשׁוֹן	550	

Practice

Focusing on New Material

A. Focus on the form of the hiphil from III Hey and Hollow roots.

Parse the following.

Verb	Pattern	Conj.	Person	Gender	Number	Root
1. הִגְלִיתָ						
2. הֲקִימוֹתָ						
3. הֵכִינוּ						
4. יָנִיחוּ						
5. יַגְלֶה						
6. הַגְלוֹת						
7. מֵקִים						
8. מַגְלִים						
9. הָכִין						
10. הִגְלֵה						

B. Focus on the form of the hiphil from roots that are doubly weak.

Parse the following.

Verb	Pattern	Conj.	Person	Gender	Number	Root
1. הִכָּה						
2. הוֹדָה						

#	Verb					
3.	יַכֶּה					
4.	יוֹדֶה					
5.	מוֹדֶה					
6.	מַכֶּה					
7.	הַכּוֹת					
8.	הוֹדוֹת					
9.	הוֹדֶה					
10.	הַכֶּה					

Reviewing Previous Lessons

C. Focus on the pronoun suffixes on nouns. Translate the following.

1. סוּסוֹ   2. סוּסָה   3. סוּסֶיהָ   4. סוּסֵנוּ   5. סוּסָם

6. סוּסְךָ   7. סוּסֵךְ   8. סוּסְכֶם   9. סוּסֶיךָ   10. סוּסָן

D. Focus on the pronoun suffixes on prepositions. Translate the following.

1. עִמְּךָ   2. עִמָּנוּ   3. עִמָּהּ   4. עִמּוֹ   5. עִמֵּךְ

6. עִמָּן   7. עִמָּכֶם   8. עִמָּכֶן   9. עִמִּי   10. עִמָּם

E. Focus on the form of all verbs learned to this point. Parse the following.

Verb	Pattern	Conj.	Person	Gender	Number	Root
1. יוֹרִיד						
2. יְכַסֶּה						
3. בָּאתָ						
4. שֹׁלֵחַ						
5. דִּבַּרְתִּי						
6. יִתְּנוּ						
7. תֵּלֵד						
8. קַחַת						

Putting It All Together

F. Translate the following.

	1.	הֵנִיחַ אֱלֹהֵינוּ לָנוּ מִכָּל־אֹיְבֵינוּ וַיּוֹשֶׁב אוֹתָנוּ בְּאֶרֶץ טוֹבָה וְאֶת־שְׁמוֹ נְהַלֵּל לְעוֹלָם
1. Our God gave us rest from all our enemies and settled us in a good land. And we will praise his name forever.	2.	אַחֲרֵי הַגְלוֹת יְהוָה אֶת־עַמּוֹ אֶל־אֶרֶץ אַחֶרֶת וַיָּשׁוּבוּ מִכָּל־עֲוֹנוֹתֵיהֶם וַיָּשֶׁב אוֹתָם אֶל־אַרְצָם
2. After the LORD exiled his people to another country, they repented of all their sins. So he returned them to their land.	3.	וּבַיּוֹם הַהוּא יוֹרוּ הָאָבוֹת אֶת־בְּנֵיהֶם לָדַעַת אֶת יְהוָה לֵאמֹר הוּא אֲדוֹנֵנוּ וַעֲבָדָיו אֲנַחְנוּ כִּי הוֹשִׁיעַ אוֹתָנוּ
3. And in that day the fathers will teach their sons to know the LORD saying, "He is our lord and we are his servants, because he has delivered us."	4.	הִכָּה הַשֹּׁמֵר אֶת־הָאִישׁ עַל־הַפֶּה כִּי דִבֶּר עַל־הַכֹּהֵן הַגָּדוֹל אֲשֶׁר בְּבֵית יְהוָה וַיָּסֶר אוֹתוֹ
4. The guard struck the man on the mouth, because he spoke against the High Priest, who was in the temple of the LORD. Then he removed him.		

Reading Your Hebrew Bible

G. Translate the following from Psalm 136:1–3, 26.

כִּי לְעוֹלָם חַסְדּוֹ	הוֹדוּ לַיהוָה כִּי־טוֹב
כִּי לְעוֹלָם חַסְדּוֹ	הוֹדוּ לֵאלֹהֵי הָאֱלֹהִים
כִּי לְעוֹלָם חַסְדּוֹ	הוֹדוּ לַאֲדֹנֵי הָאֲדֹנִים
כִּי לְעוֹלָם חַסְדּוֹ	הוֹדוּ לְאֵל הַשָּׁמַיִם

MORE ON PRONOUN SUFFIXES

Pronoun Suffixes on כֹּל

35.1 Form of כֹּל with Suffixes

➤ The word כֹּל was introduced in Lesson 13, where you learned that the construct form is כָּל־ (*qamets-chatuf*). The form to which pronoun suffixes are added is כֻּל, resulting in forms such as כֻּלָּם, כֻּלָּה, כֻּלּוֹ, and כֻּלָּנוּ.

35.2 Use of כֹּל with Suffixes

➤ Emphasis: כֹּל with a suffix is often placed after a noun it modifies to add emphasis.

"Israel, all of you!"	יִשְׂרָאֵל כֻּלְּךָ
"Listen, nations, all of them!"	שִׁמְעוּ עַמִּים כֻּלָּם
"The king's whole house, all of it!"	כָּל־בֵּית הַמֶּלֶךְ כֻּלּוֹ

➤ "Everyone": With the *3ms* suffix, understood as referring to the totality of persons or things, the sense is "all of them" or "everyone."

"Everyone says, 'Glory'."	כֻּלּוֹ אֹמֵר כָּבוֹד
"Everyone loves the king."	כֻּלּוֹ אָהֵב אֶת־הַמֶּלֶךְ

Pronoun Suffixes on Verbs

➤ In Lesson 22, you learned that when a direct object is a pronoun it is added to the direct object marker אֶת/אֵת־.

"The king sent the prophets."	שָׁלַח הַמֶּלֶךְ אֶת־הַנְּבִיאִים
"The king sent them."	שָׁלַח הַמֶּלֶךְ אוֹתָם

➤ A pronoun used as a direct object can also be added directly to the verb.

"The king sent them."   שְׁלָחָם הַמֶּלֶךְ

"The king sent us."   שְׁלָחָנוּ הַמֶּלֶךְ

➤ When a suffix is added, the accent moves to the left, so vowels will change according to the rules learned previously. Here are some examples.

"He sent us."   שְׁלָחָנוּ   שָׁלַח

"You (*ms*) sent us."   שְׁלַחְתָּנוּ   שָׁלַחְתָּ

"I sent you (*ms*)."   שְׁלַחְתִּיךָ   שָׁלַחְתִּי

"They sent you (*ms*)."   שְׁלָחוּךָ   שָׁלְחוּ

"He will send us."   יִשְׁלָחֵנוּ   יִשְׁלַח

"He will send you (*fs*)."   יִשְׁלָחֵךְ   יִשְׁלַח

➤ Most of the time, the suffix added to the verb is the same as the suffix added to the direct object marker, but two forms are different:

○ For the *3ms*, in addition to וֹ, as in קְטָלוֹ, ◌ָהוּ occurs, as in קְטָלָהוּ. The connection between ◌ָהוּ and the independent personal pronoun הוּא is obvious.

○ For the *1cs* the form is ◌ַנִי or ◌ֵנִי, as in קְטָלַנִי and יִקְטָלֵנִי. The connection between נִי and the independent personal pronoun אֲנִי is obvious.

➤ A pronoun suffix as direct object may also be added to participles.

"sending her"   שֹׁלְחָהּ   שֹׁלֵחַ

"sending them"   שֹׁלְחָם   שֹׁלֵחַ

Vocabulary

oil	שֶׁמֶן (שָׁמֶן)	560	vine *f*	גֶּפֶן (גֶּפֶן)	601
	לָחַם	89	honey	דְּבַשׁ	604
Niph: fight	נִלְחַם				
Qal: anoint	מָשַׁח	168	wine	יַיִן (יֵין)	509
Qal: open	פָּתַח	100	vineyard	כֶּרֶם (כֶּרֶם)	518
Qal: ask	שָׁאַל	112	fruit	פְּרִי	543

Practice

Focusing on New Material

A. Focus on כֹּל **with the pronoun suffixes.** Translate the following.

3. כָּל־הַמְּלָכִים כֻּלָּם	2. הַמְּלָכִים כֻּלְּכֶם	1. הַמְּלָכִים כֻּלָּם
6. כָּל־הָעִיר כֻּלָּהּ	5. הָעִיר כֻּלָּהּ	4. כָּל־מֶלֶךְ כֻּלּוֹ
9. כֻּלּוֹ יִרְאֶה	8. שָׁמַע כֻּלּוֹ	7. כֻּלּוֹ יֵלֵךְ

B. Focus on verbs with pronoun suffixes. Identify the person, gender, and number of the suffix.

5. נְתָנְכֶם	4. זְכַרְתָּהוּ	3. תִּשְׁלָחֵם	2. יִשְׁמְרוּנוּ	1. שְׁמָרְךָ
10. יְרַשְׁתִּים	9. דְּרַשְׁנוּהוּ	8. נְבַקְשֶׁהוּ	7. תַּמְלִיכוּנִי	6. יִשָּׂאֶהָ
15. יַצִּילֵהוּ	14. יִשְׁפְּטֵנוּ	13. תַּעַבְדֵךְ	12. מְצָאַתָה	11. מְצָאַתְנִי

C. Focus on verbs with pronoun suffixes. Translate the following.

5. נְתָנְכֶם	4. זְכַרְתָּהוּ	3. תִּשְׁלָחֵם	2. יִשְׁמְרוּנוּ	1. שְׁמָרְךָ
10. יְרַשְׁתִּים	9. דְּרַשְׁנוּהוּ	8. נְבַקְשֶׁהוּ	7. תַּמְלִיכוּנִי	6. יִשָּׂאֶהָ
15. יַצִּילֵהוּ	14. יִשְׁפְּטֵנוּ	13. תַּעַבְדֵךְ	12. מְצָאַתָה	11. מְצָאַתְנִי

Reviewing Previous Lessons

D. Focus on sentences with volitives. Review Lesson 24 before translating these sentences.

	1.	נְהַלְלָה אֶת־שֵׁם יְהוָה
1. Let us praise the name of the LORD.	2.	הַלְלוּ אֶת־שֵׁם יְהוָה
2. Praise (*mp*) the name of the LORD.	3.	יִבֶן מִזְבֵּחַ לַיהוָה
3. Let him build an altar for the LORD.	4.	יָקֹם הַנַּעַר לִפְנֵי הַזְּקֵנִים
4. Let the boy rise before the elders.	5.	קוּם לִפְנֵי הַזְּקֵנִים

5. Rise before the elders.	6.	אַל־תָּקֻם לִפְנֵי הָרְשָׁעִים
6. Don't rise before the wicked.	7.	אַל־תַּשְׁלֵךְ אֶת־תּוֹרַת יְהֹוָה
7. Don't reject the law of the LORD.	8.	אֶקְרָאָה בַּתּוֹרָה וְאֵדְעָה אֶת־יְהֹוָה
8. Let me read in the Law, so that I may know the LORD.	9.	שְׁמַע וְתָשֻׁב מֵחַטָּאתֶךָ
9. Listen, so that you may turn from your sin.	10.	אַל־תֶּחֱטָא פֶּן תֹּאבֵד
10. Don't sin, lest you perish.		

E. Parse the following.

Verb	Pattern	Conj.	Person	Gender	Number	Root
1. שָׁלַחְתָּ						
2. דִּבַּרְתָּ						
3. הִשְׁלַכְתָּ						
4. יִכְתֹּב						
5. יַמְלִיךְ						
6. יְמַלֵּא						
7. נְבַקֵּשׁ						
8. הִשְׁאִירָה						

Putting It All Together

F. Translate the following.

	1.	יַגֵּד מַלְאַךְ־הָאֹיֵב לְמַלְכֵּנוּ אֶת־הַדָּבָר אֲשֶׁר דִּבֶּר שָׂרוֹ לוֹ וְנֵדְעָה מָה נַעֲשֶׂה וַיְבִיאוּהוּ לִפְנֵי הַמֶּלֶךְ וַיַּגֵּד אֶת־הַדָּבָר
1. Let the messenger of the enemy tell our king the message which his leader spoke to him, so that we may know what we should do. Then they brought him before the king, and he told the matter.	2.	יָצְאוּ שִׁבְעַת גִּבּוֹרִים לַמִּלְחָמָה אֲשֶׁר בַּשָּׂדֶה וַיִּרְאוּ אֶת־מַחֲנֵה־הָאֹיֵב וַיָּבוֹאוּ בוֹ וַיָּמִיתוּ אֶת־כָּל־הָאֲנָשִׁים כֻּלָּם

| 2. Seven mighty men went out to the battle which was in the field, and they saw the enemy camp. So they entered it and killed absolutely every man. | 3. בְּרֵאשִׁית הַשָּׁנָה וַיַּמְלִיכוּהוּ וַיִּמְלֹךְ בַּשָּׁנָה הַהִיא וַיָּמָת וַיַּמְלִיכוּ אֶת־בְּנוֹ הֶחָכָם תַּחְתָּיו וַיִּמְלֹךְ שָׁנוֹת רַבּוֹת וְהוּא מֶלֶךְ טוֹב וְגָדוֹל |
| 3. At the beginning of the year, they made him king. He reigned during that year, then he died. So they made his wise son king in place of him, and he reigned for many years. He was a good and great king. | |

Reading Your Hebrew Bible

G. Translate the following from Genesis 2:2–3

(2) וַיְכַל [a] אֱלֹהִים בַּיּוֹם הַשְּׁבִיעִי מְלַאכְתּוֹ [b] אֲשֶׁר עָשָׂה וַיִּשְׁבֹּת [c] בַּיּוֹם

הַשְּׁבִיעִי מִכָּל־מְלַאכְתּוֹ אֲשֶׁר עָשָׂה: (3) וַיְבָרֶךְ [a] אֱלֹהִים אֶת־יוֹם הַשְּׁבִיעִי

וַיְקַדֵּשׁ [a] אֹתוֹ כִּי בוֹ שָׁבַת מִכָּל־מְלַאכְתּוֹ אֲשֶׁר־בָּרָא אֱלֹהִים לַעֲשׂוֹת:

[a] Strong *dagesh* is often lost when the vowel under the consonant is vocal *sheva*.

[b] The noun מְלָאכָה means "work."

[c] The verb שָׁבַת means "rest" and is related to the noun שַׁבָּת ("Sabbath").

THE NIPHAL:
STRONG ROOTS

The Meaning of the Niphal

➤ The niphal is the fourth of the seven major verb patterns you will learn. The niphal makes up 6% of all verbs in the Hebrew Bible.[1] The qal, piel, hiphil, and niphal make up 97% of all verbs.

➤ Most niphal verbs are the passive of the qal.

Niphal	Qal	Root
"be remembered"	"remember"	זכר
"be cut"	"cut"	כרת
"be given"	"give"	נתן
"be guarded"	"guard"	שמר

➤ Sometimes the niphal is the reflexive of the qal.

"guard himself"	"guard"	שמר

➤ A few verbs occur only (or mainly) in the niphal, without a corresponding qal and with a qal-like action sense.

"fight"		לחם
"swear an oath"		שבע

The niphal is abbreviated niph.

---

1. B. K. Waltke and M. O'Connor, *Syntax*, §21.2.3e.

Form of the Niphal

➤ The primary characteristic of the niphal is a prefixed *nun* (נ).

36.1 Perfect

Niphal	Qal	
נִקְטַל	קָטַל	3ms
נִקְטְלָה	קָטְלָה	3fs
נִקְטַלְתָּ	קָטַלְתָּ	2ms
נִקְטַלְתְּ	קָטַלְתְּ	2fs
נִקְטַלְתִּי	קָטַלְתִּי	1cs

Niphal	Qal	
נִקְטְלוּ	קָטְלוּ	3cp
נִקְטַלְתֶּם	קְטַלְתֶּם	2mp
נִקְטַלְתֶּן	קְטַלְתֶּן	2fp
נִקְטַלְנוּ	קָטַלְנוּ	1cp

36.2 Imperfect

Niphal	Qal	
יִקָּטֵל (> יִנְקָטֵל)	יִקְטֹל	3ms
תִּקָּטֵל	תִּקְטֹל	3fs
תִּקָּטֵל	תִּקְטֹל	2ms
תִּקָּטְלִי	תִּקְטְלִי	2fs
אֶקָּטֵל	אֶקְטֹל	1cs
יִקָּטְלוּ	יִקְטְלוּ	3mp
תִּקָּטַלְנָה	תִּקְטֹלְנָה	3fp
תִּקָּטְלוּ	תִּקְטְלוּ	2mp
תִּקָּטַלְנָה	תִּקְטֹלְנָה	2fp
נִקָּטֵל	נִקְטֹל	1cp

36.3   Imperative

(הִנָּקֵטֵל <)

Imperative	Imperfect	
הִקָּטֵל	תִּקָּטֵל	2ms
הִקָּטְלִי	תִּקָּטְלִי	2fs
הִקָּטְלוּ	תִּקָּטְלוּ	2mp
הִקָּטַלְנָה	תִּקָּטַלְנָה	2fp

36.4   Infinitives

(הִנָּקֵטֵל <)

Infinitive Construct	Imperative
הִקָּטֵל	הִקָּטֵל

Infinitive Absolute
הִקָּטֹל / נִקְטֹל

36.5   Participle

Niphal	Qal	
נִקְטָל	קֹטֵל	ms
נִקְטֶלֶת	קֹטֶלֶת	fs
נִקְטָלִים	קֹטְלִים	mp
נִקְטָלוֹת	קֹטְלוֹת	fp

36.6   Cohortative

(אֶנָּקֵטֵל <)

Niphal	Qal	
אֶקָּטְלָה	אֶקְטְלָה	1cs
נִקָּטְלָה	נִקְטְלָה	1cp

36.7   Jussive

(יִנָּקֵטֵל <)

Jussive	Imperfect	
יִקָּטֵל	יִקָּטֵל	3ms

36.8   Vav-relative

Vav-relative	Jussive	
וַיִּקָּטֵל	יִקָּטֵל	*3ms*

(> וַיִּנְקָטֵל)

Vocabulary

copper, bronze	נְחֹשֶׁת (נְחֹשֶׁת)	531	iron	בַּרְזֶל	592
sun	שֶׁמֶשׁ	562	hill	גִּבְעָה	596
	נָבָא	91	valley	גַּיְא	599
Niph: prophesy	נִבָּא				
Qal: gather	קָבַץ	101	river	נָהָר	529
Qal: pasture, tend	רָעָה	108	wadi	נַחַל (נַחַל)	530

Note:

○ Usually, a נָהָר has water flowing all year round, but a נַחַל has water only during the rainy season.

Practice

Focusing on New Material

A. Focus on the form of the niphal. Parse the following.

Verb	Pattern	Conj.	Person	Gender	Number	Root
1. נִקְטַל						
2. נִקְטָל						
3. נִלְחַמְתֶּם						
4. יִכָּתֵב						
5. נִשְׁמֵר						
6. הִשָּׁמְרוּ						
7. תִּקָּטְלִי						

8. נִקְטֶלֶת					
9. נִשְׁמְרוּ					
10. הָקְטַל					

B. Focus on the difference in meaning when a verb occurs in both the qal and the niphal. Translate the following verb forms.

5. כָּתַב   4. נִגְאַל   3. גָּאַל   2. נִמְשַׁח   1. מָשַׁח

10. נִזְכַּר   9. זָכַר   8. נִדְרַשׁ   7. דָּרַשׁ   6. נִכְתַּב

Reviewing Previous Lessons

C. Focus on qal and hiphil verbs from I Guttural and I Nun roots. Parse the following.

Verb	Pattern	Conj.	Person	Gender	Number	Root
1. עֲמַדְתֶּם						
2. יַעֲמֹד						
3. יַעֲמִיד						
4. הֶעֱמִיד						
5. הֶעֱמִידוּ						
6. מַעֲמִידִים						
7. יִפֹּל						
8. יִפְּלוּ						
9. תִּפֹּל						

D. Focus on the difference between attributive and predicate adjectives. Read the following phrases and sentences, and fill in the blanks for use of adjective (*a* for attributive and *p* for predicative) and for gender and number.

Use	Gender	Number		
a	f	s	1.	הָאִשָּׁה הַטּוֹבָה
			2.	קָדוֹשׁ הַכֹּהֵן
			3.	הַזֶּבַח הַטָּמֵא

			.4	טוֹבָה הָאָרֶץ
			.5	גְּדוֹלִים הַגִּבּוֹרִים
			.6	הָאֱלֹהִים הַחַיִּים
			.7	הַמִּשְׁפָּחוֹת הָרַבּוֹת
			.8	רְשָׁעָה הַמַּלְכוּת
			.9	לֵב חָכָם
			.10	הַנָּשִׁים הַטּוֹבוֹת

Putting It All Together

E. Translate the following.

	1. נִשְׁלְחוּ מִפָּנָיו הָאֲנָשִׁים אֲשֶׁר לֹא בִקְשׁוּ אֶת יְהוָה אֱלֹהֵיהֶם כָּל־יְמֵי־חַיֵּיהֶם
1. The men who did not seek the LORD their God all the days of their lives were sent from his presence.	2. וַיְהִי כְּהִלָּקְחוֹ אֶל־הָעִיר וַיִּקָּבְצוּ הַזְּקֵנִים וְהָאֲנָשִׁים וְהַנָּשִׁים וּבְנֵיהֶם וּבְנוֹתֵיהֶם לוֹ וַיֹּאמֶר לָהֶם יְהִי יְהוָה עִמָּכֶם
2. When he was taken to the city, the elders, the men, the women, and their sons and their daughters were gathered to him. Then he said to them, "May the LORD be with you."	3. דִּרְשׁוּ אֶת־שְׁלוֹם־עִיר־אֱלֹהֵינוּ כִּי יְבָרֵךְ יְהוָה אֶת־דֹּרְשֵׁי שְׁלוֹם עִירוֹ וְנִשְׁמְרוּ מִכָּל־אֹיְבֵיהֶם
3. Seek the peace of the city of our God, for the LORD will bless those who seek the peace of his city, and they will be guarded from all their enemies.	4. הוֹרוּ אֶת־בְּנֵיכֶם אֶת־מִצְוֹת יְהוָה וְתִזָּכַרְנָה וְיוֹרוּ אֶת־בְּנֵיהֶם וְאֶת־בְּנֵי בְנֵיהֶם לָדַעַת אֶת־יְהוָה וְאֶת־מִצְוֹתָיו
4. Teach (*mp*) your sons the commandments (*fp*) of the LORD, so that they (*fp*) may be remembered, and so that they (*mp*) may teach their sons and their grandsons to know the LORD and his commandments.	

Reading Your Hebrew Bible

F. Translate the following from Zechariah 13:1-2.

(1) בַּיּוֹם הַהוּא יִהְיֶה מָקוֹר ᵃ נִפְתָּח לְבֵית דָּוִיד ᵇ וּלְיֹשְׁבֵי יְרוּשָׁלַם ᶜ

לְחַטַּאת. . . . (2) וְהָיָה בַיּוֹם הַהוּא נְאֻם יְהוָה צְבָאוֹת אַכְרִית

אֶת־שְׁמוֹת הָעֲצַבִּים ᵈ מִן־הָאָרֶץ וְלֹא יִזָּכְרוּ עוֹד וְגַם אֶת־הַנְּבִיאִים

וְאֶת־רוּחַ הַטֻּמְאָה ᵉ אַעֲבִיר מִן־הָאָרֶץ:

ᵃ"A well"

ᵇ"David"

ᶜ"Jerusalem"

ᵈ"The idols"

ᵉ"Uncleanness;" טָמֵא = "unclean"

37

THE NIPHAL: WEAK ROOTS

I Guttural

➤ The niphal of verbs from I Guttural roots vary from the standard paradigm: (1) by replacing the *sheva* under the first root letter with *chatef-segol* ($\square$) or (2) by having compensatory lengthening of the initial *chireq* ($\square$) to *tsere* ($\square$) because the initial guttural does not take strong *dagesh*.

I Guttural Imperfect	Strong Imperfect	I Guttural Perfect	Strong Perfect
יֵעָמֵד	יִקָּטֵל	נֶעֱמַד	נִקְטַל

I Guttural Participle	Strong Participle	I Guttural Imperative	Strong Imperative
נֶעֱמָד	נִקְטָל	הֵעָמֵד	הִקָּטֵל

I Guttural Vav-rel.	Strong Vav-rel.	I Guttural Inf const	Strong Inf const
וַיֵּעָמֵד	וַיִּקָּטֵל	הֵעָמֵד	הִקָּטֵל

I Nun

➤ The niphal of verbs from I Nun roots vary from the standard paradigm only in the *pf* and the *ptc*, where the initial *nun* of the root assimilates to the second root letter.

I Nun Participle	Strong Participle	I Nun Perfect	Strong Perfect
נִצָּל	נִקְטָל	נִצַּל	נִקְטַל

I Yod (Vav)

➤ The niphal of verbs from I Yod (Vav) roots vary from the standard paradigm: (1) by having the original *vav* preserved because of the strong *dagesh*, or (2) by having a vestige of the original *vav* in the form of *cholem-vav* (וֹ).

I Yod (Vav) Imperfect	Strong Imperfect	I Yod (Vav) Perfect	Strong Perfect
יִוָּשֵׁב	יִקָּטֵל	נוֹשַׁב	נִקְטַל

I Yod (Vav) Participle	Strong Participle	I Yod (Vav) Imperative	Strong Imperative
נוֹשָׁב	נִקְטָל	הִוָּשֵׁב	הִקָּטֵל

I Yod (Vav) Vav-rel.	Strong Vav-rel.	I Yod (Vav) Inf const	Strong Inf const
וַיִּוָּשֵׁב	וַיִּקָּטֵל	הִוָּשֵׁב	הִקָּטֵל

III Hey

➤ The niphal of verbs from III Hey roots vary from the standard paradigm with basically the same endings as in the qal, piel, and hiphil. In the *pf*, the niphal usually has ־ִי (נִגְלֵינוּ) in place of ־ִי (גָּלֵינוּ).

III Hey Niphal Imperfect	III Hey Qal Imperfect	III Hey Niphal Perfect	III Hey Qal Perfect
יִגָּלֶה	יִגְלֶה	נִגְלָה	גָּלָה

III Hey Niphal Participle	III Hey Qal Participle	III Hey Niphal Imperative	III Hey Qal Imperative
נִגְלֶה	גֹּלֶה	הִגָּלֵה	גְּלֵה

III Hey Niphal Inf abs	III Hey Qal Inf abs	III Hey Niphal Inf const	III Hey Qal Inf const
הִגָּלֵה	גָּלֹה	הִגָּלוֹת	גְּלוֹת

III Hey Niphal Vav-rel.	III Hey Niphal Jussive	III Hey Niphal Imperfect
וַיִּגָּל	יִגָּל	יִגָּלֶה

Vocabulary

south, Negeb	נֶגֶב (נֶגֶב)	528	behind, west	אַחֲרוֹן	573
Qal: bury	קָבַר	102	cubit	אַמָּה	452
	קָטַר	104	wheat	חִטָּה	616
Piel: burn a sacrifice	קִטֵּר				
Hiphil: burn a sacrifice	הִקְטִיר				
Qal: burn	שָׂרַף	111	fat	חֵלֶב (חֵלֶב)	617
	שָׁרַת	123	pasture land	מִגְרָשׁ	520
Piel: serve, minister	שֵׁרֶת				

Practice

Focusing on New Material

A. Focus on the form of the niphal from weak roots. Parse the following.

Verb		Pattern	Conj.	Person	Gender	Number	Root
1.	יֵאָמֵן						
2.	נִדַּחְתִּי						
3.	יִוָּלְדוּ						
4.	יִבָּנֶה						
5.	נִבְנָה						
6.	יֵעָנֶה						
7.	נוֹדַעְנוּ						
8.	הִוָּתְרוּ						
9.	נֶאֱסַפְתֶּם						

10. הֵרָאוֹת						
11. נִצַּל						
12. נֶעֱנֵיתָ						
13. הֵהָרְגִי						
14. תִּוָּדְעוּ						
15. נִבְאוּ						

B. Focus on the meaning of niphal verbs from weak roots. Translate the following.

5. נוֹלַדְנוּ   4. נִבְנָה   3. יִוָּתְרוּ   2. נִדְּחוּ   1. נֶאֶסְפוּ

10. יֵרָאֶה   9. נִבָּא   8. נוֹדַעְנוּ   7. נֶאֱמַן   6. נִרְאָה

Reviewing Previous Lessons

C. Focus on the difference between attributive and predicate participles. Read the following phrases and sentences, and fill in the blanks for use of participle (*a* for attributive and *p* for predicative) and for gender and number.

Use	Gender	Number		
a	m	s	1.	הָאִישׁ הַיּשֵׁב
			2.	הַכֹּהֵן ישֵׁב
			3.	הַנַּעַר הַמְדַבֵּר
			4.	הַנָּבִיא מְדַבֵּר
			5.	יֹצְאִים הַגִּבּוֹרִים
			6.	הַגִּבּוֹרִים הַיֹּרְדִים
			7.	הַנָּשִׁים הַמוֹדִיעוֹת
			8.	הַנָּשִׁים בָּאוֹת
			9.	הָעַמִּים הַנֶּאֱסָפִים
			10.	נִדָּח הָעָם

Putting It All Together

D. Translate the following.

	1. וַיִּנָּצְלוּ הָאֲנָשִׁים הַקְּדוֹשִׁים מִן־הָאֲנָשִׁים הָרְשָׁעִים הַנִּלְחָמִים עֲלֵיהֶם וַיֵּשְׁבוּ בְּאֶרֶץ טוֹבָה וַיִּבָּנוּ בָתִּים לָהֶם בֶּהָרִים וּבַגֵּיאוֹת
1. The holy men were delivered from the wicked men who were fighting against them. Then they dwelled in a good land, and houses were built for them in the mountains and in the valleys.	2. וַיְהִי כַּאֲשֶׁר הִנָּבֵא הַנְּבִיאִים אֶל הַזְּקֵנִים וַיָּשׁוּבוּ הַזְּקֵנִים וְכָל־הָעָם וְלֹא נִגְלוּ מֵאַרְצָם וַיִּדְבְּקוּ לִבְרִית אֲבוֹתָם
2. When the prophets prophesied to the elders, the elders and all the people repented, and were not exiled from their land. Then they clung to the covenant of their fathers.	3. יֵאָמְנוּ דִבְרֵי־יְהוָה וּמִשְׁפָּטָיו וְתוֹרוֹתָיו לְמַעַן תַּאֲמִינוּ בָם וְלֹא תִּירָאוּ כִּי לֹא תֵּעָזְבוּ בַּיהוָה לְעוֹלָם
3. The words of the LORD and his judgments and his laws are firm, so that you (*mp*) may trust in them and not be afraid. For you (*mp*) will never be abandoned by the LORD.	

Reading Your Hebrew Bible

E. Translate the following from 1 Kings 18:36.

וַיְהִי בַּעֲלוֹת[a] הַמִּנְחָה וַיִּגַּשׁ אֵלִיָּהוּ[b] הַנָּבִיא וַיֹּאמַר יְהוָה[c]

אֱלֹהֵי אַבְרָהָם[d] יִצְחָק[e] וְיִשְׂרָאֵל[f] הַיּוֹם יִוָּדַע[g] כִּי־אַתָּה אֱלֹהִים

בְּיִשְׂרָאֵל וַאֲנִי עַבְדֶּךָ וּבִדְבָרְךָ עָשִׂיתִי אֵת כָּל־הַדְּבָרִים הָאֵלֶּה:

[a]The form is the qal *inf. const.* of עלה (go up, ascend) with the preposition בְּ = "in" in the sense of "at the time of" > "At the time of the ascending of."

[b]"Elijah"

[c]"O LORD"; a vocative

[d]"Abraham"

[e]"Isaac"

[f]"Israel"

[g]Jussive in sense

38

MORE PASSIVE VERBS:
QAL, PUAL, AND HOPHAL

Qal Passive Participle

➤ In addition to the active participle, the qal has a passive participle (abbreviated *pass ptc*).

38.1   Form of the Qal Passive Participle

	Plural	Singular
Masculine	קְטוּלִים	קָטוּל
Feminine	קְטוּלוֹת	קְטוּלָה

38.2   Use of the Qal Passive Participle

➤ The *pass ptc* has the same three uses as the *ptc*.

• Attributive: "the man who was guarded"   הָאִישׁ הַשָּׁמוּר

• Predicative: "The man was guarded."   שָׁמוּר הָאִישׁ

• Substantive: "the guarded man"   הַשָּׁמוּר

Pual

➤ The pual is the fifth of the seven major verb patterns; it makes up only 0.6% of the verbs in Hebrew[1] and is the passive of the piel.

➤ To change verb pattern is to *change the meaning* of the verb.

Pual	Piel	Root
"be blessed"	"bless"	ברך
"be praised"	"praise"	הלל

1. Waltke and O'Connor, *Syntax*, §21.2.3e.

Pual	Piel	Root
"be atoned for"	"atone for"	כפר
"be sent away"	"send away"	שלח

- Occasionally, the niphal serves as the passive of the piel.

Niphal	Piel	Root
"be defiled"	"defile"	חלל

➤ The pual is formed like the piel, with strong *dagesh* in the middle root letter, but the vowel pattern is *qibbuts* (◌ֻ) followed by *patach* (◌ַ).

Perfect:	Pual	Piel	
	קֻטַּל	קִטֵּל	3ms
	קֻטְּלָה	קִטְּלָה	3fs
	קֻטַּלְתָּ	קִטַּלְתָּ	2ms

Imperfect:	Pual	Piel	
	יְקֻטַּל	יְקַטֵּל	3ms
	תְּקֻטַּל	תְּקַטֵּל	3fs
	תְּקֻטַּל	תְּקַטֵּל	2ms

Participle:	Pual	Piel	
	מְקֻטָּל	מְקַטֵּל	ms

Hophal

➤ The hophal is the sixth of seven major verb patterns and makes up only 0.6% of the verbs in Hebrew;[2] it is the passive of the hiphil.

---

2. Waltke and O'Connor, *Syntax*, §21.2.3e.

➤ To change verb pattern is to *change the meaning* of the verb.

Hophal	Hiphil	Root
"be brought down"	"bring down"	יָרַד
"be made king"	"make king"	מָלַךְ
"be told"	"tell"	נָגַד
"be thrown"	"throw"	שָׁלַךְ

• Occasionally, the niphal serves as the passive of the hiphil.

Niphal	Hiphil	Root
"be saved"	"save"	יָשַׁע

➤ The hophal is formed like the hiphil, but the vowel pattern is *qamets-chatuf* (ָ) followed by *patach* (ַ).

Perfect:	Hophal	Hiphil	
	הָקְטַל	הִקְטִיל	*3ms*
	הָקְטְלָה	הִקְטִילָה	*3fs*
	הָקְטַלְתָּ	הִקְטַלְתָּ	*2ms*

Imperfect:	Hophal	Hiphil	
	יָקְטַל	יַקְטִיל	*3ms*
	תָּקְטַל	תַּקְטִיל	*3fs*
	תָּקְטַל	תַּקְטִיל	*2ms*

Participle:	Hophal	Hiphil	
	מָקְטָל / מֻקְטָל	מַקְטִיל	*ms*

The hophal is abbreviated hoph.

Vocabulary

doorway, door	פֶּתַח (פֶּתַח)	544	treasure, treasury	אוֹצָר	570
	פָּלַל	188	door	דֶּלֶת (דֶּלֶת)	605
Hith: pray	הִתְפַּלֵּל				
Qal: pursue	רָדַף	106	palace, temple	הֵיכָל	607
Qal: break	שָׁבַר	115	seat, throne	כִּסֵּא	517
Qal: forget	שָׁכַח	118	tower	מִגְדָּל	637

Practice

Focusing on New Material

A. Focus on qal *pass. ptc.*, pual, and hophal verbs. Parse the following.

Verb	Pattern	Conj.	Person	Gender	Number	Root
1. כָּתוּב						
2. הֻלַּל						
3. הָמְלַךְ						
4. יְכֻפַּר						
5. יֻשְׁלַךְ						
6. נָשְׁלַךְ						
7. יְהֻלְלוּ						
8. שְׁמוּרִים						
9. כֻּפַּרְנוּ						
10. הָמְלַכְתָּ						
11. מָשְׁלָךְ						
12. מְהֻלָּל						
13. קְבוּרָה						

B. Focus on the meaning of the qal *pass. ptc.*, pual, and hophal verbs. Translate the following.

5. יְשֻׁלְכוּ   4. הֻלַּלְנוּ   3. יְכֻפַּר   2. הָמְלַכְתִּי   1. כָּתוּב הוּא

10. יְהֻלַּל   9. קָבוּר הוּא   8. כֻּפַּר   7. הָשְׁלַכְתֶּם   6. תֻּמְלַךְ

Reviewing Previous Lessons

C. Focus on temporal clauses. Translate the following, paying attention to the various ways temporal clauses are expressed (see Lesson 27).

	1.	וַיְהִי כִּשְׁלֹחַ הָאִישׁ אֶת־הַנְּעָרִים וַיֵּלְכוּ
1. When the man sent the boys, they went.	2.	וְהָיָה כִּשְׁלֹחַ הָאִישׁ אֶת־הַנְּעָרִים וְהָלְכוּ
2. When the man sends the boys, they will go.	3.	וַיְהִי כִּי שָׁלַח הָאִישׁ אֶת־הַנְּעָרִים וַיֵּלְכוּ
3. When the man sent the boys, they went.	4.	וְהָיָה כִּי יִשְׁלַח הָאִישׁ אֵת הַנְּעָרִים וְהָלְכוּ
4. When the man sends the boys, they will go.	5.	וַיְהִי בַּבֹּקֶר וַיִּשְׁלַח הָאִישׁ אֶת הַנְּעָרִים וַיֵּלְכוּ
5. In the morning, the man sent the boys, and they went.	6.	וְהָיָה בַּבֹּקֶר וְשָׁלַח הָאִישׁ אֵת הַנְּעָרִים וְהָלְכוּ
6. In the morning, the man will send the boys, and they will go.		

D. Focus on interrogative clauses. Translate the following (see Lesson 27).

	1.	מָה אַתָּה עֹשֶׂה
1. What are you doing?	2.	מִי שָׁלַח אֶת־הַנְּעָרִים
2. Who sent the boys?	3.	הֲשָׁלַח אֶת־הַנְּעָרִים
3. Did he send the boys?	4.	הַאַתָּה שָׁלַחְתָּ אֶת־הַנְּעָרִים
4. Did you send the boys?	5.	מִי יֵלֵךְ לָנוּ
5. Who will go for us?	6.	מָה תֹּאמַר אֲלֵיהֶם
6. What will she/you (*ms*) say to them?		

Putting It All Together

E. Translate the following.

	1.	וַיְהִי כְּזֹבֵחַ הַכֹּהֵן אֶת־הַזְּבָחִים עַל־הַמִּזְבֵּחַ וַתְּכֻפַּרְנָה חַטֹּאותֵינוּ וַיְהֻלַּל יְהוָה אֱלֹהֵינוּ כִּי טוֹב הוּא וּלְעוֹלָם חַסְדּוֹ
1. When the priest offered the sacrifices on the altar, our sins were atoned for and the LORD our God was praised, for he is good and his loyalty endures forever.	2.	וַיָּבִיאוּ אֶת־דָּוִיד אֶל־הָעִיר הַגְּדוֹלָה וַיַּמְלַךְ שָׁם לִפְנֵי כָל־הָעָם וַיִּשְׂמְחוּ מְאֹד וַיִּשְׁלְחוּ אֶל־בָּתֵּיהֶם וַיֵּלֶךְ דָּוִיד אֶל־בֵּיתוֹ
2. They brought David to the great city and he was made king there before all the people. Then they were very glad and were sent to their homes. And David went to his house.	3.	בָּרוּךְ אַתָּה יְהוָה אֱלֹהֵינוּ מֶלֶךְ־הָעוֹלָם בֹּרֵא הָאֲדָמָה וְכֹל אֲשֶׁר עָלֶיהָ גֹּאֵל־עַמֶּךָ
3. Blessed are you, O LORD our God, King of eternity, Creator of the land and everything on it, Redeemer of your people.		

Reading Your Hebrew Bible

F. Translate the following from the Hebrew Bible.

Psalm 48:1   .1   גָּדוֹל יְהוָה וּמְהֻלָּל מְאֹד בְּעִיר אֱלֹהֵינוּ הַר־קָדְשׁוֹ

1 Chronicles 29:10   .2   וַיְבָרֶךְ דָּוִיד[a] אֶת־יְהוָה לְעֵינֵי כָל־הַקָּהָל[b] וַיֹּאמֶר

דָּוִיד בָּרוּךְ אַתָּה יְהוָה אֱלֹהֵי יִשְׂרָאֵל[c] אָבִינוּ

מֵעוֹלָם וְעַד־עוֹלָם:

[a] "David"

[b] "The assembly"

[c] "Israel"

THE VERB:
THE HITHPAEL

The Meaning of the Hithpael

➤ The hithpael is the seventh of the seven major verb patterns. The hithpael makes up 1.2% of all verbs in the Hebrew Bible.[1]

➤ A common use of the hithpael is to express the reflexive—that is, action done to oneself.

Hithpael	Piel or Qal	Root
"praise oneself"	"praise"	הלל
"prostrate oneself"	"fall"	נפל
"sanctify oneself"	"sanctify"	קדשׁ

➤ Some verbs occur only (or mainly) in the hithpael, without a corresponding qal or piel.

"pray"		פלל
"prophesy"		נבא

> *The hithpael is abbreviated hith.*

---

1. Waltke and O'Connor, *Syntax*, §21.2.3e.

The Form of the Hithpael

➤ The hithpael is easily recognized by (1) its long prefixes, e.g., יִתְ, הִתְ, and מִתְ, and (2) its similarity to the piel—the doubling of the middle root letter and similar vowel patterns.

Imperative	Imperfect	Perfect	
	יִתְקַטֵּל	הִתְקַטֵּל	3ms
	תִּתְקַטֵּל	הִתְקַטְּלָה	3fs
הִתְקַטֵּל	תִּתְקַטֵּל	הִתְקַטַּלְתָּ	2ms
הִתְקַטְּלִי	תִּתְקַטְּלִי	הִתְקַטַּלְתְּ	2fs
	אֶתְקַטֵּל	הִתְקַטַּלְתִּי	1cs

	יִתְקַטְּלוּ	הִתְקַטְּלוּ	3cp/mp
	תִּתְקַטֵּלְנָה		3fp
הִתְקַטְּלוּ	תִּתְקַטְּלוּ	הִתְקַטַּלְתֶּם	2mp
הִתְקַטֵּלְנָה	תִּתְקַטֵּלְנָה	הִתְקַטַּלְתֶּן	2fp
	נִתְקַטֵּל	הִתְקַטַּלְנוּ	1cp

Inf abs	Inf const	Participle	
הִתְקַטֵּל	הִתְקַטֵּל	מִתְקַטֵּל	ms
		מִתְקַטֶּלֶת	fs
		מִתְקַטְּלִים	mp
		מִתְקַטְּלוֹת	fp

The Verb הִשְׁתַּחֲוָה

➤ The verb הִשְׁתַּחֲוָה (169×) means "to prostrate oneself" or "to worship."

   ➤ *Vocabulary Card #116*

➤ Older dictionaries treat the verb הִשְׁתַּחֲוָה as a hithpael of שׁחה. More recent dictionaries treat הִשְׁתַּחֲוָה as a hishtafel of חוה. The latter is adopted in this grammar.

> *The hishtafel is abbreviated hish.*

➤ Some of the frequent forms are.

Imperative	Imperfect	Perfect	
	תִּשְׁתַּחֲוֶה	הִשְׁתַּחֲוִיתָ	*2ms*
		הִשְׁתַּחֲווּ	*3cp*
הִשְׁתַּחֲווּ			*2mp*

Wci	Inf const	Participle	
	הִשְׁתַּחֲוֹת	מִשְׁתַּחֲוִים	*mp*
וַיִּשְׁתַּחוּ			*3ms*
וַיִּשְׁתַּחֲווּ			*3mp*

Vocabulary

Qal: curse	אָרַר	127	ram	אַיִל (אֱיָל)	449
Qal: be gracious	חָנַן	145	lion	אֲרִי	584
Qal: be terrified	חָתַת	150	camel	גָּמָל	600
Qal: measure	מָדַד	164	lamb	כֶּבֶשׂ (כֶּבֶשׂ)	514
Qal: go/turn around	סָבַב	96	wing, extremity	כָּנָף	516

Practice

Focusing on New Material

A. Focus on the form of the _hith._ and _hish._ Parse the following.

Verb	Pattern	Conj.	Person	Gender	Number	Root
1. יִתְהַלְלוּ						
2. הִתְקַדַּשְׁתִּי						
3. מִתְנַפֵּל						
4. הִשְׁתַּחֲוִיתָ						
5. נִתְפַּלֵּל						
6. הִתְנַבֵּאתֶם						
7. וַיִּשְׁתַּחוּ						
8. וַיִּשְׁתַּחֲווּ						
9. מִתְהַלְלִים						
10. אֶתְקַדֵּשׁ						

B. Focus on the difference in meaning between the qal or piel and the _hith._ Translate the following.

4. הִתְקַדַּשְׁתִּי	3. קִדַּשְׁתִּי	2. הִתְהַלַלְתִּי	1. הִלַּלְתִּי
8. הִתְגַּדַּלְתִּי	7. גִּדַּלְתִּי	6. הִתְנַפַּלְתִּי	5. נָפַלְתִּי

Reviewing Previous Lessons

C. Focus on nouns and adjectives from geminate roots. Match the plural form of the right column with the corresponding singular form in the left column.

a. אֵם	____	1. דָּמִים
b. לֵבָב	____	2. עַמִּים
c. חֹק	____	3. אִמּוֹת
d. יָם	____	4. לְבּוֹת
e. כַּף	____	5. חַיִּים

6. לְבָבוֹת ____   f. דָּם

7. הָרִים ____   g. עַם

8. חֻקִּים ____   h. הַר

9. יָמִים ____   i. חַי

10. כַּפּוֹת ____   j. לֵב

D. Focus on the verb from hollow roots. Parse the following.

Verb	Pattern	Conj.	Person	Gender	Number	Root
1. קָם						
2. יָקוּם						
3. יָקִים						
4. הֵקִים						
5. הֲקִימוֹתָ						
6. תָּקוּמִי						
7. הֲקִימוֹנוּ						
8. קַמְתֶּם						
9. הָקִימוּ						
10. מֵקִים						

Putting It All Together

E. Translate the following.

	1.	וַיְהִי בַבֹּקֶר וַיָּבֹאוּ הָאֲנָשִׁים אֶל־הַהֵיכָל אֲשֶׁר בָּעִיר וַיְהִי כְּבוֹאָם וַיִּשְׁתַּחֲווּ לִפְנֵי הַהֵיכָל וַיָּקוּמוּ וַיֵּצְאוּ מִן־הָעִיר וְלֹא שָׁבוּ
1. In the morning, the men came to the temple in the city. And when they came, they prostrated themselves in front of the temple. Then they got up, went out from the city, and did not return.	2.	וַיֵּרְדוּ הַגִּבּוֹרִים אֶל־הַיָּם לְהִלָּחֵם עַל־אֹיְבֵיהֶם וְהֵם הֵמִיתוּ אוֹתָם וַיִּתְהַלְלוּ לֵאמֹר גְּדוֹלִים אֲנַחְנוּ מִכָּל־אֹיְבֵינוּ כִּי לֹא הֵמִיתוּ אוֹתָנוּ בִּידֵיהֶם

2. The warriors went down to the sea to fight against their enemies. They themselves killed them, then praised themselves by saying, "We are greater than all our enemies, for they did not kill us with their own hands."	3. וְהָיָה בַּיּוֹם הַהוּא וְהִתְפַּלֵּל וְהִתְנַבֵּא הַנָּבִיא הַקָּדוֹשׁ וְשָׁמְעוּ עַבְדֵי הַמֶּלֶךְ וְדָבְקוּ לַמִּצְוֹת וְלַחֻקִּים הַכְּתוּבִים בְּסֵפֶר־תּוֹרַת־אֱלֹהִים
3. In that day, the holy prophet will pray and prophesy, and the servants of the king will listen. Then they will cling to the commandments and statutes which are written in the book of the law of God.	

Reading Your Hebrew Bible

F. Translate the following from the Hebrew Bible.

1. הִשְׁתַּחֲווּ לְהַר קָדְשׁוֹ כִּי־קָדוֹשׁ יְהוָה אֱלֹהֵינוּ׃   Psalm 99:9

2. כִּי־אַתָּה יְהוָה צְבָאוֹת אֱלֹהֵי יִשְׂרָאֵל גָּלִיתָה[a] אֶת־אֹזֶן   2 Samuel 7:27
עַבְדְּךָ לֵאמֹר בַּיִת אֶבְנֶה־לָךְ[b] עַל־כֵּן מָצָא עַבְדְּךָ
אֶת־לִבּוֹ לְהִתְפַּלֵּל אֵלֶיךָ

3. וַיַּאַסְפוּ אֶת־אֲחֵיהֶם וַיִּתְקַדְּשׁוּ וַיָּבֹאוּ כְמִצְוַת־הַמֶּלֶךְ   2 Chronicles 29:15

[a] Sometimes a word usually spelled with a final *qamets* (ָ) is spelled with a final *qamets-hey* (הָ).

[b] An alternate spelling of לְךָ.

40

THE VERB: GEMINATE ROOTS

Characteristics of Geminate Verbs

➤ The second and third root letters occur in three ways.

❍ Normal: within a word and marked by strong *dagesh*, e.g., סַבּוֹתָ.

❍ Reduced: at the end of a word and only one letter showing, e.g., יָסֹב.

❍ Dissociated: both letters written with a vowel in between, e.g., סָבַב.

Qal

Imperative	Imperfect	Perfect	
	יָסֹב	סָבַב	*3ms*
	תָּסֹב	סָבְבָה	*3fs*
סֹב	תָּסֹב	סַבּוֹתָ	*2ms*
סֹבִּי	תָּסֹבִּי	סַבּוֹת	*2fs*
	אָסֹב	סַבּוֹתִי	*1cs*

Imperative	Imperfect	Perfect	
	יָסֹבּוּ	סָבְבוּ	*3cp/mp*
	תְּסֻבֶּינָה		*3fp*
סֹבּוּ	תָּסֹבּוּ	סַבּוֹתֶם	*2mp*
סֻבֶּינָה	תְּסֻבֶּינָה	סַבּוֹתֶן	*2fp*
	נָסֹב	סַבּוֹנוּ	*1cp*

Inf. abs.	Inf. const.	Participle	
סָבוֹב	סֹב/סְבֹב	סֹבֵב	*ms*
		סֹבְבָה	*fs*
		סֹבְבִים	*mp*
		סֹבְבוֹת	*fp*

> *With stative verbs the 3ms and 3fs of the perfect are usually not dissociated, e.g., תַּם "he is perfect," and תַּמָּה "she is perfect." The imperfect has the stative theme vowel and tsere under the prefix, e.g., יֵתַם "he will be perfect," and תֵּתַם "she will be perfect."*

Hiphil

Imperative	Imperfect	Perfect	
	יָסֵב	הֵסֵב	*3ms*
	תָּסֵב	הֵסֵבָּה	*3fs*
הָסֵב	תָּסֵב	הֲסִבּוֹתָ	*2ms*
הָסֵבִּי	תָּסֵבִּי	הֲסִבּוֹת	*2fs*
	אָסֵב	הֲסִבּוֹתִי	*1cs*

	יָסֵבּוּ	הֵסֵבּוּ	*3cp/mp*
	תְּסִבֶּינָה		*3fp*
הָסֵבּוּ	תָּסֵבּוּ	הֲסִבּוֹתֶם	*2mp*
הֲסִבֶּינָה	תְּסִבֶּינָה	הֲסִבּוֹתֶן	*2fp*
	נָסֵב	הֲסִבּוֹנוּ	*1cp*

Inf. abs.	Inf. const.	Participle	
הָסֵב	הָסֵב	מֵסֵב	*ms*
		מְסִבִּים	*mp*

Niphal

Imperative	Imperfect	Perfect	
	יִסַּב	נָסַב	*3ms*
	תִּסַּב	נָסַבָּה	*3fs*
הִסַּב	תִּסַּב	נְסַבּוֹתָ	*2ms*
הִסַּבִּי	תִּסַּבִּי	נְסַבּוֹת	*2fs*
	אֶסַּב	נְסַבּוֹתִי	*1cs*

	יִסַּבּוּ	נָסַבּוּ	*3cp/mp*
	תִּסַּבֶּינָה		*3fp*
הִסַּבּוּ	תִּסַּבּוּ	נְסַבּוֹתֶם	*2mp*
הִסַּבֶּינָה	תִּסַּבֶּינָה	נְסַבּוֹתֶן	*2fp*
	נִסַּב	נְסַבּוֹנוּ	*1cp*

Inf. abs.	Inf. const.	Participle	
הִסּוֹב	הִסַּב	נָסָב	*ms*

Vocabulary

evil, trouble, *f*	רָעָה	204	man	גֶּבֶר (גֶּבֶר)	597
Qal: seize	אָחַז	125	resident alien	גֵּר	602
Qal: be unclean	טָמֵא	81	male	זָכָר	609
Qal: destroy	שָׁחַת	117	foreigner	זָר	610
Qal: be complete	שָׁלֵם	121	evil, bad	רַע	204
Piel: repay	שִׁלֵּם				

Practice

Focusing on New Material

A. Focus on the form of verbs from geminate roots. Parse the following.

	Verb	Pattern	Conj.	Person	Gender	Number	Root
1.	אָסֹב						
2.	סַבּוֹנוּ						
3.	סֹבּוּ						
4.	יִמַּדּוּ						
5.	אָרוֹר						
6.	יָחֹן						
7.	אֲרוֹתִי						
8.	מַדּוֹתֶם						
9.	יִתְחַנֵּן						
10.	תָּמֹד						

Reading Your Hebrew Bible

B. Translate the following from Deuteronomy 6:4–9.

(4) שְׁמַע יִשְׂרָאֵל יְהוָה אֱלֹהֵינוּ יְהוָה אֶחָד: (5) וְאָהַבְתָּ[a] אֵת יְהוָה אֱלֹהֶיךָ
בְּכָל־לְבָבְךָ וּבְכָל־נַפְשְׁךָ וּבְכָל־מְאֹדֶךָ: (6) וְהָיוּ הַדְּבָרִים הָאֵלֶּה אֲשֶׁר
אָנֹכִי מְצַוְּךָ הַיּוֹם עַל־לְבָבֶךָ: (7) וְשִׁנַּנְתָּם[b] לְבָנֶיךָ וְדִבַּרְתָּ בָּם בְּשִׁבְתְּךָ
בְּבֵיתֶךָ וּבְלֶכְתְּךָ בַדֶּרֶךְ וּבְשָׁכְבְּךָ וּבְקוּמֶךָ: (8) וּקְשַׁרְתָּם[c] לְאוֹת[d] עַל־יָדֶךָ
וְהָיוּ לְטֹטָפֹת[e] בֵּין עֵינֶיךָ: (9) וּכְתַבְתָּם עַל־מְזוּזֹת[f] בֵּיתֶךָ וּבִשְׁעָרֶיךָ:

[a]When a *wcp* is in sequence with an *impv*, here the *impv* שְׁמַע, the *wcp* has the force of an *impv*. The initial verbs in verses 6-9 are all in sequence and used in this same way.

[b]Piel *vav consecutive perfect 2ms* + *3mp* suffix form שָׁנַן, meaning "repeat"; related to שְׁנַיִם "two"

[c]Qal *wcp 2ms* + *3mp* suffix from קָשַׁר, meaning "tie"

[d]"As a sign"

[e]"Phylacteries"

[f]"Doorposts of"

PARADIGMS

Purpose of Paradigm Charts

These paradigms are designed to aid the student in the initial memorization of the Hebrew verbal paradigms and to provide a convenient means for the continual review of the verb forms until mastery is attained.

Each page contains a full paradigm. The left-hand columns list the perfect and imperfect in parallel, followed by the jussive and cohortative. The right-hand column completes the volitive forms with the imperative, followed by the participle. The vav-relative imperfect form is placed to the immediate right of the jussive, because these forms are morphologically related. The infinitives conclude the paradigm.

Scope of the Paradigms

These paradigms include all of the paradigms a student would do well to commit to memory by the end of first-year Hebrew. These paradigms are identical to the paradigms found in the text of the grammar.

The paradigms for all seven major patterns/stems of the regular verb are provided. Two criteria determined the paradigms included for the irregular verbs: (1) only the paradigms of the affected conjugations and (2) only those of relatively high frequency have been included. Not all of the included forms occur in the root that has been employed. Forms that do not occur in any root in a given pattern/stem have not been created; XXXs are used in such slots.

Mastery of these paradigms will enable the student to recognize the majority of verbal forms encountered in the Hebrew Bible.

QAL   REGULAR

Perfect		Imperfect
קָטַל	3ms	יִקְטֹל
קָטְלָה	3fs	תִּקְטֹל
קָטַלְתָּ	2ms	תִּקְטֹל
קָטַלְתְּ	2fs	תִּקְטְלִי
קָטַלְתִּי	1cs	אֶקְטֹל
קָטְלוּ	3mp	יִקְטְלוּ
קָטְלוּ	3fp	תִּקְטֹלְנָה
קְטַלְתֶּם	2mp	תִּקְטְלוּ
קְטַלְתֶּן	2fp	תִּקְטֹלְנָה
קָטַלְנוּ	1cp	נִקְטֹל

Imperative	
ms	קְטֹל
fs	קִטְלִי
mp	קִטְלוּ
fp	קְטֹלְנָה

Participle	
ms	קֹטֵל
fs	קֹטֶלֶת / קֹטְלָה
mp	קֹטְלִים
fp	קֹטְלוֹת

Jussive	
3ms	יִקְטֹל

Vav-relative	
3ms	וַיִּקְטֹל

Cohortative	
1cs	אֶקְטְלָה
1cp	נִקְטְלָה

Infinitives	
Inf const	קְטֹל
Inf abs	קָטוֹל

NIPHAL

REGULAR

Perfect		Imperfect
נִקְטַל	3ms	יִקָּטֵל
נִקְטְלָה	3fs	תִּקָּטֵל
נִקְטַלְתָּ	2ms	תִּקָּטֵל
נִקְטַלְתְּ	2fs	תִּקָּטְלִי
נִקְטַלְתִּי	1cs	אֶקָּטֵל
נִקְטְלוּ	3mp	יִקָּטְלוּ
נִקְטְלוּ	3fp	תִּקָּטַלְנָה
נִקְטַלְתֶּם	2mp	תִּקָּטְלוּ
נִקְטַלְתֶּן	2fp	תִּקָּטַלְנָה
נִקְטַלְנוּ	1cp	נִקָּטֵל

Imperative	
ms	הִקָּטֵל
fs	הִקָּטְלִי
mp	הִקָּטְלוּ
fp	הִקָּטַלְנָה

Participle	
ms	נִקְטָל
fs	נִקְטֶלֶת / נִקְטָלָה
mp	נִקְטָלִים
fp	נִקְטָלוֹת

Jussive	
3ms	יִקָּטֵל

Vav-relative	
3ms	וַיִּקָּטֵל

Cohortative	
1cs	אֶקָּטְלָה
1cp	נִקָּטְלָה

Infinitives	
Inf const	הִקָּטֵל
Inf abs	הִקָּטֹל / נִקְטֹל

PIEL   REGULAR

Perfect		Imperfect		Imperative	
קִטֵּל	3ms	יְקַטֵּל	ms	קַטֵּל	
קִטְּלָה	3fs	תְּקַטֵּל	fs	קַטְּלִי	
קִטַּלְתָּ	2ms	תְּקַטֵּל	mp	קַטְּלוּ	
קִטַּלְתְּ	2fs	תְּקַטְּלִי	fp	קַטֵּלְנָה	
קִטַּלְתִּי	1cs	אֲקַטֵּל			

				Participle	
קִטְּלוּ	3mp	יְקַטְּלוּ	ms	מְקַטֵּל	
קִטְּלוּ	3fp	תְּקַטֵּלְנָה	fs	מְקַטֶּלֶת / מְקַטְּלָה	
קִטַּלְתֶּם	2mp	תְּקַטְּלוּ	mp	מְקַטְּלִים	
קִטַּלְתֶּן	2fp	תְּקַטֵּלְנָה	fp	מְקַטְּלוֹת	
קִטַּלְנוּ	1cp	נְקַטֵּל			

Jussive			Vav-Relative		
3ms		יְקַטֵּל	3ms	וַיְקַטֵּל	

Cohortative			Infinitives		
1cs		אֲקַטְּלָה	Inf const	קַטֵּל	
1cp		נְקַטְּלָה	Inf abs	קַטֵּל / קַטֹּל	

PUAL　　　　　　　　　　　　　　　　　　　　　　　　　　REGULAR

Perfect		Imperfect			Imperative	
קֻטַּל	3ms	יְקֻטַּל		ms		XXX
קֻטְּלָה	3fs	תְּקֻטַּל		fs		XXX
קֻטַּלְתָּ	2ms	תְּקֻטַּל		mp		XXX
קֻטַּלְתְּ	2fs	תְּקֻטְּלִי		fp		XXX
קֻטַּלְתִּי	1cs	אֲקֻטַּל				

Perfect		Imperfect			Participle	
קֻטְּלוּ	3mp	יְקֻטְּלוּ		ms		מְקֻטָּל
קֻטְּלוּ	3fp	תְּקֻטַּלְנָה		fs		מְקֻטֶּלֶת / מְקֻטָּלָה
קֻטַּלְתֶּם	2mp	תְּקֻטְּלוּ		mp		מְקֻטָּלִים
קֻטַּלְתֶּן	2fp	תְּקֻטַּלְנָה		fp		מְקֻטָּלוֹת
קֻטַּלְנוּ	1cp	נְקֻטַּל				

Jussive			Vav-Relative	
3ms	יְקֻטַּל		3ms	וַיְקֻטַּל

Cohortative			Infinitives	
1cs	אֲקֻטְּלָה		Inf const	XXX
1cp	נְקֻטְּלָה		Inf abs	קֻטֹּל

HIPHIL

REGULAR

Perfect		Imperfect
הִקְטִיל	3ms	יַקְטִיל
הִקְטִילָה	3fs	תַּקְטִיל
הִקְטַלְתָּ	2ms	תַּקְטִיל
הִקְטַלְתְּ	2fs	תַּקְטִילִי
הִקְטַלְתִּי	1cs	אַקְטִיל
הִקְטִילוּ	3mp	יַקְטִילוּ
הִקְטִילוּ	3fp	תַּקְטֵלְנָה
הִקְטַלְתֶּם	2mp	תַּקְטִילוּ
הִקְטַלְתֶּן	2fp	תַּקְטֵלְנָה
הִקְטַלְנוּ	1cp	נַקְטִיל

Imperative	
ms	הַקְטֵל
fs	הַקְטִילִי
mp	הַקְטִילוּ
fp	הַקְטֵלְנָה

Participle	
ms	מַקְטִיל
fs	מַקְטֶלֶת / מַקְטִילָה
mp	מַקְטִילִים
fp	מַקְטִילוֹת

Jussive	
3ms	יַקְטֵל

Vav-Relative	
3ms	וַיַּקְטֵל

Cohortative	
1cs	אַקְטִילָה
1cp	נַקְטִילָה

Infinitives	
Inf const	הַקְטִיל
Inf abs	הַקְטֵל

HOPHAL   REGULAR

Perfect		Imperfect		Imperative	
הָקְטַל	3ms	יָקְטַל	ms	XXX
הָקְטְלָה	3fs	תָּקְטַל	fs	XXX
הָקְטַלְתָּ	2ms	תָּקְטַל	mp	XXX
הָקְטַלְתְּ	2fs	תָּקְטְלִי	fp	XXX
הָקְטַלְתִּי	1cs	אָקְטַל		

Perfect		Imperfect		Participle	
הָקְטְלוּ	3mp	יָקְטְלוּ	ms	מָקְטָל (מֻקְטָל)
חָקְטְלוּ	3fp	תָּקְטַלְנָה	fs	מָקְטֶלֶת / מָקְטָלָה
הָקְטַלְתֶּם	2mp	תָּקְטְלוּ	mp	מָקְטָלִים
הָקְטַלְתֶּן	2fp	תָּקְטַלְנָה	fp	מָקְטָלוֹת
הָקְטַלְנוּ	1cp	נָקְטַל		

Jussive			Vav-Relative	
3ms	יָקְטַל	3ms	וַיָּקְטַל

Cohortative			Infinitives	
1cs	אָקְטְלָה	Inf const	XXX
1cp	נָקְטְלָה	Inf abs	הָקְטֵל

HITHPAEL

REGULAR

Perfect		Imperfect
הִתְקַטֵּל	3ms	יִתְקַטֵּל
הִתְקַטְּלָה	3fs	תִּתְקַטֵּל
הִתְקַטַּלְתָּ	2ms	תִּתְקַטֵּל
הִתְקַטַּלְתְּ	2fs	תִּתְקַטְּלִי
הִתְקַטַּלְתִּי	1cs	אֶתְקַטֵּל
הִתְקַטְּלוּ	3mp	יִתְקַטְּלוּ
הִתְקַטְּלוּ	3fp	תִּתְקַטֵּלְנָה
הִתְקַטַּלְתֶּם	2mp	תִּתְקַטְּלוּ
הִתְקַטַּלְתֶּן	2fp	תִּתְקַטֵּלְנָה
הִתְקַטַּלְנוּ	1cp	נִתְקַטֵּל

Imperative	
ms	הִתְקַטֵּל
fs	הִתְקַטְּלִי
mp	הִתְקַטְּלוּ
fp	הִתְקַטֵּלְנָה

Participle	
ms	מִתְקַטֵּל
fs	מִתְקַטֶּלֶת / מִתְקַטְּלָה
mp	מִתְקַטְּלִים
fp	מִתְקַטְּלוֹת

Jussive	
3ms	יִתְקַטֵּל

Vav-Relative	
3ms	וַיִּתְקַטֵּל

Cohortative	
1cs	אֶתְקַטְּלָה
1cp	נִתְקַטְּלָה

Infinitives	
Inf const	הִתְקַטֵּל
Inf abs	הִתְקַטֵּל

QAL

I GUTTURAL

Perfect		Imperfect
עָמַד	3ms	יַעֲמֹד
עָמְדָה	3fs	תַּעֲמֹד
עָמַדְתָּ	2ms	תַּעֲמֹד
עָמַדְתְּ	2fs	תַּעַמְדִי
עָמַדְתִּי	1cs	אֶעֱמֹד
עָמְדוּ	3mp	יַעַמְדוּ
עָמְדוּ	3fp	תַּעֲמֹדְנָה
עֲמַדְתֶּם	2mp	תַּעַמְדוּ
עֲמַדְתֶּן	2fp	תַּעֲמֹדְנָה
עָמַדְנוּ	1cp	נַעֲמֹד

Imperative	
ms	עֲמֹד
fs	עִמְדִי
mp	עִמְדוּ
fp	עֲמֹדְנָה

Participle	
ms	עֹמֵד
fs	עֹמֶדֶת / עֹמְדָה
mp	עֹמְדִים
fp	עֹמְדוֹת

Jussive	
3ms	יַעֲמֹד

Vav-Relative	
3ms	וַיַּעֲמֹד

Cohortative	
1cs	אֶעֱמְדָה
1cp	נַעַמְדָה

Infinitives	
Inf const	עֲמֹד
Inf abs	עָמוֹד

NIPHAL

I GUTTURAL

Perfect		Imperfect
נֶעֱמַד	3ms	יֵעָמֵד
נֶעֶמְדָה	3fs	תֵּעָמֵד
נֶעֱמַדְתָּ	2ms	תֵּעָמֵד
נֶעֱמַדְתְּ	2fs	תֵּעָמְדִי
נֶעֱמַדְתִּי	1cs	אֵעָמֵד
נֶעֶמְדוּ	3mp	יֵעָמְדוּ
נֶעֶמְדוּ	3fp	תֵּעָמַדְנָה
נֶעֱמַדְתֶּם	2mp	תֵּעָמְדוּ
נֶעֱמַדְתֶּן	2fp	תֵּעָמַדְנָה
נֶעֱמַדְנוּ	1cp	נֵעָמֵד

Imperative	
ms	הֵעָמֵד
fs	הֵעָמְדִי
mp	הֵעָמְדוּ
fp	הֵעָמַדְנָה

Participle	
ms	נֶעֱמָד
fs	נֶעֱמֶדֶת / נֶעֱמָדָה
mp	נֶעֱמָדִים
fp	נֶעֱמָדוֹת

Jussive	
3ms	יֵעָמֵד

Vav-Relative	
3ms	וַיֵּעָמֵד

Cohortative	
1cs	אֵעָמְדָה
1cp	נֵעָמְדָה

Infinitives	
Inf const	הֵעָמֵד
Inf abs	הֵעָמוֹד / נַעֲמוֹד

HIPHIL   I GUTTURAL

Perfect		Imperfect
הֶעֱמִיד	3ms	יַעֲמִיד
הֶעֱמִידָה	3fs	תַּעֲמִיד
הֶעֱמַדְתָּ	2ms	תַּעֲמִיד
הֶעֱמַדְתְּ	2fs	תַּעֲמִידִי
הֶעֱמַדְתִּי	1cs	אַעֲמִיד
הֶעֱמִידוּ	3mp	יַעֲמִידוּ
הֶעֱמִידוּ	3fp	תַּעֲמֵדְנָה
הֶעֱמַדְתֶּם	2mp	תַּעֲמִידוּ
הֶעֱמַדְתֶּן	2fp	תַּעֲמֵדְנָה
הֶעֱמַדְנוּ	1cp	נַעֲמִיד

Imperative	
ms	הַעֲמֵד
fs	הַעֲמִידִי
mp	הַעֲמִידוּ
fp	הַעֲמֵדְנָה

Participle	
ms	מַעֲמִיד
fs	מַעֲמֶדֶת / מַעֲמִידָה
mp	מַעֲמִידִים
fp	מַעֲמִידוֹת

Jussive	
3ms	יַעֲמֵד

Vav-Relative	
3ms	וַיַּעֲמֵד

Cohortative	
1cs	אַעֲמִידָה
1cp	נַעֲמִידָה

Infinitives	
Inf const	הַעֲמִיד
Inf abs	הַעֲמֵד

QAL   II GUTTURAL

Perfect		Imperfect
רָחַץ	3ms	יִרְחַץ
רָחֲצָה	3fs	תִּרְחַץ
רָחַצְתָּ	2ms	תִּרְחַץ
רָחַצְתְּ	2fs	תִּרְחֲצִי
רָחַצְתִּי	1cs	אֶרְחַץ
רָחֲצוּ	3mp	יִרְחֲצוּ
רָחֲצוּ	3fp	תִּרְחַצְנָה
רְחַצְתֶּם	2mp	תִּרְחֲצוּ
רְחַצְתֶּן	2fp	תִּרְחַצְנָה
רָחַצְנוּ	1cp	נִרְחַץ

Imperative	
ms	רְחַץ
fs	רַחֲצִי
mp	רַחֲצוּ
fp	רְחַצְנָה

Participle	
ms	רֹחֵץ
fs	רֹחֶצֶת / רֹחֲצָה
mp	רֹחֲצִים
fp	רֹחֲצוֹת

Jussive	
3ms	יִרְחַץ

Vav-Relative	
3ms	וַיִּרְחַץ

Cohortative	
1cs	אֶרְחֲצָה
1cp	נִרְחֲצָה

Infinitives	
Inf const	רְחֹץ
Inf abs	רָחוֹץ

PIEL   II GUTTURAL

Perfect		Imperfect
בֵּרֵךְ	3ms	יְבָרֵךְ
בֵּרְכָה	3fs	תְּבָרֵךְ
בֵּרַכְתָּ	2ms	תְּבָרֵךְ
בֵּרַכְתְּ	2fs	תְּבָרְכִי
בֵּרַכְתִּי	1cs	אֲבָרֵךְ
בֵּרְכוּ	3mp	יְבָרְכוּ
בֵּרְכוּ	3fp	תְּבָרֵכְנָה
בֵּרַכְתֶּם	2mp	תְּבָרְכוּ
בֵּרַכְתֶּן	2fp	תְּבָרֵכְנָה
בֵּרַכְנוּ	1cp	נְבָרֵךְ

Imperative	
ms	בָּרֵךְ
fs	בָּרְכִי
mp	בָּרֲכוּ
fp	בָּרֵכְנָה

Participle	
ms	מְבָרֵךְ
fs	מְבָרֶכֶת / מְבָרֵכָה
mp	מְבָרְכִים
fp	מְבָרְכוֹת

Jussive	
3ms	יְבָרֵךְ

Vav-Relative	
3ms	וַיְבָרֶךְ

Cohortative	
1cs	אֲבָרֲכָה
1cp	נְבָרֲכָה

Infinitives	
Inf const	בָּרֵךְ
Inf abs	בָּרֵךְ / בָּרוֹךְ

QAL   I NUN

Perfect		Imperfect		Imperative	
נָפַל	3ms	יִפֹּל	ms	נְפֹל	
נָפְלָה	3fs	תִּפֹּל	fs	נִפְלִי	
נָפַלְתָּ	2ms	תִּפֹּל	mp	נִפְלוּ	
נָפַלְתְּ	2fs	תִּפְּלִי	fp	נְפֹלְנָה	
נָפַלְתִּי	1cs	אֶפֹּל			
נָפְלוּ	3mp	יִפְּלוּ		Participle	
נָפְלוּ	3fp	תִּפֹּלְנָה	ms	נֹפֵל	
נְפַלְתֶּם	2mp	תִּפְּלוּ	fs	נֹפֶלֶת / נֹפְלָה	
נְפַלְתֶּן	2fp	תִּפֹּלְנָה	mp	נֹפְלִים	
נָפַלְנוּ	1cp	נִפֹּל	fp	נֹפְלוֹת	

Jussive			Vav-Relative	
3ms	יִפֹּל		3ms	וַיִּפֹּל

Cohortative			Infinitives	
1cs	אֶפְּלָה		Inf const	נְפֹל
1cp	נִפְּלָה		Inf abs	נָפוֹל

NIPHAL I NUN

Perfect		Imperfect
נִצַּל	3ms	יִנָּצֵל
נִצְּלָה	3fs	תִּנָּצֵל
נִצַּלְתָּ	2ms	תִּנָּצֵל
נִצַּלְתְּ	2fs	תִּנָּצְלִי
נִצַּלְתִּי	1cs	אֶנָּצֵל
נִצְּלוּ	3mp	יִנָּצְלוּ
נִצְּלוּ	3fp	תִּנָּצַלְנָה
נִצַּלְתֶּם	2mp	תִּנָּצְלוּ
נִצַּלְתֶּן	2fp	תִּנָּצַלְנָה
נִצַּלְנוּ	1cp	נִנָּצֵל

Imperative	
ms	הִנָּצֵל
fs	הִנָּצְלִי
mp	הִנָּצְלוּ
fp	הִנָּצַלְנָה

Participle	
ms	נִצָּל
fs	נִצֶּלֶת / נִצָּלָה
mp	נִצָּלִים
fp	נִצָּלוֹת

Jussive	
3ms	יִנָּצֵל

Vav-Relative	
3ms	וַיִּנָּצֵל

Cohortative	
1cs	אֶנָּצְלָה
1cp	נִנָּצְלָה

Infinitives	
Inf const	הִנָּצֵל
Inf abs	הִנָּצֵל / הִנָּצֹל / נִצֹּל

HIPHIL I NUN

Perfect		Imperfect
הִצִּיל	3ms	יַצִּיל
הִצִּילָה	3fs	תַּצִּיל
הִצַּלְתָּ	2ms	תַּצִּיל
הִצַּלְתְּ	2fs	תַּצִּילִי
הִצַּלְתִּי	1cs	אַצִּיל
הִצִּילוּ	3mp	יַצִּילוּ
הִצִּילוּ	3fp	תַּצֵּלְנָה
הִצַּלְתֶּם	2mp	תַּצִּילוּ
הִצַּלְתֶּן	2fp	תַּצֵּלְנָה
הִצַּלְנוּ	1cp	נַצִּיל

Imperative	
ms	הַצֵּל
fs	הַצִּילִי
mp	הַצִּילוּ
fp	הַצֵּלְנָה

Participle	
ms	מַצִּיל
fs	מַצֶּלֶת / מַצִּילָה
mp	מַצִּילִים
fp	מַצִּילוֹת

Jussive	
3ms	יַצֵּל

Vav-Relative	
3ms	וַיַּצֵּל

Cohortative	
1cs	אַצִּילָה
1cp	נַצִּילָה

Infinitives	
Inf const	הַצִּיל
Inf abs	הַצֵּל

QAL

I YOD (YOD)

Perfect		Imperfect
יָטֵב	3ms	יִיטַב
יָטְבָה	3fs	תִּיטַב
יָטַבְתָּ	2ms	תִּיטַב
יָטַבְתְּ	2fs	תִּיטְבִי
יָטַבְתִּי	1cs	אִיטַב
יָטְבוּ	3mp	יִיטְבוּ
יָטְבוּ	3fp	תִּיטַבְנָה
יְטַבְתֶּם	2mp	תִּיטְבוּ
יְטַבְתֶּן	2fp	תִּיטַבְנָה
יָטַבְנוּ	1cp	נִיטַב

Imperative	
ms	XXX
fs	XXX
mp	XXX
fp	XXX

Participle	
ms	XXX
fs	XXX
mp	XXX
fp	XXX

Jussive	
3ms	יִיטַב

Vav-Relative	
3ms	וַיִּיטַב

Cohortative	
1cs	אִיטְבָה
1cp	נִיטְבָה

Infinitives	
Inf const	XXX
Inf abs	XXX

HIPHIL   I YOD (YOD)

Perfect		Imperfect
הֵיטִיב	3ms	יֵיטִיב
הֵיטִיבָה	3fs	תֵּיטִיב
הֵיטַבְתָּ	2ms	תֵּיטִיב
הֵיטַבְתְּ	2fs	תֵּיטִיבִי
הֵיטַבְתִּי	1cs	אֵיטִיב
הֵיטִיבוּ	3mp	יֵיטִיבוּ
הֵיטִיבוּ	3fp	תֵּיטֵבְנָה
הֵיטַבְתֶּם	2mp	תֵּיטִיבוּ
הֵיטַבְתֶּן	2fp	תֵּיטֵבְנָה
הֵיטַבְנוּ	1cp	נֵיטִיב

Imperative	
ms	הֵיטֵב
fs	הֵיטִיבִי
mp	הֵיטִיבוּ
fp	הֵיטֵבְנָה

Participle	
ms	מֵיטִיב
fs	מֵיטֶבֶת / מֵיטִיבָה
mp	מֵיטִיבִים
fp	מֵיטִיבוֹת

Jussive	
3ms	יֵיטֵב

Vav-Relative	
3ms	וַיֵּיטֶב

Cohortative	
1cs	אֵיטִיבָה
1cp	נֵיטִיבָה

Infinitives	
Inf const	הֵיטִיב
Inf abs	הֵיטֵב

QAL

I YOD (VAV)

Perfect		Imperfect
יָשַׁב	3ms	יֵשֵׁב
יָשְׁבָה	3fs	תֵּשֵׁב
יָשַׁבְתָּ	2ms	תֵּשֵׁב
יָשַׁבְתְּ	2fs	תֵּשְׁבִי
יָשַׁבְתִּי	1cs	אֵשֵׁב
יָשְׁבוּ	3mp	יֵשְׁבוּ
יָשְׁבוּ	3fp	תֵּשַׁבְנָה
יְשַׁבְתֶּם	2mp	תֵּשְׁבוּ
יְשַׁבְתֶּן	2fp	תֵּשַׁבְנָה
יָשַׁבְנוּ	1cp	נֵשֵׁב

Imperative	
ms	שֵׁב
fs	שְׁבִי
mp	שְׁבוּ
fp	שֵׁבְנָה

Participle	
ms	יֹשֵׁב
fs	יֹשֶׁבֶת / יֹשְׁבָה
mp	יֹשְׁבִים
fp	יֹשְׁבוֹת

Jussive	
3ms	יֵשֵׁב

Vav-Relative	
3ms	וַיֵּשֶׁב

Cohortative	
1cs	אֵשְׁבָה
1cp	נֵשְׁבָה

Infinitives	
Inf const	שֶׁבֶת
Inf abs	יָשׁוֹב

HIPHIL   I YOD (VAV)

Perfect		Imperfect
הוֹשִׁיב	3ms	יוֹשִׁיב
הוֹשִׁיבָה	3fs	תּוֹשִׁיב
הוֹשַׁבְתָּ	2ms	תּוֹשִׁיב
הוֹשַׁבְתְּ	2fs	תּוֹשִׁיבִי
הוֹשַׁבְתִּי	1cs	אוֹשִׁיב
הוֹשִׁיבוּ	3mp	יוֹשִׁיבוּ
הוֹשִׁיבוּ	3fp	תּוֹשַׁבְנָה
הוֹשַׁבְתֶּם	2mp	תּוֹשִׁיבוּ
הוֹשַׁבְתֶּן	2fp	תּוֹשַׁבְנָה
הוֹשַׁבְנוּ	1cp	נוֹשִׁיב

Imperative	
ms	הוֹשֵׁב
fs	הוֹשִׁיבִי
mp	הוֹשִׁיבוּ
fp	הוֹשֵׁבְנָה

Participle	
ms	מוֹשִׁיב
fs	מוֹשֶׁבֶת / מוֹשִׁיבָה
mp	מוֹשִׁיבִים
fp	מוֹשִׁיבוֹת

Jussive	
3ms	יוֹשֵׁב

Vav-Relative	
3ms	וַיּוֹשֶׁב

Cohortative	
1cs	אוֹשִׁיבָה
1cp	נוֹשִׁיבָה

Infinitives	
Inf const	הוֹשִׁיב
Inf abs	הוֹשֵׁב

NIPHAL

I YOD (VAV)

Perfect		Imperfect
נוֹשַׁב	3ms	יִוָּשֵׁב
נוֹשְׁבָה	3fs	תִּוָּשֵׁב
נוֹשַׁבְתָּ	2ms	תִּוָּשֵׁב
נוֹשַׁבְתְּ	2fs	תִּוָּשְׁבִי
נוֹשַׁבְתִּי	1cs	אִוָּשֵׁב
נוֹשְׁבוּ	3mp	יִוָּשְׁבוּ
נוֹשְׁבוּ	3fp	תִּוָּשַׁבְנָה
נוֹשַׁבְתֶּם	2mp	תִּוָּשְׁבוּ
נוֹשַׁבְתֶּן	2fp	תִּוָּשַׁבְנָה
נוֹשַׁבְנוּ	1cp	נִוָּשֵׁב

Imperative	
ms	הִוָּשֵׁב
fs	הִוָּשְׁבִי
mp	הִוָּשְׁבוּ
fp	הִוָּשַׁבְנָה

Participle	
ms	נוֹשָׁב
fs	נוֹשֶׁבֶת / נוֹשָׁבָה
mp	נוֹשָׁבִים
fp	נוֹשָׁבוֹת

Jussive	
3ms	יִוָּשֵׁב

Vav-Relative	
3ms	וַיִּוָּשֵׁב

Cohortative	
1cs	אִוָּשְׁבָה
1cp	נִוָּשְׁבָה

Infinitives	
Inf const	הִוָּשֵׁב
Inf abs	הִוָּשֵׁב

QAL   III HEY

Perfect		Imperfect
גָּלָה	3ms	יִגְלֶה
גָּלְתָה	3fs	תִּגְלֶה
גָּלִיתָ	2ms	תִּגְלֶה
גָּלִית	2fs	תִּגְלִי
גָּלִיתִי	1cs	אֶגְלֶה
גָּלוּ	3mp	יִגְלוּ
גָּלוּ	3fp	תִּגְלֶינָה
גְּלִיתֶם	2mp	תִּגְלוּ
גְּלִיתֶן	2fp	תִּגְלֶינָה
גָּלִינוּ	1cp	נִגְלֶה

Imperative	
ms	גְּלֵה
fs	גְּלִי
mp	גְּלוּ
fp	גְּלֶינָה

Participle	
ms	גֹּלֶה
fs	גֹּלָה
mp	גֹּלִים
fp	גֹּלוֹת

Jussive	
3ms	יִגֶל

Vav-Relative	
3ms	וַיִּגֶל

Cohortative	
1cs	אֶגְלֶה
1cp	נִגְלֶה

Infinitives	
Inf const	גְּלוֹת
Inf abs	גָּלֹה

NIPHAL   III HEY

Perfect		Imperfect		Imperative	
נִגְלָה	3ms	יִגָּלֶה	ms	הִגָּלֵה	
נִגְלְתָה	3fs	תִּגָּלֶה	fs	הִגָּלִי	
נִגְלֵיתָ	2ms	תִּגָּלֶה	mp	הִגָּלוּ	
נִגְלֵית	2fs	תִּגָּלִי	fp	XXX	
נִגְלֵיתִי	1cs	אֶגָּלֶה			
נִגְלוּ	3mp	יִגָּלוּ		Participle	
נִגְלוּ	3fp	תִּגָּלֶינָה	ms	נִגְלֶה	
נִגְלֵיתֶם	2mp	תִּגָּלוּ	fs	נִגְלָה	
נִגְלֵיתֶן	2fp	תִּגָּלֶינָה	mp	נִגְלִים	
נִגְלֵינוּ	1cp	נִגָּלֶה	fp	נִגְלוֹת	

Jussive			Vav-Relative	
3ms	יִגָּל		3ms	וַיִּגָּל

Cohortative			Infinitives	
1cs	אֶגָּלֶה		Inf const	הִגָּלוֹת
1cp	נִגָּלֶה		Inf abs	הִגָּלֵה / נִגְלֹה

PIEL

III HEY

Perfect		Imperfect
גִּלָּה	3ms	יְגַלֶּה
גִּלְּתָה	3fs	תְּגַלֶּה
גִּלִּיתָ	2ms	תְּגַלֶּה
גִּלִּית	2fs	תְּגַלִּי
גִּלִּיתִי	1cs	אֲגַלֶּה
גִּלּוּ	3mp	יְגַלּוּ
גִּלּוּ	3fp	תְּגַלֶּינָה
גִּלִּיתֶם	2mp	תְּגַלּוּ
גִּלִּיתֶן	2fp	תְּגַלֶּינָה
גִּלִּינוּ	1cp	נְגַלֶּה

Imperative	
ms	גַּלֵּה
fs	גַּלִּי
mp	גַּלּוּ
fp	XXX

Participle	
ms	מְגַלֶּה
fs	מְגַלָּה
mp	מְגַלִּים
fp	מְגַלּוֹת

Jussive	
3ms	יְגַל

Vav-Relative	
3ms	וַיְגַל

Cohortative	
1cs	אֲגַלֶּה
1cp	נְגַלֶּה

Infinitives	
Inf const	גַּלּוֹת
Inf abs	גַּלֵּה / גַּלֹּה

QAL   III ALEPH

Perfect			Imperfect
מָצָא	3ms		יִמְצָא
מָצְאָה	3fs		תִּמְצָא
מָצָאתָ	2ms		תִּמְצָא
מָצָאת	2fs		תִּמְצְאִי
מָצָאתִי	1cs		אֶמְצָא
מָצְאוּ	3mp		יִמְצְאוּ
מָצְאוּ	3fp		תִּמְצֶאנָה
מְצָאתֶם	2mp		תִּמְצְאוּ
מְצָאתֶן	2fp		תִּמְצֶאנָה
מָצָאנוּ	1cp		נִמְצָא

Imperative	
ms	מְצָא
fs	מִצְאִי
mp	מִצְאוּ
fp	מְצֶאנָה

Participle	
ms	מֹצֵא
fs	מֹצֵאת
mp	מֹצְאִים
fp	מֹצְאוֹת

Jussive	
3ms	יִמְצָא

Vav-Relative	
3ms	וַיִּמְצָא

Cohortative	
1cs	אֶמְצְאָה
1cp	נִמְצְאָה

Infinitives	
Inf const	מְצֹא
Inf abs	מָצוֹא

QAL   HOLLOW

Perfect		Imperfect		Imperative	
קָם	3ms	יָקוּם	ms	קוּם
קָמָה	3fs	תָּקוּם	fs	קוּמִי
קַמְתָּ	2ms	תָּקוּם	mp	קוּמוּ
קַמְתְּ	2fs	תָּקוּמִי	fp	קֹמְנָה
קַמְתִּי	1cs	אָקוּם		

Perfect		Imperfect		Participle	
קָמוּ	3mp	יָקוּמוּ	ms	קָם
קָמוּ	3fp	תְּקוּמֶינָה	fs	קָמָה
קַמְתֶּם	2mp	תָּקוּמוּ	mp	קָמִים
קַמְתֶּן	2fp	תְּקוּמֶינָה	fp	קָמוֹת
קַמְנוּ	1cp	נָקוּם		

Jussive		Vav-Relative	
3ms	יָקֹם	3ms	וַיָּקָם

Cohortative		Infinitives	
1cs	אָקוּמָה	Inf const	קוּם
1cp	נָקוּמָה	Inf abs	קוֹם

HIPHIL   HOLLOW

Perfect		Imperfect
הֵקִים	3ms	יָקִים
הֵקִימָה	3fs	תָּקִים
הֲקִימֹ֫תָ	2ms	תָּקִים
הֲקִימֹות	2fs	תָּקִימִי
הֲקִימֹ֫תִי	1cs	אָקִים
הֵקִ֫ימוּ	3mp	יָקִ֫ימוּ
הֵקִ֫ימוּ	3fp	תְּקִימֶ֫ינָה
הֲקִימֹותֶם	2mp	תָּקִ֫ימוּ
הֲקִימֹותֶן	2fp	תְּקִימֶ֫ינָה
הֲקִימֹ֫ונוּ	1cp	נָקִים

Imperative	
ms	הָקֵם
fs	הָקִ֫ימִי
mp	הָקִ֫ימוּ
fp	הָקֵ֫מְנָה

Participle	
ms	מֵקִים
fs	מְקִימָה
mp	מְקִימִים
fp	מְקִימֹות

Jussive	
3ms	יָקֵם

Vav-Relative	
3ms	וַיָּ֫קֶם

Cohortative	
1cs	אָקִ֫ימָה
1cp	נָקִ֫ימָה

Infinitives	
Inf const	הָקִים
Inf abs	הָקֵם

QAL

GEMINATE

Perfect		Imperfect
סָבַב	3ms	יָסֹב
סָבְבָה	3fs	תָּסֹב
סַבּוֹתָ	2ms	תָּסֹב
סַבּוֹת	2fs	תָּסֹבִּי
סַבּוֹתִי	1cs	אָסֹב
סָבְבוּ	3mp	יָסֹבּוּ
סָבְבוּ	3fp	תְּסֻבֶּינָה
סַבּוֹתֶם	2mp	תָּסֹבּוּ
סַבּוֹתֶן	2fp	תְּסֻבֶּינָה
סַבּוֹנוּ	1cp	נָסֹב

Imperative	
ms	סֹב
fs	סֹבִּי
mp	סֹבּוּ
fp	סֻבֶּינָה

Participle	
ms	סֹבֵב
fs	סֹבְבָה
mp	סֹבְבִים
fp	סֹבְבוֹת

Jussive	
3ms	יָסֹב

Vav-Relative	
3ms	וַיָּסָב

Cohortative	
1cs	אָסֹבָּה
1cp	נָסֹבָּה

Infinitives	
Inf const	סֹב / סְבֹב
Inf abs	סָבוֹב

HIPHIL   GEMINATE

Perfect		Imperfect
הֵסֵב	3ms	יָסֵב
הֵסֵבָּה	3fs	תָּסֵב
הֲסִבּוֹתָ	2ms	תָּסֵב
הֲסִבּוֹת	2fs	תָּסֵבִּי
הֲסִבּוֹתִי	1cs	אָסֵב
הֵסֵבּוּ	3mp	יָסֵבּוּ
הֵסֵבּוּ	3fp	תְּסִבֶּינָה
הֲסִבּוֹתֶם	2mp	תָּסֵבּוּ
הֲסִבּוֹתֶן	2fp	תְּסִבֶּינָה
הֲסִבּוֹנוּ	1cp	נָסֵב

Imperative	
ms	הָסֵב
fs	הָסֵבִּי
mp	הָסֵבּוּ
fp	הֲסִבֶּינָה

Participle	
ms	מֵסֵב
fs	מְסִבָּה
mp	מְסִבִּים
fp	מְסִבּוֹת

Jussive	
3ms	יָסֵב

Vav-Relative	
3ms	וַיָּסֵב

Cohortative	
1cs	אָסֵבָּה
1cp	נָסֵבָּה

Infinitives	
Inf const	הָסֵב
Inf abs	הָסֵב

VOCABULARY

➤ Words are listed alphabetically.

➤ Verbs are listed in the form of the Qal perfect third person masculine singular, except in the case of verbs from hollow roots, which are listed according to the Qal infinitive construct.

➤ The number in parentheses refers to the lesson in which the vocabulary was first introduced.

א

אָב	father, ancestor (2)
אָבַד	Qal perish, be lost; Piel destroy (18)
אָבָה	Qal be willing, want (18)
אֶבֶן	stone *f* (25)
אָדוֹן	lord, master (12)
אָדָם	man, mankind, Adam (5)
אֲדָמָה	ground, land (20)
אָהַב	Qal love (20)
אֹהֶל	tent, dwelling (11)
אוֹצָר	treasure, treasury, store-house (38)
אוֹר	light *f* (20)
אָז	then (19)
אֹזֶן	ear *f* (15)
אָח	brother (2)
אֶחָד	one *m* (29)
אָחוֹת	sister (2)
אָחַז	Qal seize (40)

אַחֵר	other, another (10)
אַחַר	behind, after, west (16)
אַחֲרוֹן	behind, latter, west (37)
אַחֲרֵי	after, behind (26)
אַחֲרִית	end, outcome, latter part (34)
אַחֶרֶת	other, another *f* (10)
אַחַת	one *f* (29)
אַיִל	ram (39)
אֹיֵב	enemy (16)
אֵין	there is not (22)
אִישׁ	man, husband, each (5)
אָכַל	Qal eat; Hiph feed (2)
אֶל	toward, unto, to, for the sake of (8)
אֵל	God, god (3)
אֵלֶּה	these (16)
אֱלֹהִים	God, gods (3)
אֶלֶף	one thousand (29)
אֵם	mother *f* (2)

אִם	if (19)
אַמָּה	cubit (37)
אָמֵן	Niph be firm; Hiph believe, trust (31)
אָמַר	say (11)
אֱמֶת	faithfulness, truth (31)
אֱנוֹשׁ	man (16)
אֲנַחְנוּ	we (4)
אָנֹכִי	I (4)
אֲנִי	I (4)
אָסַף	Qal gather (25)
אָסַר	Qal imprison, bind (21)
אַף	nose, anger (15)
אַרְבַּע	four f (29)
אַרְבָּעָה	four m (29)
אָרוֹן	ark (27)
אֲרִי	lion (39)
אֹרֶךְ	length (34)
אֶרֶץ	land, earth f (3)
אָרַר	Qal curse (39)
אֵשׁ	fire f (32)
אִשֶּׁה	offering by fire (32)
אִשָּׁה	woman, wife (5)
אֲשֶׁר	who, whom, which, what, where, that, etc. (17)
אֵת	with (32)
אַתְּ	you fs (4)
אַתָּה	you ms (4)
אַתֶּם	you mp (4)
אַתֵּן	you fp (4)
אַתֵּנָה	you fp (4)

ב

בְּ	at, in, with, on, as (8)

בֶּגֶד	garment, clothing (6)
בְּהֵמָה	animal, beast, cattle (17)
בּוֹא	Qal go in, enter; Hiph bring in (24)
בּוֹשׁ	Qal be ashamed (24)
בָּחַר	Qal choose (23)
בָּטַח	Qal trust (6)
בֶּטֶן	belly, womb (33)
בִּין	Qal & Hiph understand (24)
בֵּין	between (20)
בַּיִת	house, household, temple (5)
בָּכָה	Qal cry, weep (14)
בִּלְתִּי	so that not (19)
בֵּן	son, descendant (2)
בָּנָה	Qal build, rebuild, fortify (14)
בֹּקֶר	morning (13)
בָּקָר	cattle, herd, ox (17)
בָּקַשׁ	Piel seek, inquire (27)
בָּרָא	Qal create (13)
בַּרְזֶל	iron (36)
בָּרַח	Qal flee (23)
בְּרִית	covenant (10)
בָּרַךְ	Piel bless (27)
בָּשָׂר	flesh, meat (32)
בַּת	daughter (2)
בְּתוֹךְ	within, in the midst of (8)

ג

גָּאַל	Qal redeem, claim, ransom; act as a kinsman (12)
גְּבוּל	border, boundary (25)
גִּבּוֹר	mighty man, warrior (21)
גִּבְעָה	hill (36)
גֶּבֶר	man (40)

גָּדַל   Qal be great, wealthy, important; Piel & Hiph cause to grow, magnify; Hith boast (26)

גָּדוֹל   large, great (9)

גּוֹי   nation, people, Gentile (18)

גּוּר   Qal sojourn, stay as a foreigner (34)

גַּיְא   valley (36)

גָּלָה   Qal uncover, reveal, go away; Piel uncover, reveal; Hiph take into exile (14)

גַּם   also, even (19)

גָּמָל   camel (39)

גֶּפֶן   vine f (35)

גֵּר   resident alien (40)

ד

דָּבַק   Qal cling to (23)

דָּבַר   Piel speak (27)

דָּבָר   word, matter, thing (3)

דְּבַשׁ   honey (35)

דּוֹר   period, generation, age (21)

דֶּלֶת   door (38)

דָּם   blood (18)

דֶּרֶךְ   way, road, journey, custom, conduct (5)

דָּרַשׁ   Qal seek, inquire (7)

ה

הוּא   he (4)

הִיא   she (4)

הָיָה   Qal be, happen (18)

הֵיכָל   palace, temple (38)

הָלַךְ   Qal walk, go, come (5)

הָלַל   Piel praise; Hith praise oneself (27)

הֵם   they mp (4)

הֵמָּה   they mp (4)

הִנֵּה   behold! look! (20)

הֵנָּה   they fp (4)

הַר   mountain, hill country (18)

הָרַג   Qal kill (34)

ז

זֹאת   this f (16)

זָבַח   Qal sacrifice, slaughter (7)

זֶבַח   sacrifice (7)

זֶה   this m (16)

זָהָב   gold (12)

זָכַר   Qal remember, mention; Hiph remind (2)

זָכָר   male (40)

זָקֵן   old, elder (10)

זָר   foreigner (40)

זְרוֹעַ   arm, strength f (15)

זֶרַע   seed, offspring (25)

ח

חֹדֶשׁ   new moon, month (13)

חוֹמָה   wall (21)

חָזָה   Qal see, see a vision, perceive (14)

חָזַק   Qal be strong, take courage; Hiph seize, grasp (12)

חָזָק   firm, strong (10)

חָטָא   Qal offend, sin (13)

חַטָּאת   sin, sin offering (23)

חִטָּה   wheat (37)

חַי alive, living (9)

חָיָה Qal be alive, live (18)

חַיִל strength, virtue, ability, wealth (30)

חָכָם wise, skillful, shrewd (9)

חֵלֶב fat (37)

חָלַל Piel & Hiph pollute, defile, profane, begin (28)

חֵמָה heat, anger (21)

חָמֵשׁ five *f* (29)

חֲמִשָּׁה five *m* (29)

חָנָה Qal camp (21)

חָנַן Qal be gracious (39)

חֶסֶד loyalty, faithfulness (20)

חָפֵץ Qal want, desire (23)

חֹק decree, law (23)

חֶרֶב sword *f* (28)

חָרָה Qal be hot, angry (21)

חָרַשׁ Hiph be silent, silence (31)

חָשַׁב Qal think (25)

חֹשֶׁךְ darkness (20)

חָתַת Qal be terrified (39)

ט

טָהוֹר clean, pure (9)

טוֹב good, pleasing (9)

טָמֵא Qal be unclean (40)

טָמֵא unclean, impure (9)

י

יָבֵשׁ Qal be dry, dry up, wither; Hiph cause to dry up (17)

יָד hand *f* (3)

I יָדָה Qal & Piel throw, shoot (33)

II יָדָה Hiph praise, confess (33)

יָדַע Qal know, care about, choose; Hiph make known (7)

יוֹם day, time, lifetime, today (when definite) (3)

יָטַב Qal be good, pleasing (17)

יַיִן wine (35)

יָכַח Hiph rebuke (32)

יָכֹל Qal be able, conquer (16)

יָלַד Qal give birth to; Hiph father (17)

יָם sea (18)

יָמִין right, right hand, south *f* (34)

יָסַף Qal & Hiph add, continue, do again (25)

יָצָא Qal go out; Hiph bring out (16)

יָצַק Qal pour out, dish up, spread (20)

יָצַר Qal form, fashion, create (17)

יָרֵא Qal fear, be afraid (17)

יָרַד Qal go down; Hiph bring down (16)

I יָרָה Qal throw, shoot (33)

II יָרָה Hiph teach (33)

יָרַשׁ Qal inherit; Hiph dispossess (17)

יֵשׁ there is (22)

יָשַׁב Qal sit, dwell, inhabit; Hiph make sit, settle (7)

יָשַׁע Niph be victorious, receive help; Hiph help, save (32)

יָשָׁר straight, right, upright (9)

יָתַר Niph remain; Hiph leave behind (32)

כ

כְּ like, as, according to (8)

כַּאֲשֶׁר just as, when (26)

כָּבֵד — Qal be heavy, dull; Niph have honor, glory, respect; Piel make dull, honor (2)

כָּבוֹד — glory, honor (22)

כֶּבֶשׁ — lamb (39)

כֹּה — thus (19)

כֹּהֵן — priest (5)

כוּן — Niph stand firm; Hiph prepare, make firm (33)

כִּי — because, that, surely (19)

כִּי־אִם — unless, except (19)

כֹּל — all, every, the whole (12)

כָּלָה — Qal cease, end, waste away, be finished; Piel complete, finish (14)

כְּלִי — article, implement, utensil, vessel (28)

כָּנָף — wing, extremity (39)

כִּסֵּא — seat, throne (38)

כָּסָה — Piel conceal, cover (28)

כֶּסֶף — money, silver (12)

כָּעַס — Qal be provoked; Hiph provoke (30)

כַּף — palm, sole (33)

כָּפַר — Piel atone (27)

כֶּרֶם — vineyard (35)

כָּרַת — Qal cut; Hiph cut off (10)

כָּתַב — Qal write (6)

כָּתֵף — shoulder, shoulder blade, side *f* (15)

ל

לְ — to, toward, for (8)

לֹא — no, not (7)

לֵב — heart, mind, will (7)

לֵבָב — heart, mind, will (7)

לָבַשׁ — Qal clothe, dress, wear; Hiph clothe (26)

לָחַם — Niph fight (35)

לֶחֶם — bread, food (10)

לַיְלָה — night (13)

לָכַד — Qal capture, catch (21)

לָכֵן — therefore (19)

לָמַד — Qal learn; Piel teach (32)

לְמַעַן — in order to, for the sake of (19)

לִפְנֵי — before (8)

לָקַח — Qal take, seize, acquire (5)

לָשׁוֹן — tongue, language (33)

מ

מְאֹד — very, abundance, strength (22)

מֵאָה — one hundred (29)

מִגְדָּל — tower (38)

מִגְרָשׁ — pasture land (37)

מָדַד — Qal measure (39)

מָה — what? (26)

מוֹעֵד — meeting, appointed time (28)

מוּת — Qal die; Hiph put to death (24)

מִזְבֵּחַ — altar (7)

מַחֲנֶה — camp (31)

מַטֶּה — staff, tribe (30)

מִי — who? (26)

מַיִם — water, waters (10)

מָלֵא — Qal be full; Piel fill (22)

מַלְאָךְ — messenger, angel (22)

מִלְחָמָה — battle, war (3)

מָלַךְ — Qal rule, be king; Hiph make king (10)

מֶלֶךְ   king (3)

מַלְכוּת   kingdom (3)

מִן   from (8)

מִנְחָה   gift, tribute, grain offering (26)

מַעֲשֶׂה   work, product (31)

מָצָא   Qal find (13)

מִצְוָה   commandment (23)

מָקוֹם   place (12)

מָשַׁח   Qal anoint (35)

מִשְׁפָּחָה   clan, family (6)

מִשְׁפָּט   judgment, decision, custom (7)

נ

נְאֻם   declaration, utterance (32)

נָבָא   Niph & Hith prophesy (36)

נָבַט   Hiph look (31)

נָבִיא   prophet (6)

נֶגֶב   south, Negeb (37)

נָגַד   Hiph tell, make known

נֶגֶד   in front of, opposite (23)

נָגַע   Qal touch, hurt (14)

נָגַשׁ   Qal approach, step forth (14)

נָדַח   Niph be scattered; Hiph scatter (31)

נָהָר   river (36)

נוּחַ   Qal rest; Hiph give rest, settle (33)

נוּס   Qal flee (34)

נַחַל   wadi (36)

נַחֲלָה   inheritance, portion (30)

נְחֹשֶׁת   copper, bronze (36)

נָטָה   Qal reach out, extend (26)

נָכָה   Hiph strike (33)

נָסַע   Qal start out, break camp; Hiph take away, remove (14)

נַעַר   boy (6)

נָפַל   Qal fall; Hith prostrate oneself (12)

נֶפֶשׁ   soul, self, emotions *f* (6)

נָצַל   Hiph deliver (31)

נָשָׂא   Qal lift, carry, pardon, forgive (13)

נָתַן   Qal give, present, put (5)

ס

סָבַב   Qal go around, turn around; Niph encircle; Hiph make go around (39)

סָבִיב   around (23)

סוּס   horse (3)

סוּסָה   mare (4)

סוּר   Qal turn aside; Hiph remove (24)

סָפַר   Qal count, measure, register; Piel report, tell (28)

סֵפֶר   book, document (11)

ע

עָבַד   Qal serve, work, be a slave, worship (12)

עֶבֶד   slave, servant (12)

עָבַר   Qal pass through, go across, transgress; Hiph make pass through, make go across, remove (11)

עַד   until, as far as (20)

עֵדָה   congregation (28)

עוֹד   yet, still (28)

עוֹלָה   burnt offering (26)

עוֹלָם   forever, antiquity (6)

עָוֹן   sin, guilt, punishment (23)

עָזַב   Qal abandon, leave, forsake (22)

עַיִן   eye, spring *m* and *f* (15)

עִיר   city, town *f* (3)

עַל   on, upon, on account of, unto, against (8)

עָלָה   Qal go up; Hiph bring up (16)

עַל־כֵּן   therefore (25)

עִם   with (8)

עַם   people (7)

עָמַד   Qal stand; Hiph cause to stand, station (11)

I עָנָה   Qal answer (25)

II עָנָה   Niph be humble, afflicted (25)

עֵץ   tree, wood (25)

עֶצֶם   bone (33)

עֶרֶב   evening (13)

עָשָׂה   Qal make, do (14)

עֶשֶׂר   ten *f* (29)

עֲשָׂרָה   ten *m* (29)

עֵת   time (13)

עַתָּה   now (21)

פ

פֶּה   mouth (15)

פָּלַל   Hith pray (38)

פֶּן   so that not (19)

פָּנָה   Qal turn (34)

פָּנִים   face, presence *m* and *f* (15)

פָּקַד   Qal visit, take care of, commission, call to account; Hiph appoint (11)

פַּר   bull, steer (17)

פְּרִי   fruit (35)

פָּתַח   Qal open (35)

פֶּתַח   doorway, door (38)

צ

צֹאן   flock, sheep, goats *f* (17)

צָבָא   army (18)

צַדִּיק   righteous (27)

צֶדֶק   righteousness (27)

צָוָה   Piel command (27)

צָפוֹן   north (34)

ק

קָבַץ   Qal gather (36)

קָבַר   Qal bury (37)

קָדַשׁ   Qal be holy; Piel & Hiph sanctify; Hith sanctify oneself (27)

קָדוֹשׁ   holy, sacred (9)

קֹדֶשׁ   holiness, sacredness (11)

קָטַר   Piel & Hiph burn a sacrifice (37)

קוֹל   voice, sound, noise (11)

קוּם   Qal arise, stand; Hiph set up, establish (24)

קָרָא   Qal call, read aloud (13)

קָרַב   Qal approach (22)

קֶרֶב   midst (31)

ר

רָאָה   Qal see, know; Hiph appear, become visible; Hiph show (14)

רֹאשׁ   head, first, chief (15)

רִאשׁוֹן   first, former, chief (34)

רֵאשִׁית   beginning (15)

רָבָה   Qal be much, many, numerous, great; Hiph multiply (26)

רַב   much, great, many (9)

רֶגֶל   foot *f* (15)

רָדַף   Qal pursue, persecute (38)

רוּחַ   breath, wind, spirit *f* (18)

רוּם   Qal be high, exalted, haughty (24)

רוּץ   Qal run (24)

רֹחַב   width, breadth (34)

רַע   evil, bad (40)

רֵעַ   friend (32)

רָעָה   evil, trouble (40)

רָעָה   Qal pasture, tend (36)

רַק   only (28)

רָשָׁע   guilty, wicked, criminal (9)

שׂ

שָׂדֶה   field (25)

שִׂים   Qal put, place (24)

שָׂמַח   Qal be glad; Piel make glad (28)

שָׂנֵא   Qal hate (20)

שָׂפָה   lip, language (33)

שַׂר   leader (30)

שָׂרַף   Qal burn (37)

שׁ

שָׁאַל   Qal ask (35)

שָׁאַר   Qal remain; Hiph leave as a remnant (30)

שָׁבַע   Niph swear an oath; Hiph make swear an oath (30)

שֶׁבַע   seven *f* (29)

שִׁבְעָה   seven *m* (29)

שָׁבַר   Qal break (38)

שַׁבָּת   sabbath (30)

שׁוּב   Qal turn, return (intransitive); Hiph return (transitive) (24)

שָׁחַת   Qal destroy (40)

שָׁכַב   Qal lie down, have intercourse with (10)

שָׁכַח   Qal forget (38)

שָׁלוֹם   peace (22)

שָׁלַח   Qal send, reach out, stretch (2)

שָׁלַךְ   Hiph throw, reject (30)

שָׁלַם   Qal be complete, stay healthy; Piel repay (40)

שָׁלֹשׁ   three *f* (29)

שְׁלֹשָׁה   three *m* (29)

שֵׁם   name, reputation (7)

שָׁם   there (21)

שָׁמַיִם   sky, heaven, heavens (10)

שֶׁמֶן   oil (35)

שְׁמֹנֶה   eight *f* (29)

שְׁמֹנָה   eight *m* (29)

שָׁמַע   Qal hear, listen to (5)

שָׁמַר   Qal guard, watch, observe (6)

שֶׁמֶשׁ   sun (36)

שָׁנָה   year (11)

שְׁנַיִם   two *m* (29)

שַׁעַר   gate (30)

שָׁפַט   Qal judge, decide, punish (6)

שָׁפַךְ   Qal pour out, shed (20)

שָׁרַת   Piel serve, minister (37)

שֵׁשׁ   six *f* (29)

שִׁשָּׁה   six *m* (29)

שָׁתָה   Qal drink (22)

שְׁתַּיִם   two *f* (29)

תַּחַת   under (8)

תֵּשַׁע   nine *f* (29)

תִּשְׁעָה   nine *m* (29)

ת

תּוֹרָה   teaching, law, instruction (11)

ANSWERS TO PRACTICE DRILLS

Lesson 1

A. **Memorize the names and letters** of the alphabet so well that you can write them out as fast as you can say and write your ABCs!

B. Make the sound and say the name of the following letters, reading from right to left.

נ ת כ ס מ ג א ף ע פ ל ח ד ←

ש ץ ז ב ז פ ר ק ה ס ו ב ←

C. Read the two previous lines again and circle the letters in a special final form.

D. Read the two previous lines again and underline the gutturals + *resh*.

E. Read the two previous lines again and draw a box around the *begadkefat*s.

F. Match the letters that sound alike.

291

Lesson 2

A. Focus on the sounds of the vowels. The following are not Hebrew words, but they sound like English words. Pronounce the Hebrew word, then write the English word that sounds the same.

1.	fall	7.	feel	13.	fought	19.	bell	25.	boot
2.	fall	8.	feel	14.	fought	20.	bed	26.	boot
3.	fall	9.	foam	15.	ball	21.	bead	27.	bought
4.	fail	10.	foam	16.	ball	22.	bead	28.	bought
5.	fell	11.	food	17.	ball	23.	boat	29.	bet
6.	fell	12.	food	18.	bail	24.	boat	30.	beat

B. Focus on the class of the vowels. Memorize the vertical columns on the chart on p. 8 before doing this exercise.

1. Circle the "a" vowels:
2. Circle the "i" vowels:
3. Circle the "u" vowels:

C. Focus on the length of the vowels. Memorize the horizontal rows on the chart on p. 8 before doing this exercise.

1. Circle the long vowels:
2. Circle the medium vowels:
3. Circle the short vowels:
4. Circle the very short vowels:

D. Focus on letters with two pronunciations. The following are not Hebrew words, but they sound like English words. Pronounce the Hebrew word, then write the English word that sounds the same.

1.	bet	3.	pool	5.	balk	7.	base	9.	pace
2.	vet	4.	fool	6.	Bach	8.	vase	10.	face

E. Focus on letters that look alike. The following are not Hebrew words, but they sound like English words. Pronounce the Hebrew word, then write the English word that sounds the same.

1.	case	4.	read	7.	tall	10.	car	13.	paw
2.	base	5.	red	8.	veal	11.	loom	14.	pots
3.	deed	6.	hall	9.	zeal	12.	loose	15.	zoom

F. Focus on letters that sound alike. The following are not Hebrew words, but they sound like English words. Pronounce the Hebrew word, then write the English word that sounds the same.

1.	vase	3.	Bach	5.	tall	7.	car	9.	same
2.	vase	4.	Bach	6.	tall	8.	car	10.	same

G. The following are not Hebrew words, but they sound like English words. Pronounce the Hebrew word, then write the English word that sounds the same.

1.	game	7.	sane	13.	zoo	19.	see/a	25.	soul
2.	rain	8.	hen	14.	you	20.	oats	26.	need
3.	ball	9.	egg	15.	nod	21.	vet	27.	near
4.	safe	10.	she	16.	bake	22.	lean	28.	roof
5.	key	11.	row	17.	cake	23.	aim	29.	gate
6.	note	12.	vote	18.	see/a	24.	aim	30.	cots

Lesson 3

A. Focus on *sheva*. Identify each *sheva* as vocal or silent and give the reason.

1. Silent, preceded by short vowel
2. Silent, preceded by short vowel
3. Silent, preceded by short vowel
4. Silent, preceded by short vowel
5. Silent, preceded by short vowel
6. Vocal, not preceded by short vowel
7. Vocal, not preceded by short vowel
8. Vocal, not preceded by short vowel
9. First is silent, preceded by short vowel; second is vocal, not preceded by short vowel
10. Vocal, not preceded by short vowel
11. Vocal, not preceded by short vowel
12. Silent, preceded by short vowel
13. Silent, preceded by short vowel
14. Vocal, not preceded by short vowel
15. Both are vocal, not preceded by short vowel

B. Focus on *dagesh*. Identify each *dagesh* as weak or strong and give the reason.

1. Weak, preceded by consonant
2. Strong, preceded by vowel
3. Strong, preceded by vowel
4. Weak, preceded by consonant
5. Weak, preceded by consonant
6. Strong, preceded by vowel
7. Strong, preceded by vowel
8. Weak, preceded by consonant
9. Weak, preceded by consonant

10. Strong, preceded by vowel
11. Strong, preceded by vowel
12. Weak, preceded by consonant
13. Weak, preceded by consonant
14. Strong, preceded by vowel
15. Strong, preceded by vowel

C. Focus on syllables. Divide the following into syllables, pronouncing each word as you go. If there is a strong *dagesh* in a letter, draw a line through that letter (marked here, in the answer key, with a colored letter).

5. מִנְ|חָה   4. מְקֻ|טָל   3. נֶגְ|דּוֹ   2. יַקְ|טִיל   1. מְדַ|בֵּר

10. דּוֹ|רְ|כִים   9. מִזְ|בְּ|חוֹת   8. דְּ|בָ|רִים   7. בֶּ|רְ|כָה   6. כּוֹ|תְ|בִים

15. יְ|דַ|בְּ|רוּ   14. יְ|דַ|בֵּר   13. סִפְ|רוּ   12. עוֹ|לָ|מִים   11. קְ|טַ|לוּ

D. Focus on the class of the vowels.

1. Circle the "a" vowels:
2. Circle the "i" vowels:
3. Circle the "u" vowels:

E. Focus on the length of the vowels.

1. Circle the long vowels:
2. Circle the medium vowels:
3. Circle the short vowels:
4. Circle the very short vowels:

F. The following are not Hebrew words, but they sound like English words. Pronounce the Hebrew word, then write the English word that sounds the same.

1.	soon	4.	let's	7.	coats	10.	she	13.	zero
2.	gate	5.	key	8.	target	11.	seal	14.	letter
3.	doll	6.	root	9.	vista	12.	history	15.	nod

Lesson 4

A. Focus on gender. Read the following Hebrew words; circle the masculine words and underline the feminine words.

1. אֵלִים מֶלֶךְ דָּבָר יוֹם מַלְכוּת בֵּן בַּת אָב מִלְחָמוֹת

2. מְדַבֵּר מִנְחָה סֵפֶר דַּלִים טוֹבוֹת שָׁלוֹם אֱמֶת עַמִּים

B. Focus on number. Read the Following Hebrew words; circle the singular words, underline the plural words, and draw a box around the dual words.

1. אֵלִים ‏‎ יָדַיִם ‏‎ דָּבָר ‏‎ אֱלֹהִים ‏‎ מַלְכוּת ‏‎ אָבוֹת ‏‎ בַּת ‏‎ בֵּן ‏‎ מִלְחָמוֹת

2. מִזְבְּחוֹת ‏‎ עוֹלָמִים ‏‎ עֵינַיִם ‏‎ מִשְׁפַּחַת ‏‎ אֲרָצוֹת ‏‎ אֱמֶת ‏‎ טוֹבִים

C. Focus on number and gender. Read the following Hebrew words and circle the word that is out of place in terms of number or gender.

1. יוֹם ‏‎ מֶלֶךְ ‏‎ מַלְכוּת   2. אֵלִים ‏‎ סוּסוֹת ‏‎ טוֹבִים

3. סוּס ‏‎ דָּבָר ‏‎ אֵלִים   4. בַּת ‏‎ אָב ‏‎ אֵם

5. יָדַיִם ‏‎ מַיִם ‏‎ יָמִים   6. אֶרֶץ ‏‎ מֶלֶךְ ‏‎ דֶּרֶךְ

D. Focus on sheva. Identify each sheva as vocal or silent, and give the reason.

    1. Vocal, not preceded by short vowel
    2. Silent, preceded by short vowel
    3. First is silent, preceded by short vowel; second is vocal, not preceded by short vowel
    4. Silent, preceded by short vowel
    5. Silent, preceded by short vowel

E. Focus on dagesh. Identify each dagesh as weak or strong, and give the reason.

    1. Strong, preceded by vowel
    2. Strong, preceded by vowel
    3. Weak, preceded by consonant
    4. Strong, preceded by vowel
    5. Weak, preceded by consonant

F. Focus on pronunciation. Read the following English words, written in Hebrew.

    1. moon   2. garden   3. severe   4. also   5. better

G. Focus on meaning. Circle the word that does not belong in terms of meaning.

2. אֵל ‏‎ אֵם ‏‎ אֱלֹהִים   1. יוֹם ‏‎ מֶלֶךְ ‏‎ מַלְכוּת

4. בַּת ‏‎ אָב ‏‎ עִיר   3. יָד ‏‎ אָח ‏‎ אָחוֹת

6. אָכַל ‏‎ מֶלֶךְ ‏‎ מִלְחָמָה   5. בֵּן ‏‎ אֶרֶץ ‏‎ בַּת

H. The following is Gen 1:1-3.

1. בְּרֵאשִׁית ‏‎ בָּרָא ‏‎ אֱלֹהִים ‏‎ אֵת ‏‎ הַשָּׁמַיִם ‏‎ וְאֵת ‏‎ הָאָרֶץ

2. וְהָאָרֶץ ‏‎ הָיְתָה ‏‎ תֹהוּ ‏‎ וָבֹהוּ ‏‎ וְחֹשֶׁךְ ‏‎ עַל ‏‎ פְּנֵי ‏‎ תְהוֹם

וְרוּחַ ‏‎ אֱלֹהִים ‏‎ מְרַחֶפֶת ‏‎ עַל ‏‎ פְּנֵי ‏‎ הַמָּיִם

3. וַיֹּאמֶר ‏‎ אֱלֹהִים ‏‎ יְהִי ‏‎ אוֹר ‏‎ וַיְהִי ‏‎ אוֹר

Lesson 5

A. Focus on the personal pronoun. Translate the following Hebrew sentences.

1. He is a father.	5. You are a mother.	9. They are mares.
2. You are a father.	6. I am a mother.	10. You are God/a god.
3. I am a father.	7. It is a horse.	11. You are gods.
4. She is a mother.	8. They are horses.	12. We are gods.

B. Focus on the definite article. Translate the following Hebrew words, paying attention to the presence or absence of the definite article.

1. a day	6. a daughter	11. a sister
2. the day	7. the king	12 a city
3. God/gods	8. a king	13. the city
4. (the) God	9. hand	14. the word
5. the daughter	10. the hand	15. a word

C. Focus on letters that sound alike. Circle the letters that sound alike.

5. צ ח כ   4. כ כ ק   3. ט ת ה   2. ש ש ס   1. ב כ ו

D. Focus on gutturals and resh. Circle the gutturals or resh.

5. ל ח ו   4. מ א ג   3. ה ת ב   2. ע צ ט   1. ד ר ך

E. Focus on gender and number. Identify the gender and number of the following.

1. *ms*   2. *fs*   3. *fp*   4. *mp*   5. *fs*

F. Translate the following.

1. I am a father.	5. They are mares.	9. He sent.
2. I am the father.	6. He remembered.	10. You are gods.
3. You are the king.	7. It is the earth.	11. He gave.
4. It is the battle.	8. You are the daughter.	12. It/he is heavy.

G. The following is 2 Samuel 7:1-2.

1. וַיְהִי כִּי יָשַׁב הַמֶּלֶךְ בְּבֵיתוֹ

וַיהוָה הֵנִיחַ לוֹ מִסָּבִיב מִכָּל אֹיְבָיו

2. וַיֹּאמֶר הַמֶּלֶךְ אֶל נָתָן הַנָּבִיא

רְאֵה נָא אָנֹכִי יוֹשֵׁב בְּבֵית אֲרָזִים

וַאֲרוֹן הָאֱלֹהִים יֹשֵׁב בְּתוֹךְ הַיְרִיעָה

Lesson 6

A. Focus on roots. Write the Hebrew root of the following.

5. דרך   4. דבר   3. ארץ   2. אכל   1. אדם

10. שלח   9. לחם   8. שפח   7. מלך   6. מלך

B. Parse the following.

	Verb	Pattern	Conj.	Person	Gender	Number	Root
1.	שָׁלַח	qal	pf	3	m	s	שלח
2.	לָקְחָה	qal	pf	3	f	s	לקח
3.	הָלַכְתָּ	qal	pf	2	m	s	הלך
4.	זְכַרְתֶּם	qal	pf	2	m	p	זכר
5.	שָׁמַעְנוּ	qal	pf	1	c	p	שמע
6.	כָּתַבְתִּי	qal	pf	1	c	s	כתב
7.	בְּטַחְתֶּן	qal	pf	2	f	p	בטח
8.	אָכְלוּ	qal	pf	3	c	p	אכל
9.	קָטַלְתְּ	qal	pf	2	f	s	קטל
10.	קָטַל	qal	pf	3	m	s	קטל

E. The following is Psalm 1:1.

1. אַשְׁרֵי הָאִישׁ אֲשֶׁר

לֹא הָלַךְ בַּעֲצַת רְשָׁעִים

וּבְדֶרֶךְ חַטָּאִים לֹא עָמָד

וּבְמוֹשַׁב לֵצִים לֹא יָשָׁב

Lesson 7

E. Focus on parsing. Parse the following Hebrew verbs.

Verb	Pattern	Conj.	Person	Gender	Number	Root
1. נָתְנָה	qal	pf	3	f	s	נתן
2. כָּתְבוּ	qal	pf	3	c	p	כתב
3. שְׁמַרְתֶּם	qal	pf	2	m	p	שׁמר
4. שָׁפַטְנוּ	qal	pf	1	c	p	שׁפט
5. אָכַלְתָּ	qal	pf	2	m	s	אכל
6. זָכַרְתִּי	qal	pf	1	c	s	זכר
7. כָּבֵד	qal	pf	3	m	s	כבד

F. Focus on the class of the vowels. Review the vertical columns on the chart on p. 8 before doing this exercise.

1. Circle the "a" vowels:
2. Circle the "i" vowels:
3. Circle the "u" vowels:

G. Focus on the length of the vowels. Review the horizontal rows on the chart on p. 8 before doing this exercise.

1. Circle the long vowels:
2. Circle the medium vowels:
3. Circle the short vowels:
4. Circle the very short vowels:

I. The following are from Genesis 1:1, 4, 27.

1 בְּרֵאשִׁית בָּרָא אֱלֹהִים אֵת הַשָּׁמַיִם וְאֵת הָאָרֶץ

4 וַיַּרְא אֱלֹהִים אֶת־הָאוֹר כִּי־טוֹב

27 וַיִּבְרָא אֱלֹהִים אֶת־הָאָדָם בְּצַלְמוֹ

Lesson 8

A. Focus on the accent. Circle the accented syllable.

5. הַבֵּן	4. מְלָכִים	3. מֶלֶךְ	2. יָשַׁב	1. אָדָם
10. נַעַר	9. עוֹלָם	8. זֶבַח	7. נֶפֶשׁ	6. כָּתְבוּ

B. Focus on the syllable. Circle the closed syllables and underline the open syllables.

5. עוֹלָם	4. מְלָכִים	3. מֶלֶךְ	2. מַלְכוּת	1. אָדָם
10. נַעַר	9. יוֹם	8. מִלְחָמָה	7. נֶפֶשׁ	6. מִשְׁפָּט

C. Focus on vowel changes in the plural. Match the plural form of the right column with the corresponding singular form in the left column.

a. דָּבָר		h.	1. נְעָרִים
b. לֵבָב		f.	2. מְלָכִים
c. נָבִיא		i.	3. מִשְׁפָּטִים
d. עוֹלָם		a.	4. דְּבָרִים
e. דֶּרֶךְ		j.	5. זְבָחִים
f. מֶלֶךְ		b.	6. לְבָבוֹת
g. נֶפֶשׁ		e.	7. דְּרָכִים
h. נַעַר		c.	8. נְבִיאִים
i. מִשְׁפָּט		l.	9. אֲרָצוֹת
j. זֶבַח		d.	10. עוֹלָמִים
k. מִזְבֵּחַ		g.	11. נְפָשׁוֹת
l. אֶרֶץ		k.	12. מִזְבְּחוֹת

D. Parse the following.

	Verb	Pattern	Conj.	Person	Gender	Number	Root
1.	כָּבֵד	qal	pf	3	m	s	כבד
2.	הָלַכְתִּי	qal	pf	1	c	s	הלך
3.	יָשַׁבְתָּ	qal	pf	2	m	s	ישב

4. לְקַחְתֶּם	qal	pf	2	m	p	לקח
5. שָׁמְעוּ	qal	pf	3	c	p	שמע
6. שָׁמְעָה	qal	pf	3	f	s	שמע
7. אָכַלְנוּ	qal	pf	1	c	p	אכל

F. The following is 1 Kings 1:11.

וַיֹּאמֶר נָתָן אֶל־בַּת־שֶׁבַע אֵם־שְׁלֹמֹה לֵאמֹר

הֲלוֹא שָׁמַעַתְּ כִּי מָלַךְ אֲדֹנִיָּהוּ בֶן־חַגִּית

וַאֲדֹנֵינוּ דָוִד לֹא יָדָע

Lesson 9

A. Focus on prepositions. Translate the following prepositional phrases.

1. to an altar
2. within an altar
3. on an altar
4. before an altar
5. under an altar
6. with an altar
7. like an altar
8. like the altar
9. to an altar
10. to the altar
11. in the altar
12. in an altar
13. from the altar
14. from an altar
15. from a city
16. in a city
17. to a city
18. to the city
19. like a land
20. like the land

B. Focus on vav conjunction. Translate the following.

1. you and he
2. altar and sacrifice
3. priest and prophet
4. heart and soul
5. a city and a house
6. a priest and a king
7. son and daughter
8. they and we

D. Focus on gender. Read the following Hebrew words; circle the masculine words and underline the feminine words.

1. סוּס סוּסָה סוּסִים סוּסוֹת בֶּגֶד אָחוֹת מִלְחָמָה מִשְׁפָּחָה מִשְׁפָּט

2. אֵם אֲרָצוֹת אֶרֶץ זֶבַח נַעַר נְפָשׁוֹת נֶפֶשׁ אִשָּׁה נָשִׁים בַּיִת

E. Focus on number. Read the following Hebrew words; circle the singular words and underline the plural words.

1. סוּס סוּסָה סוּסִים סוּסוֹת בְּגָדִים אָחוֹת אָבוֹת עוֹלָם מִלְחָמוֹת

2. אַתֶּם אַתָּה אַתְּ הֵם הֵנָּה יוֹם כֹּהֵן מַלְכוּת מִשְׁפָּטִים אֲרָצוֹת שָׁם

F. Parse the following.

Verb		Pattern	Conj.	Person	Gender	Number	Root
1.	זָבְחוּ	qal	pf	3	c	p	זבח
2.	שְׁפַטְנוּ	qal	pf	1	c	p	שׁפט
3.	הָלַכְתָּ	qal	pf	2	m	s	הלך
4.	כָּבַדְתִּי	qal	pf	1	c	s	כבד
5.	זָכְרָה	qal	pf	3	f	s	זכר
6.	כְּתַבְתֶּם	qal	pf	2	m	p	כתב

H. Translate the following verses from the Hebrew Bible.

Joshua 2:5	I do not know where the men went.	1.
Judges 21:22	We did not take a man.	2.
1 Samuel 4:18	And he judged Israel.	3.
Jeremiah 34:17	You did not hear.	4.

Lesson 10

A. Focus on attributive adjectives. Translate the following phrases.

1. a great king
2. many boys
3. a good family
4. living souls
5. the straight way
6. the many wars
7. the clean earth
8. a wise mother
9. a wicked judgment
10. the holy priests
11. a pure heart
12. the good cities

B. Focus on predicative adjectives. Translate the following sentences.

1. the altar is unclean
2. the daughter is wise
3. the women are many
4. the sacrifices are holy
5. the boys are wicked
6. the days are good
7. the word is alive
8. the house is big

C. Focus on the difference between attributive and predicate adjectives. Read the following phrases and sentences and fill in the blanks for use of adjective (*a* for attributive and *p* for predicative) and for gender and number.

Use	Gender	Number		
a	f	s	.1	הָאִשָּׁה הַטּוֹבָה
p	m	s	.2	יָשָׁר הָאָדָם
a	m	s	.3	הַמִּזְבֵּחַ הַטָּהוֹר
a	f	s	.4	הַבַּת הַטּוֹבָה
p	m	p	.5	טְמֵאִים הָאֵלִים
a	m	p	.6	הָאֱלֹהִים הַחַיִּים
p	m	p	.7	גְּדוֹלִים הַבְּגָדִים
p	f	s	.8	רְשָׁעָה הַמַּלְכוּת
a	m	s	.9	לֵב חָכָם
a	f	p	.10	הָאֲרָצוֹת הָרַבּוֹת

D. Focus on vowel changes in the plural. Match the plural form of the right column with the corresponding singular form in the left column.

a.	אִשָּׁה	d.	בְּגָדִים	.1
b.	לֵבָב	h.	אֵלִים	.2
c.	בֵּן	k.	עַמִּים	.3
d.	בֶּגֶד	i.	לִבּוֹת	.4
e.	מִזְבֵּחַ	b.	לְבָבוֹת	.5
f.	נָבִיא	l.	אֲנָשִׁים	.6
g.	עִיר	c.	בָּנִים	.7
h.	אֵל	f.	נְבִיאִים	.8
i.	לֵב	e.	מִזְבְּחוֹת	.9
j.	אֵם	g.	עָרִים	.10
k.	עַם	j	אִמּוֹת	.11
l.	אִישׁ	a.	נָשִׁים	.12

E. Parse the following.

	Verb	Pattern	Conj.	Person	Gender	Number	Root
1.	קְטַלְתֶּם	qal	pf	2	m	p	קטל
2.	יָשַׁבְתִּי	qal	pf	1	c	s	ישב
3.	לָקַחְתְּ	qal	pf	2	f	s	לקח
4.	יָדְעָה	qal	pf	3	f	s	ידע
5.	הָלְכוּ	qal	pf	3	c	p	הלך
6.	זָכַרְנוּ	qal	pf	1	c	p	זכר
7.	דָּרַשְׁתָּ	qal	pf	2	m	s	דרש
8.	כָּבֵד	qal	pf	3	m	s	כבד

G. Translate the following lines from the Hebrew Bible.

Deuteronomy 2:10	A great and many/numerous people.	1.
Joshua 24:19	He is a holy God.	2.
Exodus 18:17	The word/matter is not good.	3.
Jeremiah 10:10	He is a living God.	4.

Lesson 11

A. Focus on the form of the imperfect. Parse the following imperfect verbs.

	Verb	Pattern	Conj.	Person	Gender	Number	Root
1.	יִקְטֹל	qal	impf	3	m	s	קטל
2.	יִכְתְּבוּ	qal	impf	3	m	p	כתב
3.	אֶשְׁפֹּט	qal	impf	1	c	s	שפט
4.	תִּשְׁלַח	qal	impf	3 / 2	f / m	s	שלח
5.	תִּשְׁמְרוּ	qal	impf	2	m	p	שמר
6.	תִּשְׁמְעִי	qal	impf	2	f	s	שמע
7.	נִבְטַח	qal	impf	1	c	p	בטח
8.	תִּקְטֹלְנָה	qal	impf	3 / 2	f	p	קטל

B. Focus on the use of the imperfect. Translate the following imperfect forms as future imperfects.

1. he will remember	6. you will seek	11. he will sacrifice
2. I will reign	7. they will lie down	12 we will reign
3. you will guard	8. they/you will hear	13. I will trust
4. we will judge	9. he will cut	14. they will guard
5. she/you will trust	10. they will write	15. she/you will hear

D. Parse the following.

	Verb	Pattern	Conj.	Person	Gender	Number	Root
1.	כָּרְתוּ	qal	pf	3	c	p	כרת
2.	שָׁכַבְתִּי	qal	pf	1	c	s	שכב
3.	מָלַכְתָּ	qal	pf	2	m	s	מלך
4.	זָבַחְנוּ	qal	pf	1	c	p	זבח
5.	יְדַעְתֶּם	qal	pf	2	m	p	ידע
6.	יָשַׁבְתְּ	qal	pf	2	f	s	ישב
7.	דָּרְשָׁה	qal	pf	3	f	s	דרש
8.	כָּבֵד	qal	pf	3	m	s	כבד
9.	בְּטַחְתֶּן	qal	pf	2	f	p	בטח

E. Focus on the syllable. Underline the closed syllables and circle the open propretonic syllables.

5. עוֹלָם   4. מְלָכִים   3. קְדוֹשָׁה   2. מַלְכוּת   1. גָּדוֹל

10. נַעַר   9. טוֹבִים   8. רְשָׁעָה   7. יְשָׁרוֹת   6. חֲכָמִים

G. Translate the following lines from the Hebrew Bible.

Psalm 146:10	The LORD will reign forever.	1.
Ecclesiastes 3:17	And he will judge the wicked.	2.
Deuteronomy 17:1	You will not sacrifice to the LORD.	3.

Lesson 12

A. **Focus on the form of the construct.** Circle the words that are in a construct form that differs from the absolute form.

1. סוּס עַם נֶפֶשׁ (דְּבַר) (בֵּן) סֵפֶר (נְבִיא) עִיר (תּוֹרַת) (סוּסַת)

2. קוֹל (לְבַב) קֹדֶשׁ מִשְׁפַּט) (מִלְחֶמֶת) (יַד) (בֵּית) מַלְכוּת שֵׁם

B. **Focus on the form of the construct.** Match the construct form of the right-hand column with the corresponding absolute form of the left-hand column.

מִשְׁפָּחָה	a.	g.	דְּבַר 1.
שֵׁם	b.	c.	שְׁנַת 2.
שָׁנָה	c.	i.	לְבַב 3.
יָד	d.	f.	נְבִיא 4.
מִשְׁפָּט	e.	b.	שֵׁם 5.
נָבִיא	f.	a.	מִשְׁפַּחַת 6.
דָּבָר	g.	j.	בֵּן 7.
תּוֹרָה	h.	e.	מִשְׁפַּט 8.
לֵבָב	i.	d.	יַד 9.
בֵּן	j.	h.	תּוֹרַת 10.

C. **Focus on the use of the construct.** Translate the following phrases and indicate whether the use is possession (*p*) or adjectival (*a*).

the heart of the prophet	p	1.	לְבַב הַנָּבִיא
the king's law	p	2.	תּוֹרַת הַמֶּלֶךְ
a holy garment	a	3.	בֶּגֶד־קֹדֶשׁ
the prophet's word	p	4.	דְּבַר הַנָּבִיא
the prophet of the land	p	5.	נְבִיא הָאָרֶץ
the daily sacrifice	a	6.	זֶבַח־הַיּוֹם
the boy's hand	p	7.	יַד הַנַּעַר
the mother's family	p	8.	מִשְׁפַּחַת הָאֵם
the LORD's battle	p	9.	מִלְחֶמֶת־יְהוָה
the man of God	p	10.	אִישׁ הָאֱלֹהִים

D. Focus on the difference between attributive and predicate adjectives. Read the following phrases and sentences and fill in the blanks for use of adjective (*a* for attributive and *p* for predicative) and for gender and number.

Use	Gender	Number		
a	m	p	.1	הַכֹּהֲנִים הַקְּדוֹשִׁים
p	m	p	.2	קְדוֹשִׁים הַכֹּהֲנִים
p	m	s	.3	יָשָׁר הַדֶּרֶךְ
a	m	s	.4	הַמִּזְבֵּחַ הַטָּמֵא
p	f	p	.5	זְקֵנוֹת הַתּוֹרוֹת
a	f	s	.6	הָאֵם הַזְּקֵנָה
a	f	p	.7	הֶעָרִים הַגְּדוֹלוֹת
p	f	s	.8	טוֹבָה הָאָרֶץ
a	m	p	.9	הָאָבוֹת הַחֲכָמִים
p	f	s	.10	רְשָׁעָה הַמִּשְׁפָּחָה

E. Parse the following.

	Verb	Pattern	Conj.	Person	Gender	Number	Root
1.	אֶפְקֹד	qal	impf	1	c	s	פקד
2.	זָכַרְנוּ	qal	pf	1	c	p	זכר
3.	נִדְרֹשׁ	qal	impf	1	c	p	דרש
4.	תִּכְתֹּבְנָה	qal	impf	3 / 2	f	p	כתב
5.	עָמְדָה	qal	pf	3	f	s	עמד
6.	שָׁמְעוּ	qal	pf	3	c	p	שמע
7.	תִּכְרֹת	qal	impf	3 / 2	f / m	s	כרת
8.	שְׁפַטְתֶּם	qal	pf	2	m	p	שפט
9.	מָלַכְתָּ	qal	pf	2	m	s	מלך

G. Translate the following lines from the Hebrew Bible.

Genesis 21:17   God listened to the boy's voice. .1

Joshua 7:15   He broke the LORD's covenant. .2

Proverbs 21:1   A king's heart is in the LORD's hand. .3

2 Chronicles 30:16 According to the law of Moses, the man of God. .4

Lesson 13

A. Focus on the form of the construct. Circle the words that are in construct form that is different from the absolute form.

1. סוּסִים עַמֵּי נַפְשׁוֹת דְּבָרִים בְּנֵי סִפְרֵי נְבִיאִים מִשְׁפָּחוֹת

2. קוֹלוֹת לְבָבוֹת דַּרְכֵי זִקְנֵי מִלְחֲמוֹת סוּסוֹת בְּגָדִים מִזְבְּחוֹת

B. Focus on the form of the construct. Match the construct form in the right column with the corresponding absolute form in the left column.

a. מָקוֹם		f. דְּבְרֵי	1.
b. מִשְׁפָּחָה		h. מַלְכֵי	2.
c. זֶבַח		e. יְדוֹת	3.
d. דֶּרֶךְ		a. מְקוֹמוֹת	4.
e. יָד		c. זִבְחֵי	5.
f. דָּבָר		b. מִשְׁפָּחוֹת	6.
g. מִלְחָמָה		i. עַמֵּי	7.
h. מֶלֶךְ		d. דַּרְכֵי	8.
i. עַם		g. מִלְחֲמוֹת	9.

E. Parse the following.

	Verb	Pattern	Conj.	Person	Gender	Number	Root
1.	גָּאַלְתִּי	qal	pf	1	c	s	גאל
2.	יִפְקְדוּ	qal	impf	3	m	p	פקד
3.	אָמְרוּ	qal	pf	3	c	p	אמר
4.	נִשְׁכַּב	qal	impf	1	c	p	שכב
5.	מָלַכְנוּ	qal	pf	1	c	p	מלך
6.	יְדַעְתֶּם	qal	pf	2	m	p	ידע
7.	אֶזְבַּח	qal	impf	1	c	s	זבח
8.	תִּבְטְחִי	qal	impf	2	f	s	בטח
9.	תִּכְתְּבוּ	qal	impf	2	m	p	כתב
10.	שָׁמְרָה	qal	pf	3	f	s	שמר

F. Focus on the inseparable prepositions. Circle the words that have an insepar-able preposition with the definite article.

.1 כְּסוּסִים (כַּסּוּסִים) (בַּדְּבָרִים) לְבָנִים בִּסְפָרִים (לַנָּבִיא) כְּמִשְׁפָּחָה

.2 בְּקוֹל (לַלֵּבָב) (בַּדֶּרֶךְ) לִזְקֵנִים כְּמִלְחָמוֹת (כַּסּוּסוֹת) בִּבְגָדִים (לַמִּזְבְּחוֹת)

H. Translate the following from the Hebrew Bible.

Numbers 11:16   They are the elders of the people. 1.

Deuteronomy 13:4   You shall not listen to the words of the prophet. 2.

Psalm 18:22   I guarded/kept the ways of the LORD. 3.

Leviticus 16:4   They are holy garments. 4.

Lesson 14

A. Focus on weak roots. Before doing this exercise, go back and review the para-digms in Lessons 6 and 11. Underline the verbs below that vary from the standard paradigm and circle the point(s) at which the variance occurs.

.1 עֲבַרְתֶּם חֲזַקְתֶּם עָבְדָה גָּאֲלָה נָשְׂאָה מָצָא מָצָה עֲמַדְתֶּם מְצָאתִי

.2 יַעֲבֹר יִגְאֲלוּ תַּעֲמְדוּ תִּקְרָא יֶבְבָּה נַעֲבֹד תִּמְצָאִי

.3 נָשְׂאוּ אֶעֱמֹד גָּאֲלוּ מְצָאָם תַּעַבְדִי חָזְקָה חֲזַקְתֶּם

B. Focus on weak roots. Parse the following.

	Verb	Pattern	Conj.	Person	Gender	Number	Root
1.	חָטָא	qal	pf	3	m	s	חטא
2.	עֲבַרְתֶּם	qal	pf	2	m	p	עבר
3.	נַעֲמֹד	qal	impf	1	c	p	עמד
4.	תִּמְצָא	qal	impf	3 / 2	f / m	s	מצא
5.	חֲטָאתֶם	qal	pf	2	m	p	חטא
6.	יַעַבְדוּ	qal	impf	3	m	p	עבד
7.	גָּאֲלָה	qal	pf	3	f	s	גאל
8.	אֲמַרְתֶּם	qal	pf	2	m	p	אמר

C. Focus on the construct state. Translate the following construct forms.

1. prophet of
2. judgment of
3. kings of
4. years of

5. word of
6. law of
7. family of
8. son of

9. ways of
10. sacrifices of
11. families of
12. gold of

13. mare of
14. battles of
15. servants of
16. souls of

D. Focus on the form of the construct. Match the construct form of the right column with the corresponding absolute singular form of the left column.

a. סוּסָה	e.	תּוֹרַת	.1
b. מִשְׁפָּחָה	j.	יָדוֹת	.2
c. יָשָׁר	d.	כַּסְפֵּי	.3
d. כֶּסֶף	b.	מִשְׁפָּחוֹת	.4
e. תּוֹרָה	g.	אַנְשֵׁי	.5
f. מִלְחָמָה	c.	יִשְׁרֵי	.6
g. אִישׁ	i.	עַמֵּי	.7
h. זָקֵן	f.	מִלְחֶמֶת	.8
i. עַם	a.	סוּסַת	.9
j. יָד	h.	זִקְנֵי	.10

E. Parse the following.

	Verb	Pattern	Conj.	Person	Gender	Number	Root
1.	יִזְבַּח	qal	impf	3	m	s	זבח
2.	שָׁלְחוּ	qal	pf	3	c	p	שׁלח
3.	נָשָׂאנוּ	qal	pf	1	c	p	נשׂא
4.	יַעַבְדוּ	qal	impf	3	m	p	עבד
5.	הֲלַכְתֶּם	qal	pf	2	m	p	הלך
6.	מָלַכְתָּ	qal	pf	2	m	s	מלך
7.	נִשְׁפֹּט	qal	impf	1	c	p	שׁפט
8.	אֶעֱמֹד	qal	impf	1	c	s	עמד
9.	תִּמְצָא	qal	impf	3 / 2	f / m	s	מצא
10.	תִּקְטֹלְנָה	qal	impf	3 / 2	f	p	קטל

G. Translate the following from the Hebrew Bible.

Ezekiel 44:24	They will stand for judgment. 1.
1 Samuel 28:20	He did not eat . . . all day and all night. 2.
Genesis 1:1	God created the heavens and the earth. 3.

Lesson 15

A. Focus on weak roots. Before doing this exercise, go back and review the paradigms in Lessons 6 and 11. Underline the verbs that vary from the standard paradigm and circle the point(s) at which the variation occurs.

1. נָגַע חֲזִיתֶם שָׁלַחְתִּי עָשׂוּ נָפַלְנוּ גָּלִיתָ בָּכָה

2. תִּכְלִי תִּמְלְכִי נֹסַע תִּגְּשׁוּ יִבְנֶה יִשְׁפְּטוּ יִפֹּל

3. תִּכְלֶה נָסְעָה עֲשִׂיתֶם יִבְנוּ תִּפֹּלְנָה בָּכְתָה

B. Focus on weak roots. Parse the following.

	Verb	Pattern	Conj.	Person	Gender	Number	Root
1.	יִפֹּל	qal	impf	3	m	s	נפל
2.	כָּלְתָה	qal	pf	3	f	s	כלה
3.	תַּעֲשֶׂה	qal	impf	3 / 2	f / m	s	עשה
4.	נִגַּשׁ	qal	impf	1	c	p	נגשׁ
5.	חֲזִיתֶם	qal	pf	2	m	p	חזה
6.	בָּנִינוּ	qal	pf	1	c	p	בנה
7.	תִּגְּעִי	qal	impf	2	f	s	נגע
8.	רָאִיתָ	qal	pf	2	m	s	ראה

C. Focus on the construct state. Translate the following construct forms.

1. place of
2. mare of
3. sacrifices of
4. souls of
5. monies of
6. battle of
7. word of
8. law of
9. gold of
10. family of
11. families of
12. books of
13. hand of
14. ways of
15. judgments of
16. men of

D. Focus on the form of the construct. Match the construct form of the right column with the corresponding absolute singular form of the left column.

זָהָב	.a	h.	נָבִיא	1.
מִשְׁפָּט	.b	d.	דִּבְרֵי	2.
סוּסָה	.c	j.	תּוֹרַת	3.
דָּבָר	.d	e.	נַפְשׁוֹת	4.
נֶפֶשׁ	.e	i.	אַנְשֵׁי	5.
רַב	.f	b.	מִשְׁפַּט	6.
שָׁנָה	.g	f.	רַבֵּי	7.
נָבִיא	.h	c.	סוּסַת	8.
אִישׁ	.i	a.	זְהַב	9.
תּוֹרָה	.j	g.	שְׁנַת	10.

E. Parse the following.

	Verb	Pattern	Conj.	Person	Gender	Number	Root
1.	יִשְׁלְחוּ	qal	impf	3	m	p	שׁלה
2.	עָבַרְנוּ	qal	pf	1	c	p	עבר
3.	גָּאֲלָה	qal	pf	3	f	s	גאל
4.	אֶקַּח	qal	impf	1	c	s	לקח
5.	כָּלִיתִי	qal	pf	1	c	s	כלה
6.	תִּמְצָא	qal	impf	3 / 2	f / m	s	מצא
7.	נִמְלֹךְ	qal	impf	1	c	p	מלך
8.	כָּבֵד	qal	pf	3	m	s	כבד
9.	יִפְּלוּ	qal	impf	3	m	p	נפל
10.	מָצָאתָ	qal	pf	2	m	s	מצא

G. Translate the following from the Hebrew Bible.

Exodus 20:23   Gods of silver . . . you shall not make. 1.

Numbers 4:15   And they shall not touch the holy things. 2.

Leviticus 10:17   You did not eat . . . in the holy place. 3.

Psalm 78:10   They did not keep God's covenant. 4.

Lesson 16

A. Focus on words with possessive suffixes. Match the form with the possessive suffix in the right column with the corresponding absolute singular form in the left column.

אָדוֹן	.a	f.	קוֹלִי	1.
סוּסָה	.b	c.	תּוֹרָתְךָ	2.
תּוֹרָה	.c	a.	אֲדוֹנֵנוּ	3.
סֵפֶר	.d	i.	כַּסְפְּכֶם	4.
בֹּקֶר	.e	g.	לִבָּהּ	5.
קוֹל	.f	d.	סִפְרוֹ	6.
לֵב	.g	j.	אִשְׁתִּי	7.
שָׁנָה	.h	b.	סוּסָתָן	8.
כֶּסֶף	.i	e.	בָּקְרֶךָ	9.
אִשָּׁה	.j	h.	שְׁנָתוֹ	10.

B. Focus on words with possessive suffixes. Translate the following words with possessive suffixes.

1.	his horse	5.	your horse	9.	our king	13.	your gold
2.	your horse	6.	my horse	10.	your soul	14.	her house
3.	our horse	7.	your horse	11.	their holiness	15.	your garment
4.	their horse	8.	her horse	12.	his word	16.	my people

D. Focus on the personal pronouns. Translate the personal pronouns, then identify the person, gender, and number.

3fp	they	1.	הֵנָּה
2ms	you	2.	אַתָּה
1cs	I	3.	אֲנִי
3fs	she	4.	הִיא
1cp	we	5.	אֲנַחְנוּ
2mp	you	6.	אַתֶּם
3ms	he	7.	הוּא
2fs	you	8.	אַתְּ
3mp	they	9.	הֵם
1cs	I	10.	אָנֹכִי

E. Parse the following.

Verb	Pattern	Conj.	Person	Gender	Number	Root
1. הֲלַכְתֶּם	qal	pf	2	m	p	הלך
2. אֶגְלֶה	qal	impf	1	c	s	גלה
3. נִמְצָא	qal	impf	1	c	p	מצא
4. עָשִׂיתִי	qal	pf	1	c	s	עשה
5. יַעַבְדוּ	qal	impf	3	m	p	עבד
6. יִגַּשׁ	qal	impf	3	m	s	נגש
7. חָטָאתָ	qal	pf	2	m	s	חטא
8. גָּאֲלָה	qal	pf	3	f	s	גאל
9. עֲבַרְתֶּן	qal	pf	2	f	p	עבר
10. תִּשָּׂא	qal	impf	3 / 2	f / m	s	נשא

G. Translate the following from the Hebrew Bible.

2 Samuel 7:20   And you know your servant. .1

Isaiah 42:24   And they did not obey his law. .2

Joshua 24:15   And I and my house, we will serve the Lord. .3

Lesson 17

A. Focus on attributive demonstrative pronouns. Translate the following phrases.

1. this mouth
2. this family
3. these enemies
4. that head
5. that daughter
6. those servants
7. this law
8. that son
9. this bread
10. these battles
11. those good men
12. that unclean foot

B. Focus on predicate demonstrative pronouns. Translate the following sentences.

1. This is the house.
2. This is the woman.
3. These are the words.
4. That is the way.
5. That is the kingdom.
6. Those are the books.
7. This is the land.
8. These are the women.
9. This is the king.

C. Focus on the difference between the attributive and predicate demonstrative pronouns. Read the following lines, then indicate the use (*a* for attributive or *p* for predicate), gender, and number.

Use	Gender	Number		
a	f	s	.1	הָאִשָּׁה הַזֹּאת
p	m	s	.2	זֶה הָאָדָם
a	m	s	.3	הַמִּזְבֵּחַ הַזֶּה
a	f	s	.4	הַבַּת הַהִיא
p	c	p	.5	אֵלֶּה הָאֵלִים
a	m	p	.6	הַבְּגָדִים הָהֵם
a	m	s	.7	הָרֹאשׁ הַזֶּה
p	f	s	.8	זֹאת הַמַּלְכוּת
a	m	s	.9	הָאֹהֶל הַהוּא
a	c	p	.10	הָאֲרָצוֹת הָאֵלֶּה

D. Focus on the relative pronoun. Translate the following.

1. the king who reigned
2. the woman who sent
3. the prophets who said
4. the silver that is in the house
5. places where he lived
6. the gold that he took
7. sacrifices that are on an altar
8. the bread that he ate
9. sons who went out

E. Parse the following.

Verb	Pattern	Conj.	Person	Gender	Number	Root
1. שְׁמַרְתֶּם	qal	pf	2	m	p	שמר
2. בָּנִיתִי	qal	pf	1	c	s	בנה
3. יִפֹּל	qal	impf	3	m	s	נפל
4. תַּעֲלֶה	qal	impf	3 / 2	f / m	s	עלה
5. יִגְּעוּ	qal	impf	3	m	p	נגע
6. כָּלִינוּ	qal	pf	1	c	p	כלה
7. חֲטָאתֶם	qal	pf	2	m	p	חטא

8.	אֶגְלֶה	qal	impf	1	c	s	גלה
9.	יִשָּׂא	qal	impf	3	m	s	נשא
10.	גָּאֲלָה	qal	pf	3	f	s	גאל

F. Focus on weak verbs. Translate the following.

1. The boys cried.
2. I will see the enemy.
3. You (*ms*) read the law.
4. You (*mp*) built a house.
5. The people will start out.
6. We will find a father.
7. The brother will fall.
8. They (*mp*) will carry bread.
9. We will be finished.
10. You (*mp*) will make an altar.
11. You (*mp*) went out.
12. I sinned.

H. Translate the following from the Hebrew Bible.

Judges 4:14   This is the day in which the Lord gave Sisera into your hand.   1.

Genesis 15:18   On that day the Lord made a covenant with Abram.   2.

Genesis 17:10   This is my covenant that you shall keep.   3.

Lesson 18

A. Focus on weak roots. Parse the following.

	Verb	Pattern	Conj.	Person	Gender	Number	Root
1.	יִירַשׁ	qal	impf	3	m	s	ירשׁ
2.	יֵלֵד	qal	impf	3	m	s	ילד
3.	יֹאכַל	qal	impf	3	m	s	אכל
4.	יִיבְשׁוּ	qal	impf	3	m	p	יבשׁ
5.	אֵלֵךְ	qal	impf	1	c	s	הלך
6.	נָתַתִּי	qal	pf	1	c	s	נתן
7.	כְּרַתֶּם	qal	pf	2	m	p	כרת
8.	נֵצֵא	qal	impf	1	c	p	יצא
9.	תִּירָא	qal	impf	3 / 2	f / m	s	ירא
10.	יִתֵּן	qal	impf	3	m	s	נתן

B. Focus on weak roots. Translate the following.

1.	they will say	6.	I will inherit	11.	you cut
2.	she/you will dwell	7.	they will go out	12.	she/you will eat
3.	we will know	8.	you will fear	13.	you gave
4.	I gave	9.	you will wither	14.	I will say
5.	he will fear	10.	I will bear	15.	she/you will walk

C. Focus on possessive suffixes. Translate the following and indicate the person, gender, and number of the suffix.

Person	Gender	Number		
1	c	s	1.	my king
3	m	s	2.	his king
3	f	s	3.	her king
1	c	p	4.	our king
3	m	p	5.	their king
2	m	s	6.	your king
2	m	p	7.	your king
2	f	s	8.	your king
2	f	p	9.	your king
3	f	p	10.	their king

D. Focus on possessive suffixes. Translate the following.

1.	his judgment	5.	our book	9.	our gold	13.	my eye
2.	my God	6.	their family	10.	your house	14.	your morning
3.	her word	7.	his heart	11.	her soul	15.	our city
4.	your law	8.	his people	12.	their time		

F. Translate the following from the Hebrew Bible.

Psalms 26:5	And with wicked men I will not dwell. .1
Deuteronomy 22:16	I gave my daughter to this man. .2
Psalm 56:5	In God I trust; I will not fear. .3
Isaiah 52:6	My people will know my name. .4

Lesson 19

A. Focus on words with possessive suffixes. Match the form with the possessive suffix of the right hand column with the corresponding absolute singular form of the left hand column.

סֵפֶר .a	c.	קוֹלוֹתֵינוּ	1.
עִיר .b	f.	תּוֹרוֹתֶיךָ	2.
קוֹל .c	g.	אֲדוֹנִי	3.
מִשְׁפָּט .d	i.	כַּסְפֵּיכֶם	4.
שָׁנָה .e	h.	לִבּוֹתֵיהֶם	5.
תּוֹרָה .f	a.	סְפָרֶיהָ	6.
אָדוֹן .g	j.	דְּבָרָיו	7.
לֵב .h	d.	מִשְׁפָּטֶיךָ	8.
כֶּסֶף .i	b.	עָרֵיכֶן	9.
דָּבָר .j	e.	שְׁנוֹתַיִךְ	10.

B. Focus on words with possessive suffixes. Translate the following words with possessive suffixes.

1. his horses
2. your horses
3. our horses
4. their horses
5. your horses
6. my horses
7. your horses
8. her horses
9. your servants
10. their souls
11. our gold(s)
12. his words
13. your judgments
14. your fathers
15. my places
16. his hands

D. Parse the following.

	Verb	Pattern	Conj.	Person	Gender	Number	Root
1.	גָּאֲלוּ	qal	pf	3	c	p	גאל
2.	תַּעֲמֹד	qal	impf	3 / 2	f / m	s	עמד
3.	אֶשָּׂא	qal	impf	1	c	s	נשׂא
4.	בְּכִיתֶם	qal	pf	2	m	p	בכה
5.	יוּכַל	qal	impf	3	m	s	יכל
6.	נֹאמַר	qal	impf	1	c	p	אמר
7.	תַּעֲשׂוּ	qal	impf	2	m	p	עשׂה

8.	כָּבֵד	qal	pf	3	m	s	כבד
9.	יָכֹלְתָּ	qal	pf	2	m	s	יכל
10.	תֵּשְׁבִי	qal	impf	2	f	s	ישׁב

E. Focus on weak roots. Translate the following.

1. I created
2. they will touch
3. you did not make
4. we will know
5. we built

6. she/you will eat
7. he will not go up
8. she/you will lift
9. they will say
10. I will not bear

11. you did not give
12. we will be able
13. he will weep
14. we will not fear
15. he created

G. Translate the following from the Hebrew Bible.

1 Kings 8:48   And the house that I built for your name. .1

Psalm 18:39   They will fall under my feet. .2

Genesis 32:31   I saw God face to face. .3

Lesson 20

A. Focus on the forms of the *inf const*. Write the root of each *inf const*.

שׁמע	שְׁמֹעַ .2	קטל	קְטֹל .1
ישׁב	שֶׁבֶת .4	עמד	עֲמֹד .3
ילד	לֶדֶת .6	גלה	גְּלוֹת .5
ידע	דַּעַת .8	שׁלח	שְׁלֹחַ .7
בכה	בְּכוֹת .10	בנה	בְּנוֹת .9
הלך	לֶכֶת .12	ירד	רֶדֶת .11
יצא	צֵאת .14	נתן	תֵּת .13

B. Focus on the use of the *inf const*. Translate the following phrases.

1. to write
2. to remember
3. to sacrifice
4. to reign
5. to dwell
6. to give birth

7. when he went down
8. when he knew
9. when he built
10. when he revealed
11. to see him

12. to make it
13. to give
14. to go
15. when he went out
16. when he took

C. Focus on the use of the *inf abs.* Translate the following phrases.

1. she/you will certainly guard
2. she/you will certainly send
3. she/you will certainly remember
4. she/you will certainly go
5. she/you will certainly dwell
6. she/you will certainly know
7. she/you will certainly build
8. she/you will certainly weep
9. she/you will certainly be finished
10. she/you will certainly give
11. she/you will certainly go out
12. she/you will certainly go up

D. Focus on the use of adjectives. Translate the following phrases and sentences and fill in the blanks for use of adjective (*a* for attributive and *p* for predicative) and for gender and number.

Use	Gender	Number		
a	f	s	.1	הָאִשָּׁה הַטּוֹבָה
p	m	s	.2	יָשָׁר הָאָדָם
a	m	s	.3	הַמִּזְבֵּחַ הַטָּהוֹר
a	f	s	.4	הַבַּת הַטּוֹבָה
p	m	p	.5	טְמֵאִים הָאֵלִים
a	m	p	.6	הָאֱלֹהִים הַחַיִּים
p	m	p	.7	גְּדוֹלִים הַבְּגָדִים
p	f	s	.8	רְשָׁעָה הַמַּלְכוּת
a	m	s	.9	לֵב חָכָם
a	f	p	.10	הָאֲרָצוֹת הָרַבּוֹת

E. Parse the following.

	Verb	Pattern	Conj.	Person	Gender	Number	Root
1.	קְטֹל	qal	inf const				קטל
2.	אָבַדְתִּי	qal	pf	1	c	s	אבד
3.	אֶכְתֹּב	qal	impf	1	c	s	כתב
4.	יֵרֵד	qal	impf	3	m	s	ירד
5.	שֶׁבֶת	qal	inf const				ישׁב
6.	נִרְאֶה	qal	impf	1	c	p	ראה

7.	גְּלוֹת	qal	inf const			גלה
8.	אָמוֹר	qal	inf abs			אמר
9.	לֶכֶת	qal	inf const			הלך
10.	תֵּת	qal	inf const			נתן

G. Translate the following from the Hebrew Bible.

1 Samuel 24:20   I know that you will certainly be king.   1.

1 Samuel 20:5   I will certainly sit with the king to eat.   2.

Deuteronomy 29:3   The LORD has not given to you a heart to know,   3.

or eyes to see, or ears to hear.

Lesson 21

A. Focus on the form of the active participle. Parse the following.

Verb		Pattern	Conj.	Person	Gender	Number	Root
1.	כֹּרֵת	qal	ptc		m	s	כרת
2.	הֹלֶכֶת	qal	ptc		f	s	הלך
3.	עֹבְרִים	qal	ptc		m	p	עבר
4.	שֹׁלְחוֹת	qal	ptc		f	p	שלח
5.	שֹׁולֵחַ	qal	ptc		m	s	שלח
6.	נֹשֵׂאת	qal	ptc		f	s	נשׂא
7.	בֹּונִים	qal	ptc		m	p	בנה
8.	בֹּכָה	qal	ptc		f	s	בכה
9.	גֹּולוֹת	qal	ptc		f	p	גלה
10.	רֹאֶה	qal	ptc		m	s	ראה

B. **Focus on the use of the active participle.** Translate the following (present progressive is fine, since there is no context) and indicate the use (*a* for attributive, *p* for predicate, or *s* for substantive).

Use	
a	1. the king who is sitting
p	2. The king is sitting.
s	3. the inhabitants of the city
p	4. We are eating.
p	5. We are about to eat.
p	6. The slaves are building.
a	7. the slaves who are building
p	8. The mother is crying.
p	9. The mother is going out.
s	10. the judge of wicked men

C. **Focus on possessive suffixes.** Translate the following nouns, paying attention to the number of the noun and the person, gender, and number of the suffix.

1. my light
2. your (*ms*) G/god
3. your (*ms*) arms
4. her voice
5. her voices
6. their (*mp*) family

7. their (*mp*) families
8. my word
9. my words
10. your (*mp*) sacrifices
11. his book

12. his books
13. our kings
14. our king
15. your (*fs*) eye
16. your (*fs*) eyes

D. Parse the following.

	Verb	Pattern	Conj.	Person	Gender	Number	Root
1.	עֲבַדְתֶּם	qal	pf	2	m	p	עבד
2.	אֶמְצָא	qal	impf	1	c	s	מצא
3.	יִתֵּן	qal	impf	3	m	s	נתן
4.	גָּלִינוּ	qal	pf	1	c	p	גלה
5.	שְׁפֹט	qal	inf const				שפט
6.	שֹׁמְרִים	qal	ptc		m	p	שמר

7.	בְּנוֹת	qal	inf const				בנה
8.	בֹּנוֹת	qal	ptc		f	p	בנה
9.	יֵרְדוּ	qal	impf	3	m	p	ירד
10.	שֶׁבֶת	qal	inf const				ישׁב

F. Translate the following from the Hebrew Bible.

Joshua 23:14   Today I am about to go the way of the whole earth.   .1
1 Kings 18:9   You are giving your servant into the hand of Ahab.   .2
Psalm 145:20   The LORD guards all who love him.   .3

Lesson 22

A. Focus on prepositions with pronoun suffixes. Translate the following prepositional phrases.

1.	to him	8.	with/in you	14.	to us	20	to you
2.	with/in you	9.	to/for you	15.	before them	21.	with us
3.	with her	10.	to him	16.	under us	22.	before us
4.	within me	11.	on you	17.	on you	23.	to/for me
5.	to/for you	12.	before me	18.	to you	24.	to me
6.	with them	13.	under her	19.	before them	25.	with/in us
7.	within us						

C. Focus on the construct state. Translate the following phrases.

1.	the word of the prophet	7.	the souls of the peoples
2.	the words of the prophet	8.	the day of the LORD
3.	the host/army of heaven	9.	the days of the year
4.	the law of the land	10.	the Lord of all the earth
5.	the king's family	11.	the beginning of his way
6.	the sacrifices of God	12.	the covenant of our God

D. Focus on adjectives and the construct state. Translate the following phrases, paying attention to which noun is modified by the adjective.

1.	the great day of the LORD	7.	the pure law of the LORD
2.	the great army of heaven	8.	the good covenant of our God
3.	the good beginning of his way	9.	the clean souls of the peoples
4.	the sacrifices of the unclean priest	10.	the words of the great prophet
5.	the word of the wicked prophets	11.	the great Lord of all the earth
6.	the good days of the year	12.	the family of the great king

E. Parse the following.

Verb	Pattern	Conj.	Person	Gender	Number	Root
1. כְּתַבְתֶּם	qal	pf	2	m	p	כתב
2. נֵרֵד	qal	impf	1	c	p	ירד
3. עֲשׂוֹת	qal	inf const				עשׂה
4. בֹּנִים	qal	ptc		m	p	בנה
5. מָצָאנוּ	qal	pf	1	c	p	מצא
6. אֶתֵּן	qal	impf	1	c	s	נתן
7. שֶׁבֶת	qal	inf const				ישׁב
8. כְּתֹב	qal	inf const				כתב
9. לָכוֹד	qal	inf abs				לכד
10. יַעֲלוּ	qal	impf	3	m	p	עלה

G. Translate the following from the Hebrew Bible.

Deuteronomy 1:30   the Lᴏʀᴅ your God who goes before you   .1
Joshua 22:31   Today we know that the Lᴏʀᴅ is in our midst.   .2
Genesis 41:38   a man within whom is the Spirit of God   .3

Lesson 23

A. Focus on "there is/was (not)." Translate the following, paying attention to the difference between past/present and positive/negative.

1. There was a prophet in the land.
2. There was not a prophet in the land.
3. There is not a prophet in the land.
4. There is a prophet in the land.
5. There is peace in the kingdom.
6. There is not a warrior there.
7. There was not a warrior there.
8. There is not a sacrifice on the altar.
9. There is a warrior on the way.

B. Focus on "have/had (not)." Translate the following, paying attention to the difference between past/present and positive/negative.

1. The man had cattle.
2. The man did not have cattle.
3. The man does not have cattle.
4. The man has cattle.
5. You (*ms*) have servants.
6. We do not have peace.
7. You (*mp*) did not have honor.
8. The daughter does not have a brother.
9. The city has a wall.

C. Focus on אֵין negating predicate participles. Translate the following.

1. I am not writing.
2. I am not writing.
3. You (*ms*) are not listening.
4. You (*ms*) are not listening.
5. You (*mp*) are not trusting.

6. You (*mp*) are not trusting.
7. He is not reigning.
8. He is not reigning.
9. We are not making a covenant.

E. Parse the following.

	Verb	Pattern	Conj.	Person	Gender	Number	Root
1.	כְּתַבְתֶּם	qal	pf	2	m	p	כתב
2.	נִבְטַח	qal	impf	1	c	p	בטח
3.	עֲשׂוֹת	qal	inf const				עשׂה
4.	גֹּלוֹת	qal	ptc		f	p	גלה
5.	דַּעַת	qal	inf const				ידע
6.	אֶתֵּן	qal	impf	1	c	s	נתן
7.	בָּרָאתָ	qal	pf	2	m	s	ברא
8.	תֵּצֵא	qal	impf	3 / 2	f / m	s	יצא
9.	תֹּאכְלוּ	qal	impf	2	m	p	אכל
10.	אָבוֹד	qal	inf abs				אבד

G. Translate the following from the Hebrew Bible.

Isaiah 57:21　　　　　　　"The wicked have no peace," says my God.　.1

1 Samuel 17:46　　And the whole earth will know that Israel has a God.　.2

2 Kings 17:26　　　　They do not know the custom of the god of the land.　.3

Lesson 24

A. Focus on the form of the volitives. Parse the following.

Verb	Pattern	Conj.	Person	Gender	Number	Root
1. אֶשְׁפְּטָה	qal	coh	1	c	s	שׁפט
2. זִבְחוּ	qal	impv	2	m	p	זבח
3. יִבֶן	qal	jus	3	m	s	בנה
4. שֵׁב	qal	impv	2	m	s	ישׁב
5. לֵךְ	qal	impv	2	m	s	הלך
6. נִתְּנָה	qal	coh	1	c	p	נתן
7. בְּכֵה	qal	impv	2	m	s	בכה
8. אֵדְעָה	qal	coh	1	c	s	ידע
9. קְחוּ	qal	impv	2	m	p	לקח
10. כִּתְבִי	qal	impv	2	f	s	כתב

B. Focus on the use of the volitives. Translate the following.

1. Visit! (*ms*)
2. Let us cut!
3. Let him build!
4. Don't let him go up!
5. Send! (*mp*)
6. Cling! (*fs*)
7. Don't let me go down!
8. Build! (*mp*)
9. Go out! (*mp*)
10. Go! (*mp*)
11. Let her do/make!
12. Don't let her cry!

D. Parse the following.

Verb	Pattern	Conj.	Person	Gender	Number	Root
1. מָלַכְתָּ	qal	pf	2	m	s	מלך
2. יִבְטְחוּ	qal	impf	3	m	p	בטח
3. שִׁלְחִי	qal	impv	2	f	s	שׁלח
4. זֹבְחִים	qal	ptc		m	p	זבח
5. אָבוֹד	qal	inf abs				אבד
6. לְקַחְתֶּם	qal	pf	2	m	p	לקח
7. תִּשְׁמְעוּ	qal	impf	2	m	p	שׁמע
8. שֹׁמֶרֶת	qal	ptc		f	s	שׁמר
9. נָפַלְתִּי	qal	pf	1	c	s	נפל
10. תִּפְקֹד	qal	impf	3 / 2	f / m	s	פקד

F. Translate the following from the Hebrew Bible.

Psalm 62:9   Trust in him at all times . . . pour out your heart before him.   .1

Deuteronomy 4:1   And now Israel, listen to the statutes and judgments,   .2
so that you may live.

Isaiah 2:5   Come, so that we may walk in the light of the Lord.   .3

Lesson 25

A. Focus on the forms of qal Hollow verbs. Memorize the forms of the qal Hollow verbs before parsing the following.

	Verb	Pattern	Conj.	Person	Gender	Number	Root
1.	קָם	qal	pf / ptc	3	m / m	s / s	קוּם
2.	שַׂמְנוּ	qal	pf	1	c	p	שִׂים
3.	בָּאתָ	qal	pf	2	m	s	בוֹא
4.	שָׁבוּ	qal	pf	3	c	p	שׁוּב
5.	תָּרוּץ	qal	impf	3 / 2	f / m	s	רוּץ
6.	אָבִין	qal	impf	1	c	s	בִּין
7.	תָּבוֹאוּ	qal	impf	2	m	p	בוֹא
8.	רָמִים	qal	ptc		m	p	רוּם
9.	שִׂימוּ	qal	impv	2	m	p	שִׂים
10.	בָּאוֹת	qal	ptc		f	p	בוֹא
11.	מוֹת	qal	inf abs				מוּת
12.	יֵבוֹשׁוּ	qal	impf	3	m	p	בּוֹשׁ
13.	נָסוּרָה	qal	coh	1	c	p	סוּר
14.	יָשֵׂם	qal	jus	3	m	s	שִׂים
15.	יָקֹם	qal	jus	3	m	s	קוּם
16.	רָצִים	qal	ptc		m	p	רוּץ
17.	מֵתוּ	qal	pf	3	c	p	מוּת

18.	בּוֹשִׁי	qal	impv	2	f	s	בוש
19.	מַתָּה	qal	pf	2	m	s	מות
20.	תָּרוּמוּ	qal	impf	2	m	p	רום

B. Focus on the use of the *pf* and *impf*. Translate the following verb forms.

1. He heard.
2. He is heavy.
3. He will trust.
4. I will judge.

5. They stood.
6. You (*mp*) saw.
7. We will do/make.

8. We built.
9. You (*fs*) will take.
10. They (*mp*) will go up.

C. Focus on the forms of the *pf and impf*. Parse the following.

Verb	Pattern	Conj.	Person	Gender	Number	Root
1. יֹאבֶה	qal	impf	3	m	s	אבה
2. אֹמַר	qal	impf	1	c	s	אמר
3. יֵרְדוּ	qal	impf	3	m	p	ירד
4. מָצָאתִי	qal	pf	1	c	s	מצא
5. עֲלִיתֶם	qal	pf	2	m	p	עלה
6. אֵשֵׁב	qal	impf	1	c	s	ישב
7. נָתַתָּ	qal	pf	2	m	s	נתן
8. נִקַּח	qal	impf	1	c	p	לקח
9. תֵּלְכוּ	qal	impf	2	m	p	הלך
10. תִּשְׂאִי	qal	impf	2	f	s	נשא

E. Translate the following from the Hebrew Bible.

Isaiah 6:3

1. This one called to this one and said,
"Holy, holy, holy is the Lᴏʀᴅ of Hosts,
the whole earth is full of his glory."

Deuteronomy 12:1

2. These are the statutes and the judgments that you
will be careful to do in the land that the Lᴏʀᴅ the God
of your fathers has given you to possess (it) all the days
that you are alive on the land.

Lesson 26

A. Focus on the form of the vav-relative imperfect (*wci*). Parse the following.

	Verb	Pattern	Conj.	Person	Gender	Number	Root
1.	וַיִּבְטַח	qal	wci	3	m	s	בטח
2.	וָאֶבְטַח	qal	wci	1	c	s	בטח
3.	וַנָּקָם	qal	wci	1	c	p	קום
4.	וַתִּבֶן	qal	wci	3 / 2	f / m	s	בנה
5.	וַתַּעַל	qal	wci	3 / 2	f / m	s	עלה
6.	וַיִּתֵּן	qal	wci	3	m	s	נתן
7.	וַתָּשֶׂם	qal	wci	3 / 2	f / m	s	שִׂים
8.	וַיֵּבְךְּ	qal	wci	3	m	s	בכה
9.	וַיַּעַשׂ	qal	wci	3	m	s	עשׂה
10.	וַתִּפֹּל	qal	wci	3 / 2	f / m	s	נפל

B. Focus on the use of the vav-relative perfect and the vav-relative imperfect. Translate the following forms.

1. They (*mp*) sacrificed.
2. They will sacrifice.
3. He will go up.
4. He went up.
5. She/you arose.
6. You (*ms*) will arise.
7. He said.
8. We wept.
9. They (mp) ran.
10. I stood.
11. You (*mp*) will give.
12. They (*mp*) went up.
13. We will know.
14. He lifted.
15. He fell.

D. Focus on the form of the infinitive construct. Parse the following.

	Verb	Pattern	Conj.	Person	Gender	Number	Root
1.	כְּתֹב	qal	inf const				כתב
2.	בִּין	qal	inf const				בין
3.	תֵּת	qal	inf const				נתן
4.	בְּכוֹת	qal	inf const				בכה
5.	רֶדֶת	qal	inf const				ירד
6.	קַחַת	qal	inf const				לקח

7.	לֶכֶת	qal	inf const				הלך
8.	עֲשׂוֹת	qal	inf const				עשׂה
9.	שׁוּב	qal	inf const				שׁוּב
10.	בּוֹא	qal	inf const				בּוֹא

E. Focus on the use of the infinitive construct in temporal clauses. Translate the following.

1. When the man sent the boy,
2. When he sent the boy,
3. When he sent him,
4. When our enemies arose against us,
5. When you lay down and arose,
6. When the priests went up,
7. When he went out and came in,
8. When the woman bore her son,
9. When you (*mp*) built an altar,

G. Translate the following from the Hebrew Bible.

Joshua 24:19   Joshua said to the people, "You will not be able   .1
to serve the Lord, for he is a holy God."

Joshua 24:24-25   The people said to Joshua, "We will serve the Lord   .2
our God and we will obey him." And Joshua made
a covenant for the people on that day and gave it to them
as a statute and judgment in Shechem.

Lesson 27

A. Focus on temporal clauses. Translate the following clauses.

1. When the man wrote a book
2. When the man writes a book
3. After he wrote a book
4. When he wrote a book
5. When he wrote a book
6. Before he wrote a book
7. On that day (in the future)
8. In that year (in the past)
9. When the Lord judges the nations
10. When the Lord judged his people

C. Focus on interrogative clauses. Translate the following clauses.

1. Who heard the words?
2. Did he hear the words?
3. What did he hear?
4. Will she/you listen to me?
5. Are you the king of the city?
6. Who is the king of the city?
7. What did he say to you?
8. Will he offer sacrifices?
9. What are you doing?
10. Who is walking with us?

D. Parse the following.

	Verb	Pattern	Conj.	Person	Gender	Number	Root
1.	שָׁכַבְתִּי	qal	pf	1	c	s	שכב
2.	אֶפְקֹד	qal	impf	1	c	s	פקד
3.	מָלַכְתָּ	qal	pf	2	m	s	מלך
4.	זְכַרְתֶּם	qal	pf	2	m	p	זכר
5.	נִכְתֹּב	qal	impf	1	c	p	כתב
6.	יִדְרְשׁוּ	qal	impf	3	m	p	דרשׁ
7.	תִּדְבְּקוּ	qal	impf	2	m	p	דבק
8.	אָכְלוּ	qal	pf	3	c	p	אכל
9.	אָסַפְנוּ	qal	pf	1	c	p	אסף
10.	תִּמְצְאִי	qal	impf	2	f	s	מצא

E. Focus on nouns with pronoun suffixes. Translate the following words.

1. your (*ms*) peace
2. your (*mp*) peace
3. his peace
4. my peace
5. our peace

6. their (*mp*) word
7. their (*mp*) words
8. your (*ms*) words
9. my words
10. her words

11. his sacrifice
12. his sacrifices
13. their (*mp*) sacrifices
14. our sacrifices
15. your (*fp*) sacrifices

G. Translate the following from Josh 1:1–2.

(1) After the death of Moses servant of the Lord, the Lord said to Joshua son of Nun, servant of Moses, (2) "Moses my servant is dead. Arise, cross this Jordan, you and this whole people, to the land that I am giving to them, to the sons of Israel."

Lesson 28

A. Focus on the form of the piel. Parse the following.

Verb	Pattern	Conj.	Person	Gender	Number	Root
1. דִּבַּרְתִּי	piel	pf	1	c	s	דבר
2. יְכַפֵּר	piel	impf	3	m	s	כפר
3. מְקַדֵּשׁ	piel	ptc		m	s	קדשׁ
4. הַלְלוּ	piel	impv	2	m	p	הלל
5. תְּבַקְשִׁי	piel	impf	2	f	s	בקשׁ
6. דִּבַּרְתֶּם	piel	pf	2	m	p	דבר
7. הִלְלוּ	piel	pf	3	c	p	הלל
8. נְקַדֵּשׁ	piel	impf	1	c	p	קדשׁ
9. בַּקֵּשׁ	piel	impv / inf const	2	m	s	בקשׁ
10. מְדַבְּרִים	piel	ptc		m	p	דבר
11. אֲהַלְלָה	piel	coh	1	c	s	הלל
12. כַּפֵּר	piel	inf abs				כפר
13. תְּבַקֵּשׁ	piel	impf	3 / 2	f / m	s	בקשׁ
14. קִדַּשְׁתָּ	piel	pf	2	m	s	קדשׁ
15. תְּדַבְּרוּ	piel	impf	2	m	p	דבר

B. Focus on strong verbs in the qal and piel. Parse the following.

Verb	Pattern	Conj.	Person	Gender	Number	Root
1. יִמְלֹךְ	qal	impf	3	m	s	מלך
2. יְדַבֵּר	piel	impf	3	m	s	דבר
3. הָלַכְתָּ	qal	pf	2	m	s	הלך
4. הִלַּכְתָּ	piel	pf	2	m	s	הלך
5. שִׁפְטוּ	qal	impv	2	m	p	שׁפט
6. דַּבְּרוּ	piel	impv	2	m	p	דבר
7. מְקַדֵּשׁ	piel	ptc		m	s	קדשׁ

8. שֹׁמֵר	qal	ptc		m	s	שמר
9. תְּכַפְּרוּ	piel	impf	2	m	p	כפר
10. בִּקַּשְׁתֶּם	piel	pf	2	m	p	בקשׁ

C. Focus on III Hey verbs in the qal. Parse the following.

Verb	Pattern	Conj.	Person	Gender	Number	Root
1. בָּכִינוּ	qal	pf	1	c	p	בכה
2. יִבְנֶה	qal	impf	3	m	s	בנה
3. עֹלִים	qal	ptc		m	p	עלה
4. רְאוֹת	qal	inf const				ראה
5. יִגְלוּ	qal	impf	3	m	p	גלה
6. עָשׂוּ	qal	pf	3	c	p	עשׂה
7. בְּנֵה	qal	impv	2	m	s	בנה
8. בְּכוּ	qal	impv	2	m	p	בכה
9. כְּלוֹת	qal	inf const				כלה
10. נְטִיתֶם	qal	pf	2	m	p	נטה

E. Translate the following from 1 Samuel 11.

(4) The messengers came to Gibeah of Saul and spoke the words in the ears of the people. Then all the people lifted their voices and wept. (5) Just then, Saul came behind the herd from the field, and Saul said, "What's wrong with the people, that they are weeping?" So they reported to him the words of the men of Jabesh.
(6) Then the Spirit of God rushed on Saul when he heard these words, and he was very angry.

Lesson 29

A. Focus on the form of the piel from weak roots. Parse the following.

	Verb	Pattern	Conj.	Person	Gender	Number	Root
1.	כִּסָּה	piel	pf	3	m	s	כסה
2.	בֵּרֵךְ	piel	pf	3	m	s	ברך
3.	יְגַלֶּה	piel	impf	3	m	s	גלה
4.	אֲבָרֵךְ	piel	impf	1	c	s	ברך
5.	מְכַסִּים	piel	ptc		m	p	כסה
6.	מְבָרְכוֹת	piel	ptc		f	p	ברך
7.	גִּלִּינוּ	piel	pf	1	c	p	גלה
8.	בֵּרַכְנוּ	piel	pf	1	c	p	ברך
9.	בָּרֵךְ	piel	impv / inf const/abs	2	m	s	ברך
10.	כַּסּוֹת	piel	inf const				כסה

B. Focus on the piel from strong and weak roots. Parse the following.

	Verb	Pattern	Conj.	Person	Gender	Number	Root
1.	שִׂמַּחְתֶּם	piel	pf	2	m	p	שׂמח
2.	יְהַלְלוּ	piel	impf	3	m	p	הלל
3.	יְכַסּוּ	piel	impf	3	m	p	כסה
4.	צִוִּיתָ	piel	pf	2	m	s	צוה
5.	מְבַקֶּשֶׁת	piel	ptc		f	s	בקשׁ
6.	מְגַלָּה	piel	ptc		f	s	גלה
7.	קַדְּשׁוּ	piel	impv	2	m	p	קדשׁ
8.	בָּרְכוּ	piel	impv	2	m	p	ברך
9.	צַוֹּת	piel	inf const				צוה
10.	תְּבָרֵךְ	piel	impf	3 / 2	f / m	s	ברך

C. Focus on the difference in meaning when a verb occurs in both the qal and the piel. Translate the following verb forms. If you encounter a root you have not yet learned in the qal or piel, consult the vocabulary at the back of the grammar for the meaning.

1. They are glad.
2. They made X glad.
3. I counted.
4. I told/reported.

5. He is holy.
6. He sanctified X.
7. We are great.

8. We magnified.
9. You are finished.
10. You finished.

D. Focus on the construct state. Translate the following.

1. the law of the LORD
2. the holy congregation
3. the land's peace
4. the king's judgment
5. the man's servants
6. the city's wall

7. the warrior's glory
8. the battle of the year
9. holy land
10. the God of heaven
11. the people's righteousness
12. the prophet's word

E. Focus on verbs in the qal and the piel. Parse the following.

	Verb	Pattern	Conj.	Person	Gender	Number	Root
1.	מִלֵּא	piel	pf	3	m	s	מלא
2.	זָקֵן	qal	pf	3	m	s	זקן
3.	הַלְלוּ	piel	impv	2	m	p	הלל
4.	יִשְׂמַח	qal	impf	3	m	s	שׂמח
5.	תְּסַפְּרוּ	piel	impf	2	m	p	ספר
6.	כַּסּוֹת	piel	inf const				כסה
7.	בֹּנוֹת	qal	ptc		f	p	בנה
8.	מְצַוִּים	piel	ptc		m	p	צוה
9.	דִּבַּרְתֶּם	piel	pf	2	m	p	דבר
10.	גָּלִיתִי	qal	pf	1	c	s	גלה

G. Translate the following from Joshua 22:2–3

(2) He said to them, "You yourselves have kept everything that Moses servant of the LORD commanded you. And you have obeyed me in regard to everything that I commanded you. (3) You did not abandon your brothers."

Lesson 30

A. Focus on cardinal numbers one through ten. Translate the following.

1. one king	5. three kings	9. five kings
2. one mother	6. three mothers	10. ten kings
3. two kings	7. nine mothers	11. six mothers
4. two mothers	8. seven kings	12. four mothers

B. Focus on ordinal numbers one through ten. Translate the following.

1. the first king	4. the third mother	7. the seventh king
2. the first mother	5. the fourth mother	8. the ninth mother
3. the third king	6. the eighth king	9. the sixth king

C. Focus on higher cardinal numbers. Decipher the following.

1. 30	3. 54	5. 300	7. 330	9. 3,000
2. 33	4. 96	6. 303	8. 333	10. 3,333

D. Focus on the qal and piel of strong roots. Parse the following.

Verb	Pattern	Conj.	Person	Gender	Number	Root
1. שָׁלַחְתָּ	qal	pf	2	m	s	שׁלח
2. דִּבַּרְתָּ	piel	pf	2	m	s	דבר
3. נִכְתֹּב	qal	impf	1	c	p	כתב
4. נְסַפֵּר	piel	impf	1	c	p	ספר
5. מָלְכוּ	qal	pf	3	c	p	מלך
6. אֲהַלֵּל	piel	impf	1	c	s	הלל
7. קַדְּשׁוּ	piel	impv	2	m	p	קדשׁ
8. קִדְּשׁוּ	piel	pf	3	c	p	קדשׁ
9. מְשַׂמְּחִים	piel	ptc		m	p	שׂמח
10. בִּקַּשְׁתֶּם	piel	pf	2	m	p	בקשׁ

G. Translate the following from 2 Samuel 5:4–5.

(4) David was 30 years old when he became king. He reigned forty years. (5) He reigned over Judah in Hebron seven years and six months, and he reigned over all Israel and Judah in Jerusalem thirty-three years.

Lesson 31

A. Focus on the form of the hiphil. Parse the following.

	Verb	Pattern	Conj.	Person	Gender	Number	Root
1.	הִכְעִיסוּ	hiph	pf	3	c	p	כעס
2.	הַשְׁלִיכוּ	hiph	impv	2	m	p	שלך
3.	הַשְׁאִיר	hiph	inf const				שאר
4.	אַשְׂבִּיעַ	hiph	impf	1	c	s	שבע
5.	מַכְעִיסִים	hiph	ptc		m	p	כעס
6.	הִשְׁלַכְתֶּם	hiph	pf	2	m	p	שלך
7.	תַּשְׂבִּיעוּ	hiph	impf	2	m	p	שבע
8.	וַתַּכְעֵס	hiph	wci	3 / 2	f / m	s	כעס
9.	מַשְׁאֶרֶת	hiph	ptc		f	s	שאר
10.	הִשְׁלַכְתִּי	hiph	pf	1	c	s	שלך

B. Focus on the difference in meaning when a verb occurs in both the qal and the hiphil. Translate the following verb forms. If you encounter a root that you have not yet learned in the qal or hiphil, consult the vocabulary at the back of the grammar for the meaning.

1. He is provoked.
2. He provoked.
3. I remained.
4. I left X.
5. You are holy.
6. You sanctified.
7. We remembered.
8. We reminded.
9. You are great.
10. You magnified.

C. Focus on the form of verbs in the qal from I Guttural roots. Parse the following.

	Verb	Pattern	Conj.	Person	Gender	Number	Root
1.	חֲזַקְתֶּם	qal	pf	2	m	p	חזק
2.	עֲזַבְתֶּם	qal	pf	2	m	p	עזב
3.	יֶחֱזַק	qal	impf	3	m	s	חזק
4.	אֶעֱמֹד	qal	impf	1	c	s	עמד
5.	עֲמֹד	qal	impv / inf const	2	m	s	עמד
6.	חֲשַׁבְתֶּם	qal	pf	2	m	p	חשב

D. Focus on qal verbs from I Nun roots. Parse the following.

	Verb	Pattern	Conj.	Person	Gender	Number	Root
1.	יִתֵּן	qal	impf	3	m	s	נתן
2.	אֶפֹּל	qal	impf	1	c	s	נפל
3.	אֶפְּלָה	qal	coh	1	c	s	נפל
4.	נִסַּע	qal	impf	1	c	p	נסע
5.	תִּגַּשׁ	qal	impf	3 / 2	f / m	s	נגשׁ
6.	יִשָּׂא	qal	impf	3	m	s	נשׂא
7.	יִטֶּה	qal	impf	3	m	s	נטה
8.	נְתַתֶּם	qal	pf	2	m	p	נתן

F. Translate the following from the Hebrew Bible.

1 Kings 12:20   When all Israel heard that Jeroboam had returned,   1.
they sent and called him to the assembly. Then they made
him king over all Israel

Joshua 3:6   Joshua said to the priests, "Lift the ark of the covenant   2.
and cross in front of the people." Then they lifted the ark
of the covenant and walked in front of the people.

Lesson 32

A. Focus on the the form of the hiphil from I Guttural and I Nun roots. Parse the following.

	Verb	Pattern	Conj.	Person	Gender	Number	Root
1.	הֶאֱמִינוּ	hiph	pf	3	c	p	אמן
2.	אַבִּיט	hiph	impf	1	c	s	נבט
3.	תַּגִּידוּ	hiph	impf	2	m	p	נגד
4.	הַגִּידוּ	hiph	impv	2	m	p	נגד
5.	הִגִּידוּ	hiph	pf	3	c	p	נגד
6.	נַחֲרִישׁ	hiph	impf	1	c	p	חרשׁ

	Verb		Conj.	Person	Gender	Number	Root
7.	הַאֲמִין	hiph	inf const				אמן
8.	הֶאֱמִין	hiph	pf	3	m	s	אמן
9.	הַחֲרֵשׁ	hiph	impv / inf abs	2	m	s	חרשׁ
10.	יַצֵּל	hiph	jus	3	m	s	נצל
11.	וַיַּצֵּל	hiph	wci	3	m	s	נצל
12.	הִבַּטְתֶּם	hiph	pf	2	m	p	נבט
13.	מַאֲמִין	hiph	ptc		m	s	אמן
14.	יַחֲרֵשׁ	hiph	jus	3	m	s	חרשׁ
15.	מַבִּיטִים	hiph	ptc		m	p	נבט

B. Focus on the form of all verbs learned to this point. Parse the following.

	Verb	Pattern	Conj.	Person	Gender	Number	Root
1.	מָצָאתָ	qal	pf	2	m	s	מצא
2.	גַּלּוֹת	piel	inf const				גלה
3.	יַאֲמִינוּ	hiph	impf	3	m	p	אמן
4.	מְבָרֵךְ	piel	ptc		m	s	ברך
5.	יִתֵּן	qal	impf	3	m	s	נתן
6.	בֹּנֶה	qal	ptc		m	s	בנה
7.	דַּבֵּר	piel	impv / inf const	2	m	s	דבר
8.	יֵרֵד	qal	impf	3	m	s	ירד
9.	קַמְתֶּם	qal	pf	2	m	p	קום
10.	גְּלוֹת	qal	inf const				גלה

C. Focus on qal verbs from I Yod roots. Parse the following.

	Verb	Pattern	Conj.	Person	Gender	Number	Root
1.	יֵשֵׁב	qal	impf	3	m	s	ישׁב
2.	יִיבַשׁ	qal	impf	3	m	s	יבשׁ

3.	יֵלְדוּ	qal	impf	3	m	p	ילד
4.	נִירָא	qal	impf	1	c	p	ירא
5.	יִיטַב	qal	impf	3	m	s	יטב
6.	אֵדַע	qal	impf	1	c	s	ידע
7.	תֵּצְאִי	qal	impf	2	f	s	יצא
8.	תִּירְשִׁי	qal	impf	2	f	s	ירשׁ

E. Translate the following from 2 Chronicles 9:5–6. The first verb is *3fs* and refers to the Queen of Sheba.

She said to the king, "The word that I heard in my land about your words and your wisdom is true. But I did not believe their words until I came and my eyes saw."

Lesson 33

A. Focus on the form of the hiphil from I Yod roots. Parse the following.

Verb	Pattern	Conj.	Person	Gender	Number	Root
1. הֵיטִיב	hiph	pf / inf const	3	m	s	יטב
2. הוֹשִׁיב	hiph	pf / inf const	3	m	s	ישׁב
3. יוֹשִׁיב	hiph	impf	3	m	s	ישׁב
4. יֵיטִיב	hiph	impf	3	m	s	יטב
5. מוֹלִידִים	hiph	ptc		m	p	ילד
6. הוֹרַדְתֶּם	hiph	pf	2	m	p	ירד
7. תֵּיטִיבוּ	hiph	impf	2	m	p	יטב
8. וַנּוֹשֵׁב	hiph	wci	1	c	p	ישׁב
9. הוֹשֵׁעַ	hiph	impv / inf abs	2	m	s	ישׁע
10. הוֹשִׁיבִי	hiph	impv	2	f	s	ישׁב

B. Focus on the difference in meaning when a verb occurs in both the qal and the hiphil. Translate the following verb forms. If you encounter a root that you have not yet learned in the qal or hiphil, consult the vocabulary at the back of the grammar for the meaning.

1. He went out.
2. He brought X out.
3. He is dry.
4. He dried X up.
5. He went down.
6. He brought X down.
7. He inherited.
8. He dispossessed X.
9. He knew.
10. He made known.
11. She bore.
12. He fathered.
13. You brought X out.
14. You brought X down.
15. You informed.

C. Focus on the form of qal and piel verbs from III Hey roots. Parse the following.

	Verb	Pattern	Conj.	Person	Gender	Number	Root
1.	גָּלָה	qal	pf	3	m	s	גלה
2.	גִּלָּה	piel	pf	3	m	s	גלה
3.	יְכְסֶה	qal	impf	3	m	s	כסה
4.	יְכַסֶּה	piel	impf	3	m	s	כסה
5.	גַּלּוֹת	piel	inf const				גלה
6.	גְּלוֹת	qal	inf const				גלה
7.	כִּסִּיתָ	piel	pf	2	m	s	כסה
8.	כָּסִיתָ	qal	pf	2	m	s	כסה
9.	יְגְלוּ	qal	impf	3	m	p	גלה
10.	יְגַלּוּ	piel	impf	3	m	p	גלה

D. Focus on the form of qal verbs from Hollow roots. Parse the following.

	Verb	Pattern	Conj.	Person	Gender	Number	Root
1.	קָם	qal	pf / ptc	3	m / m	s / s	קום
2.	יָקוּם	qal	impf	3	m	s	קום
3.	קוּם	qal	impv / inf const	2	m	s	קום
4.	קַמְתֶּם	qal	pf	2	m	p	קום
5.	תָּקָם	qal	jus	3 / 2	f / m	s	קום

	Verb					
6.	וַתָּקָם	qal	wci	3 / 2	f / m	s	קום
7.	קַמְתְּ	qal	pf	2	f	s	קום
8.	תָּקוּמוּ	qal	impf	2	m	p	קום
9.	קוּמוּ	qal	impv	2	m	p	קום
10.	אָקוּמָה	qal	coh	1	c	s	קום

F. Translate the following from Judges 7:4, 5, 7.

(4) The LORD said to Gideon, "The people are still too numerous. Bring them down to the water . . . (5) He brought the people down to the water. (7) The LORD said to Gideon, "With three hundred men I will save you."

Lesson 34

A. Focus on the form of the hiphil from III Hey and Hollow roots. Parse the following.

	Verb	Pattern	Conj.	Person	Gender	Number	Root
1.	הִגְלִיתָ	hiph	pf	2	m	s	גלה
2.	הֲקִימוֹתָ	hiph	pf	2	m	s	קום
3.	הֵכִינוּ	hiph	pf	3	c	p	כון
4.	יָנִיחוּ	hiph	impf	3	m	p	נוח
5.	יַגְלֶה	hiph	impf	3	m	s	גלה
6.	הַגְלוֹת	hiph	inf const				גלה
7.	מֵקִים	hiph	ptc		m	s	קום
8.	מַגְלִים	hiph	ptc		m	p	גלה
9.	הָכִין	hiph	inf const				כון
10.	הַגְלֵה	hiph	impv / inf abs	2	m	s	גלה

B. Focus on the form of the hiphil from roots that are doubly weak. Parse the following.

	Verb	Pattern	Conj.	Person	Gender	Number	Root
1.	הִכָּה	hiph	pf	3	m	s	נכה
2.	הוֹדָה	hiph	pf	3	m	s	ידה
3.	יַכֶּה	hiph	impf	3	m	s	נכה
4.	יוֹדֶה	hiph	impf	3	m	s	ידה
5.	מוֹדֶה	hiph	ptc		m	s	ידה
6.	מַכֶּה	hiph	ptc		m	s	נכה
7.	הַכּוֹת	hiph	inf const				נכה
8.	הוֹדוֹת	hiph	inf const				ידה
9.	הוֹדֵה	hiph	impv / inf abs	2	m	s	ידה
10.	הַכֵּה	hiph	impv / inf abs	2	m	s	נכה

C. Focus on the pronoun suffixes on nouns. Translate the following.

1. his horse
2. her horse
3. her horses
4. our horse
5. their horse
6. your horse
7. your horse
8. your horse
9. your horses
10. their horse

D. Focus on the pronoun suffixes on prepositions. Translate the following.

1. with you
2. with us
3. with her
4. with him
5. with you
6. with them
7. with you
8. with you
9. with me
10. with them

E. Focus on the form of all verbs learned to this point. Parse the following.

	Verb	Pattern	Conj.	Person	Gender	Number	Root
1.	יוֹרִיד	hiph	impf	3	m	s	ירד
2.	יְכַסֶּה	piel	impf	3	m	s	כסה
3.	בָּאתָ	qal	pf	2	m	s	בוא
4.	שֹׁלֵחַ	qal	ptc		m	s	שלח

5.	דִּבַּרְתִּי	piel	pf	1	c	s	דבר
6.	יִתְּנוּ	qal	impf	3	m	p	נתן
7.	תֵּלֵד	qal	impf	3 / 2	f / m	s	ילד
8.	קַחַת	qal	inf const				לקח

G. Translate the following from Psalm 136:1–3, 26.

Give thanks to the Lord, for he is good;
　for his faithfulness endures forever.
Give thanks to the God of Gods,
　for his faithfulness endures forever.
Give thanks to the Lord of lords,
　for his faithfulness endures forever
Give thanks to the God of heaven,
　for his faithfulness endures forever.

Lesson 35

A. Focus on כל with the pronoun suffixes. Translate the following.

1. the kings, all of them
2. the kings, all of you
3. all of the kings, all of them
4. every king, every one of them
5. the city, all of it
6. the whole city, all of it
7. every one will go
8. everyone heard
9. everyone will see

B. Focus on verbs with pronoun suffixes. Identify the person, gender, and number of the suffix.

1. 2ms
2. 1cp
3. 3mp
4. 3ms
5. 2mp
6. 1cs
7. 3fs
8. 3ms
9. 3ms
10. 3mp
11. 1cs
12. 3fs
13 2fs
14. 1cp
15. 3ms

C. Focus on verbs with pronoun suffixes. Translate the following.

1. He guarded you.
2. They will guard us.
3. She/you will send them.
4. You remembered him.
5. He gave you.
6. You will make me king.
7. He will lift her.
8. We will seek him.
9. We sought him.
10. I inherited them.
11. You found me.
12. You found her.
13. She will serve you.
14. He will judge us.
15. He will deliver him.

E. Parse the following.

Verb	Pattern	Conj.	Person	Gender	Number	Root
1. שָׁלַחְתָּ	qal	pf	2	m	s	שלח
2. דִּבַּרְתָּ	piel	pf	2	m	s	דבר
3. הִשְׁלַכְתָּ	hiph	pf	2	m	s	שלך
4. יִכְתֹּב	qal	impf	3	m	s	כתב
5. יַמְלִיךְ	hiph	impf	3	m	s	מלך
6. יְמַלֵּא	piel	impf	3	m	s	מלא
7. נְבַקֵּשׁ	piel	impf	1	c	p	בקש
8. הִשְׁאִירָה	hiph	pf	3	f	s	שאר

G. Translate the following from Genesis 2:2–3

(2) On the seventh day, God finished the work that he did, and on the seventh day he rested from all his work that he did. (3) So God blessed the seventh day and sanctified it, because on it he rested from all his work of creating that God did.

Lesson 36

A. Focus on the form of the niphal. Parse the following.

Verb	Pattern	Conj.	Person	Gender	Number	Root
1. נִקְטַל	niph	pf	3	m	s	קטל
2. נִקְטָל	niph	ptc		m	s	קטל
3. נִלְחַמְתֶּם	niph	pf	2	m	p	לחם
4. יִכָּתֵב	niph	impf	3	m	s	כתב
5. נִשָּׁמֵר	niph	impf	1	c	p	שמר
6. הִשָּׁמְרוּ	niph	impv	2	m	p	שמר
7. תִּקָּטְלִי	niph	impf	2	f	s	קטל
8. נִקְטֶלֶת	niph	ptc		f	s	קטל
9. נִשְׁמְרוּ	niph	pf	3	c	p	שמר
10. הִקָּטֹל	niph	inf abs				קטל

B. Focus on the difference in meaning when a verb occurs in both the qal and the niphal. Translate the following verb forms.

1. He anointed.
2. He was anointed.
3. He redeemed.
4. He was redeemed.
5. He wrote.
6. It was written.
7. He sought.
8. He was sought.
9. He remembered.
10. He was remembered.

C. Focus on qal and hiphil verbs from I Guttural and I Nun roots. Parse the following.

	Verb	Pattern	Conj.	Person	Gender	Number	Root
1.	עֲמַדְתֶּם	qal	pf	2	m	p	עמד
2.	יַעֲמֹד	qal	impf	3	m	s	עמד
3.	יַעֲמִיד	hiph	impf	3	m	s	עמד
4.	הֶעֱמִיד	hiph	pf	3	m	s	עמד
5.	הַעֲמִידוּ	hiph	impv	2	m	p	עמד
6.	מַעֲמִידִים	hiph	ptc		m	p	עמד
7.	יִפֹּל	qal	impf	3	m	s	נפל
8.	יִפְּלוּ	qal	impf	3	m	p	נפל
9.	תִּפֹּל	qal	impf	3 / 2	f / m	s	נפל

D. Focus on the difference between attributive and predicate adjectives. Read the following phrases and sentences, and fill in the blanks for use of adjective (*a* for attributive and *p* for predicative) and for gender and number.

Use	Gender	Number		
a	f	s	.1	הָאִשָּׁה הַטּוֹבָה
p	m	s	.2	קָדוֹשׁ הַכֹּהֵן
a	m	s	.3	הַזֶּבַח הַטָּמֵא
p	f	s	.4	טוֹבָה הָאָרֶץ
p	m	p	.5	גְּדוֹלִים הַגִּבּוֹרִים
a	m	p	.6	הָאֱלֹהִים הַחַיִּים
a	f	p	.7	הַמִּשְׁפָּחוֹת הָרַבּוֹת

p	f	s	.8 רִשְׁעָה הַמַּלְכוּת
a	m	s	.9 לֵב חָכָם
a	f	p	.10 הַנָּשִׁים הַטּוֹבוֹת

F. Translate the following from Zechariah 13:1-2.

(1) "And in that day a well will be opened for the house of David and for the inhabitants of Jerusalem for sin. . . ." (2) "And in that day," declares the LORD of hosts, "I will cut off the names of the idols from the land, and they will be remembered no longer. And I will also remove the prophets and the spirit of uncleanness from the land."

Lesson 37

A. Focus on the form of the niphal from weak roots. Parse the following.

Verb	Pattern	Conj.	Person	Gender	Number	Root
1. יֵאָמֵן	niph	impf	3	m	s	אמן
2. נִדַּחְתִּי	niph	pf	1	c	s	נדח
3. יִוָּלְדוּ	niph	impf	3	m	p	ילד
4. יִבָּנֶה	niph	impf	3	m	s	בנה
5. נִבְנָה	niph	pf	3	m	s	בנה
6. יֵעָנֶה	niph	impf	3	m	s	ענה
7. נוֹדַעְנוּ	niph	pf	1	c	p	ידע
8. הִוָּתְרוּ	niph	impv	2	m	p	יתר
9. נֶאֱסַפְתֶּם	niph	pf	2	m	p	אסף
10. הֵרָאוֹת	niph	inf const				ראה
11. נִצָּל	niph	ptc		m	s	נצל
12. נֶעֱנֵיתָ	niph	pf	2	m	s	ענה
13. הֵהָרְגִי	niph	impv	2	f	s	הרג
14. תִּוָּדְעוּ	niph	impf	2	m	p	ידע
15. נִבְאוּ	niph	pf	3	c	p	נבא

B. Focus on the meaning of niphal verbs from weak roots. Translate the following.

1. They were gathered.
2. They were scattered.
3. They will be left.
4. It was built.
5. We were born.
6. He appeared.
7. It was firm.
8. We were known.
9. He prophesied.
10. He will appear.

C. Focus on the difference between attributive and predicate participles. Read the following phrases and sentences, and fill in the blanks for use of participle (*a* for attributive and *p* for predicative) and for gender and number.

Use	Gender	Number		
a	m	s	1.	הָאִישׁ הַיּשֵׁב
p	m	s	2.	הַכֹּהֵן ישֵׁב
a	m	s	3.	הַנַּעַר הַמְדַבֵּר
p	m	s	4.	הַנָּבִיא מְדַבֵּר
p	m	p	5.	יֹצְאִים הַגִּבּוֹרִים
a	m	p	6.	הַגִּבּוֹרִים הַיֹּרְדִים
a	f	p	7.	הַנָּשִׁים הַמּוֹדִיעוֹת
p	f	p	8.	הַנָּשִׁים בָּאוֹת
a	m	p	9.	הָעַמִּים הַנֶּאֱסָפִים
p	m	s	10.	נִדָּח הָעָם

E. Translate the following from 1 Kings 18:36.

(36) At the time of offering the grain offering, Elijah the prophet approached and said, "O LORD, God of Abraham, Isaac, and Israel, let it be known today that you are God in Israel, that I am your servant, and that in keeping with your word I have done all these things."

Lesson 38

A. Focus on qal *pass ptc*, pual, and hophal verbs. Parse the following.

Verb	Pattern	Conj.	Person	Gender	Number	Root
1. כָּתוּב	qal	pass ptc		m	s	כתב
2. הֻלַּל	pual	pf	3	m	s	הלל
3. הָמְלַךְ	hoph	pf	3	m	s	מלך
4. יְכֻפַּר	pual	impf	3	m	s	כפר
5. יָשְׁלַךְ	hoph	impf	3	m	s	שלך
6. נָשְׁלַךְ	hoph	impf	1	c	p	שלך
7. יְהֻלְלוּ	pual	impf	3	m	p	הלל
8. שְׁמוּרִים	qal	pass ptc		m	p	שמר
9. כֻּפַּרְנוּ	pual	pf	1	c	p	כפר
10. הָמְלַכְתָּ	hoph	pf	2	m	s	מלך
11. מָשְׁלָךְ	hoph	ptc		m	s	שלך
12. מְהֻלָּל	pual	ptc		m	s	הלל
13. קְבוּרָה	qal	pass ptc		f	s	קבר

B. Focus on the meaning of the qal *pass ptc*, pual, and hophal verbs. Translate the following.

1. It is written.
2. I was made king.
3. It will be atoned for.
4. We were praised.
5. They will be thrown.
6. You will be made king.
7. You were thrown.
8. It was atoned for.
9. He was buried.
10. He will be praised.

F. Translate the following from the Hebrew Bible.

Psalm 48:1   Great is the LORD and worthy of great praise in the city .1
of our God, his holy mountain.

1 Chronicles 29:10   David blessed the LORD before the whole .2
congregation, and David said, "Blessed are you, O LORD
God of Israel, our father from everlasting to everlasting."

Lesson 39

A. Focus on the form of the hith and hish. Parse the following.

	Verb	Pattern	Conj.	Person	Gender	Number	Root
1.	יִתְהַלְלוּ	hith	impf	3	m	p	הלל
2.	הִתְקַדַּשְׁתִּי	hith	pf	1	c	s	קדש
3.	מִתְנַפֵּל	hith	ptc		m	s	נפל
4.	הִשְׁתַּחֲוִיתָ	hish	pf	2	m	s	חוה
5.	נִתְפַּלֵּל	hith	impf	1	c	p	פלל
6.	הִתְנַבֵּאתֶם	hith	pf	2	m	p	נבא
7.	וַיִּשְׁתַּחוּ	hish	wci	3	m	s	חוה
8.	וַיִּשְׁתַּחֲווּ	hish	wci	3	m	p	חוה
9.	מִתְהַלְלִים	hith	ptc		m	p	הלל
10.	אֶתְקַדֵּשׁ	hith	impf	1	c	s	קדש

B. Focus on the difference in meaning between the qal or piel and the hith. Translate the following.

1. I praised.
2. I boasted.
3. I sanctified.
4. I sanctified myself.
5. I fell.
6. I prostrated myself.
7. I magnified.
8. I boasted.

C. Focus on nouns and adjectives from geminate roots. Match the plural form of the right column with the corresponding singular form in the left column.

אֵם	.a	f.	דָּמִים	.1
לֵבָב	.b	g.	עַמִּים	.2
חֹק	.c	a.	אִמּוֹת	.3
יָם	.d	j.	לִבּוֹת	.4
כַּף	.e	i.	חַיִּים	.5
דָּם	.f	b.	לְבָבוֹת	.6
עַם	.g	h.	הָרִים	.7
הַר	.h	c.	חֻקִּים	.8
חַי	.i	d.	יָמִים	.9
לֵב	.j	e.	כַּפּוֹת	.10

D. Focus on the verb from Hollow roots. Parse the following.

Verb	Pattern	Conj.	Person	Gender	Number	Root
1. קָם	qal	pf / ptc	3	m m	s s	קוּם
2. יָקוּם	qal	impf	3	m	s	קוּם
3. יָקִים	hiph	impf	3	m	s	קוּם
4. הֵקִים	hiph	pf	3	m	s	קוּם
5. הֲקִימֹתָ	hiph	pf	2	m	s	קוּם
6. תָּקוּמִי	qal	impf	2	f	s	קוּם
7. הֲקִימֹונוּ	hiph	pf	1	c	p	קוּם
8. קַמְתֶּם	qal	pf	2	m	p	קוּם
9. הָקִימוּ	hiph	impv	2	m	p	קוּם
10. מֵקִים	hiph	ptc		m	s	קוּם

F. Translate the following from the Hebrew Bible.

Psalm 99:9 — Bow down toward his holy mountain, for the LORD our God is holy .1

2 Samuel 7:27 — For you LORD of Hosts, the God of Israel, have opened the ear of / revealed to your servant, saying, "I will build a house for you." Therefore, your servant has found it in his heart to pray to you. .2

2 Chronicles 29:15 — They gathered their brothers and sanctified themselves. Then they came according to the commands of the king. .3

Lesson 40

A. Focus on the form of verbs from geminate roots. Parse the following.

	Verb	Pattern	Conj.	Person	Gender	Number	Root
1.	אָסֹב	qal	impf	1	c	s	סבב
2.	סַבּוֹנוּ	qal	pf	1	c	p	סבב
3.	סֹבּוּ	qal	impv	2	m	p	סבב
4.	יִמַּדּוּ	niph	impf	3	m	p	מדד
5.	אָרוֹר	qal	inf abs				ארר
6.	יָחֹן	qal	impf	3	m	s	חנן
7.	אָרוֹתִי	qal	pf	1	c	s	ארר
8.	מַדּוֹתֶם	qal	pf	2	m	p	מדד
9.	יִתְחַנֵּן	hith	impf	3	m	s	חנן
10.	תָּמֹד	qal	impf	3 / 2	f / m	s	מדד

B. Translate the following from Deuteronomy 6:4–9.

(4) Hear, O Israel. The Lᴏʀᴅ our God, the Lᴏʀᴅ is one. (5) Love the Lᴏʀᴅ your God with all your heart, with all your soul, and with all your strength. (6) These words that I am commanding you today are to be on your hearts. (7) Repeat them to your children: speak of them when you sit down in your house, when you walk along the road, when you lie down, and when you rise. (8) Tie them as a sign on your hand, and they are to be phylacteries between your eyes. (9) Write them on the door posts of your house and on your gates.

INDEX OF TOPICS

INDEX OF HEBREW TERMS*

* Only Hebrew terms/words that are discussed as such in the text are included in this index.